QuestionTime3

150 Questions and Answers on the Catholic Faith

FR JOHN FLADER

Foreword by Peter Rosengren

Published in 2016 by Connor Court Publishing Pty Ltd

Copyright © John Flader 2016

ALL RIGHTS RESERVED. This book contains material protected under International and Federal Copyright Laws and Treaties. Any unauthorised reprint or use of this material is prohibited. No part of this book may be reproduced or transmitted in any form or by any means, electronic or mechanical, including photocopying, recording, or by any information storage and retrieval system without express written permission from the publisher.

Connor Court Publishing Pty Ltd
PO Box 7257
Redland Bay QLD 4165
sales@connorcourt.com
www.connorcourt.com

Imprimatur
Nihil Obstat: Rev. Peter Joseph STD
Imprimatur: + Most Reverend Anthony Fisher OP, Archbishop of Sydney
Date: 22 June 2016

The *Nihil Obstat* and *Imprimatur* are a declaration that a book or pamphlet is considered to be free from doctrinal or mmoral error. It is not necessarily implied that those who have granted them agree with the contents, opinions or statements expressed,

ISBN: 978-1-925501-20-9

The Scripture quotations are from the Revised Standard Version, Second Catholic Edition, Ignatius Edition, of the Bible, copyrighted 2006, by the Division of Christian Education of the National Council of Churches in the United States of America, and are used by permission. All rights reserved.

Cover design by Ian James

Printed in Australia

*In memory of St Josemaría Escrivá,
who taught me love for the Church*

CONTENTS

I. CATHOLIC DOCTRINE 1

God and creation 3

   301. Design in nature 3
   302. Atheism and science 6
   303. Darwin, God and evolution 7
   304. God and natural disasters 10
   305. The fall of the angels 12
   306. The devil 14
   307. Pope Francis and the devil 16

Sacred Scripture 19

   308. The unity of the Scriptures 19
   309. The interpretation of Scripture 21
   310. Who wrote Genesis? 23
   311. Is Genesis a myth? 26
   312. Apocryphal books of the Bible 28
   313. Who wrote the Gospel of Matthew? 30
   314. The historicity of the Gospels 32

Jesus Christ 35
   315. Jesus' humanity 35
   316. The birth of Christ ....;... 37
   317. When was Christ born? 39
   318. Where was Jesus born? 42
   319. The circumcision of Christ 44
   320. Jesus' "brothers and sisters" 46
   321. The "hour" of Jesus 49
   322. Veronica and the face of Jesus 51

Our Lady and St Joseph 54
   323. The bethrothal of Mary and Joseph 54
   324. St Joseph's dilemma 56
   325. St Joseph's flowering staff 59
   326. St Joseph's chastity 61

The Church 64
   327. Early Christian symbols 64
   328. More early Christian symbols 66
   329. Resignation of a Pope 68
   330. The election of a Pope 71
   331. What happens in a conclave?....................................... 73
   332. Abuses in a papal election 75
   333. The Year of Faith of Pope Paul VI 78
   334. Catholics and evangelical groups 80
   335. Rosicrucians 82

The Last Things 85

    336. Can atheists go to heaven? 85

    337. Is there time in heaven? 87

    338. Do pets go to heaven? 89

    339. Is it easy to go straight to heaven? 91

    340. God's mercy and hell 94

II. THE SACRAMENTS 97

The Liturgy 99

    341. The Liturgical Year 99

    342. Applause in the liturgy 101

    343. Silence in the church 103

    344. Who can give blessings? 105

The Mass 108

    345. Jesus' blessing in the Last Supper 108

    346. The Last Supper and the Passover 110

    347. The penitential rite and forgiveness of sins 112

    348. Who can give the homily? 115

    349. Why a new translation of the Mass? 117

    350. "And with your spirit" 119

    351. What does "consubstantial" mean? 121

    352. "My sacrifice and yours" 124

    353. "Lift up your hearts" 126

    354. "For all" – "For many" 128

    355. "The light of your face" 130

356. "From the rising of the sun to its setting" 132
357. "The Order of Bishops" 135
358. "We dare to say" 137
359. "The supper of the Lamb" 139

Holy Communion 142

360. Acolytes and ministers of Communion 142
361. Communion for all 144
362. Denying Communion 146
363. How to receive Communion 148
364. Blessings in Communion 150
365. Taking Communion to the sick 152

The Real Presence 155

366. Who has the Real Presence? 155
367. Pope Francis and a Eucharistic miracle 157
368. A Eucharistic miracle in Poland 159
369. The Eucharistic miracle of Lanciano 161

Penance 165

370. Whose sins you shall retain 165
371. The importance of individual confession 167
372. The benefits of confession 170
373. The seal of confession 172
374. Absolution without prior confession 174
375. Shedding of blood and the forgiveness of sin 176

CONTENTS

Holy Orders and Matrimony 179
   376. Is celibacy too hard? 179
   377. Why celibacy only in the West? 181
   378. Admission to the seminary of men with same-sex attraction 183
   379. Wedding matters 185

III. MORAL LIFE IN CHRIST 189

General Moral Issues 191
   380. The natural law 191
   381. Workers of the eleventh hour 193
   382. What is grace? 195
   383. What is actual grace? 198
   384. Other types of grace 200
   385. Occasions of sin 202
   386. Diminished guilt for sins 204
   387. Mortal sins 206
   388. Does God punish us for our sins? 209
   389. Cooperation in sin 211
   390. What is scandal? 213
   391. New deadly sins 216
   392. The seven deadly sins 218
   393. The value of temptations 220
   394. The influence of habits on morality 222
   395. Pride – habit and acts 224
   396. The value of suffering 227

Relations with God 230
- 397. Faith and Church teaching 230
- 398. Why study the faith 233
- 399. Can faith be lost? 235
- 400. Another kind of faith 237
- 401. What is blasphemy? 239
- 402. Catholics and halal meat 241
- 403. Catholics and Halloween 244

Relations with Our Neighbour 247
- 404. Love of self 247
- 405. Tattoos and body piercing 249
- 406. The morality of cosmetic surgery 251
- 407. The morality of in-vitro fertilisation 253
- 408. Vaccines from aborted fetuses 256
- 409. Living together outside marriage 258
- 410. Adultery and divorce 260
- 411. Impure thoughts 262
- 412. The sexual abuse scandal 264
- 413. Keeping secrets 267

IV. CHRISTIAN PRAYER 271

Prayer and Devotions 273
- 414. The Sign of the Cross 273
- 415. Distractions in prayer 275
- 416. Spiritual dryness 277
- 417. Praying in tongues 279

418. Is the Rosary boring? 281
419. The Angelus 284
420. The Hail, Holy Queen 286
421. The *Trisagium Angelicum* 288
422. The *Akathistos* hymn 290
423. What is a litany? 292
424. The Litany of Loreto 295
425. The Litany of the Saints 297

Seasons and Feast Days 300
426. The Advent wreath 300
427. Why is Christmas so important? 302
428. Nativity scenes 304
429. The feast of St Stephen 306
430. The feast of the Holy Innocents 309
431. Epiphany and the magi 311
432. The spirit of Easter 313
433. The date of Easter 315
434. The Jewish feast of Pentecost 317
435. The Octave of Prayer for Christian Unity 320
436. The Presentation of Mary in the Temple 322

Devotion to the Saints 325
437. St Michael the Archangel 325
438. Mary, Star of the Sea 327
439. The sorrows and joys of St Joseph 329
440. The Sabbatine privilege 332
441. The history of canonisations 334

442. Saints in the Roman Canon 336
443. More saints in the Roman Canon 339
444. St Christopher 341
445. St Anthony's bread 343
446. St John Paul II 345

Shrines of Our Lady 348
447. The Holy House of Loreto 348
448. The Marian shrine of Knock 350
449. Our Lady of Walsingham 352
450. Our Lady of Aparecida 354

INDEX 357

Foreword

With the publication of this third volume of his widely popular *Question Time* series in which Fr Flader answers questions on almost every conceivable aspect of the Catholic Faith, a writer who is possibly Australia's most prolific contemporary author on things Catholic has now passed a real milestone: he has answered in book form 450 questions on what the Catholic faith means and teaches and the goals Christians naturally strive for as they seek to be faithful, daily disciples of the Risen Christ rather than merely nominal members of a tribe named "Catholic".

However it would be a mistake to describe Fr Flader as merely prolific. In fact, it would be to risk doing him a disservice because, in the end, while quantity may impress, what really counts is the quality of the thing conveyed or produced. In this sense, what is far more important to note, I think, is that Fr Flader's question and answer format columns have become a ministry which has touched lives everywhere – a textbook model of how meticulously researched, precise, patient, rational and reasonable explanations can enlighten readers and, one suspects, for many, open doors in life that had previously seemed shut tight.

Interestingly, the questions in Fr Flader's book are sifted from the even more numerous questions he has answered for readers in recent years but what most people would not know is that while his weekly column began in Sydney's *The Catholic Weekly* it has grown to be so popular that it now appears regularly in Catholic publications across Australia. This says something important. The weekly *Question Time* columns which first began appearing in *The Catholic Weekly* in 2005 clearly struck a note with readers of the 21st Century, much as another Sydney priest's earlier *Radio Replies* did with listeners and readers of the early to mid 20th Century. But whereas Dr Rumble often dealt with Protestant objections to Catholicism so characteristic of one era of Australian history, Fr Flader focuses on the questions which naturally arise in the minds of Catholics and other enquirers in an Australian society vastly different from that of three quarters of a century ago.

It is probably more true now than ever before in the history of this country that the men, women and young people who make up our society are searching for answers to the most important questions of life. Yet while our society, for the time being, appears in many ways to have increasingly cut itself adrift from any deep sense of the presence of God in life, it also decreasingly fails to supply answers to the most basic questions of human existence which the human spirit always seeks.

Father Flader's answers to the questions of faith are therefore invaluable and provide points of reference and certainty which readers know will not suddenly transform or disappear like the constantly changing and dissolving perspectives of postmodern fashionable theories, here today and gone tomorrow. His articles therefore greatly help at least two groups of people I can think of: Catholics who, as a result of their faith, want to know and understand more of the remarkable invitation to life that God offers every one of us and those, not necessarily Catholic, who are searching for truth. And, I hasten to add, they help because they are so interesting. Quite apart from their usefulness for individual reading, Fr Flader's answers would be ideal for use in parish or home-based discussion groups and would also make an excellent gift for a friend or an acquaintance.

In *Question Time 3*, as in the two previous *Question Time* volumes, readers will find four general headings under which a veritable array of questions are answered: Christian doctrine, the sacraments, moral life in Christ and Christian prayer. Under these headings Fr Flader not only enlightens readers about things they will probably not know (such as question 337: Is there time in heaven? Or question 332: Abuses in a papal election), he also faces up to the difficult issues without trying to sidestep them. For a while, the existence of a spirit utterly malignant towards human beings seemed to have slipped off the radar of many in the Catholic Church, but Fr Flader frankly discusses the reality of the devil (question 306) as he does the sexual abuse scandal within the Church (question 412). Then there are those questions which, until recently, may not have arisen in the minds of many but are now increasingly encountered, such as what to think regarding Catholics and halal meat (question 402) or the issue of vaccines derived from aborted foetuses (question 408). Then there are issues many will find merely intriguing such as the morality of tattoos and body piercings (question 405), and whether pets can go to heaven (question 338). In fact, it is difficult to convey adequately the range of this latest volume other than to say that Fr Flader has allowed his pen a very wide scope in the issues it addresses with the sum effect being a book in which it is impossible to flip through the pages without constantly pausing to find out what its author has actually said. And at every turn Fr Flader is able to summarise neatly the issues and convey what the Church believes and why.

As editor of *The Catholic Weekly* I am constantly grateful to be the beneficiary of Fr Flader's scholarship and wisdom which are distilled into his weekly columns and I know our readers are too. I can only commend this latest volume of *Question Time* as an excellent companion for the home, the daily commute to work or for a holiday, and an excellent aid to all those searching for what the Church teaches and why as opposed to what so many believe.

Peter Rosengren
Editor, ***The Catholic Weekly***

Foreword to *Question Time 1*

Contrary to some stereotypes in our society, the life of the Christian is one of constant reflection and questioning. The more we learn about God, the more we read the Bible, the more we puzzle over problems in our daily lives and in our societies which seem to challenge Christian beliefs and Catholic teachings, the more questions we have. Praying and meditating regularly also gives rise to many questions as we ponder God's mercy and love, his promises to us, and the evil and suffering that frequently confront us in our daily lives.

Father John Flader's book *Question Time – 150 Questions and Answers on the Catholic Faith* is a wonderful resource for every Catholic who has ever had questions about the faith or about our life together with God. This book brings together answers from Fr. Flader's popular column in *The Catholic Weekly* and reflects the timelessness and fascination that different questions have for Christians of all ages and across all generations. The ground covered in this book is nothing if not wide ranging. Can we hurt God? What does the Church think about Evolution? Did the children of Adam and Eve commit incest? Is everyone saved? What does infallibility mean? Does limbo exist? What is an indulgence?

Fr. Flader also covers important questions about the life and teaching of Jesus, the sacraments of the Church, the Mass, Mary, and prayer. Moral problems such as suicide, the death penalty, homosexuality, and gambling are also discussed.

Question Time will be a much referenced resource for everyone who uses it. Different questions at different times of the year and at different times in our lives will bring readers back to it again and again. In its succinct and elegant explanations of Catholic teaching and belief, Catholics will find information, encouragement, reassurance, and clarity. They will probably also find some new questions to ask.

Fr. Flader has done us all an enormous service in collating his columns and in bringing them to print in this book. I have enjoyed reading it and learnt much from it and I hope you do too.

+George Cardinal Pell

ARCHBISHOP OF SYDNEY

7 March 2008

Introduction to *Question Time 1*

Soon after beginning to write the *Question Time* column for *The Catholic Weekly*, I began to receive reports of people who were cutting out the columns and pasting them on paper for future reference, or photocopying them for others. Over the years numerous people have asked if there was any plan to publish the columns as a book.

Now that three years have passed, the time has come to satisfy the desires of these people and to publish the first 150 columns.

The questions and answers are arranged systematically by topic, following the general structure of the *Catechism of the Catholic Church*. Chapter 1 deals with matters of Catholic doctrine, Chapter 2 with questions relating to the sacraments and sacramentals, Chapter 3 with matters of moral life in Christ, and Chapter 4 with questions relating to prayer and Christian devotions.

I am indebted especially to Joanne Lucas, who read most of the columns before they were sent to *The Catholic Weekly* and made helpful comments on their style and content. Also to Fr Peter Joseph and Fr Edward Barry, who made valuable suggestions to improve the final draft.

I am also grateful to Anthony Cappello of *Connor Court*, who graciously offered to publish the book.

I pray that *Question Time* will help those who read it to understand their faith better and to come to a deeper love for Jesus Christ, Our Lady and the Church.

Deo omnis gloria!

Fr John Flader

Abbreviations

CCC	*Catechism of the Catholic Church* (1992)
CCL	Pope John Paul II, *Code of Canon Law* (1983)
CDW	Congregation for Divine Worship and the Discipline of the Sacraments
DS	Denzinger-Schönmetzer, *Enchiridion Symbolorum et Definitionum* (1963)
DV	Second Vatican Council, Dogmatic Constitution *Dei Verbum* (1965)
DVitae	Congregation for the Doctrine of the Faith, Instruction *Donum Vitae* (1987)
GIRM	Congregation for Divine Worship, *General Instruction of the Roman Missal* (2012)
HV	Pope Paul VI, Encyclical *Humanae Vitae* (1968)
LG	Second Vatican Council, Dogmatic Constitution on the Church *Lumen Gentium* (1964)
MC	Pope Pius XII, Encyclical *Mystici Corporis* (1943)
PF	Pope Benedict XVI, Apostolic Letter *Porta Fidei* (2012)
PPA	Pope Paul VI, Apostolic Exhortation *Petrum et Paulum Apostolos* (1967)
RS	Congregation for Divine Worship, Instruction *Redemptionis Sacramentum* (2004)
SC	Second Vatican Council, Constitution on the Liturgy *Sacrosanctum Concilium* (1963)
STh	St Thomas Aquinas, *Summa Theologiae*
VD	Pope Benedict XVI, Apostolic Exhortation *Verbum Domini* (2010)

I. CATHOLIC DOCTRINE

God and creation

301 Design in nature

I have recently become interested in the question of intelligent design in nature. That is, whether the universe just happened by chance to be the way it is or whether it had to have been designed by some supremely intelligent being. Can you shed light on this question?

As you imply in your question, there are only two possible answers to the question. Either the universe just happened by chance, or it was given its form by a creator of supreme intelligence, who can only be God. Atheists, of course, subscribe to the view that everything came about by chance.

But if it did come about by chance we would expect to find only chaos, with random motion of bodies each with a random purposeless structure that could not be comprehended and reduced to simple formulas by the human mind. In short, there would be no universal laws of nature that would give rise to sciences like physics and chemistry.

But in fact we find a structured universe with laws, like the law of gravity, that can be formulated mathematically and which are universally valid. This moved Albert Einstein, arguably the one of the greatest minds of the twentieth century, to observe: "The most incomprehensible thing about the universe is that it is comprehensible." He went on to say that he considered this comprehensibility "a miracle" or "an eternal mystery" and it moved him to believe in God: "My religion consists in a humble admiration of the superior unlimited spirit which is revealed in the minimal details which we are able to perceive with our fragile and weak minds. This conviction, deeply emotional, of the presence of a rational superior power which is revealed in the incomprehensible universe, forms my idea of God" (*Letters to Solovine,* New York 1987, p. 131).

One of St Thomas Aquinas' five arguments for the existence of God is based precisely on order or purpose in nature. We see this purpose everywhere, especially in living things. The reproductive, digestive and immune systems of animals, especially man, are a classic example. Here everything works together according to an admirable plan.

Archbishop Michael Sheehan, in his popular *Apologetics and Catholic Doctrine,* explains this argument of St Thomas using the of a camera, which has various parts all working together to produce a photograph. No one would say that the camera put itself together by chance. Yet the human eye is far more complex than a camera. It too must have been put together by an intelligent designer, who can only be God (Baronius Press 2009, pp. 31-33).

Sir Isaac Newton reflects this thinking in his *Opticks,* written in 1721: "How are the bodies of animals to be contrived with so much art, and for what ends were their natural parts? Was the eye contrived without skill in optics, and the ear without knowledge of sounds? ... Does it not appear from phenomena that there is a Being incorporeal, living, intelligent...?"

Another aspect of nature where we see incredible design is the living cell. Microbiologist Michael Denton, in his book *Evolution, a Theory in Crisis,* describes the complexity of even the tiniest of bacterial cells, weighing less than a trillionth of a gram, as "a veritable microminiaturised factory containing thousands of exquisitely designed pieces of intricate molecular machinery, made up altogether of 100 thousand million atoms, far more complicated than any machine built by man and absolutely without parallel in the non-living world". Denton goes on to ask: "Is it really credible that random processes could have constructed a reality, the smallest element of which – a functional protein or gene – is complex beyond our own creative capacities, a reality which is the very antithesis of chance, which excels in every sense anything produced by the intelligence of man?" (Adler and Adler 1986, pp. 249-250)

The very origin of life, its first appearance in the universe billions of years ago, is another clear argument for design. In the early 1980s two non-believers, Sir Frederick Hoyle and Chandra Wickramasinghe, set out to calculate the probability of the first living organism putting itself together by chance in the earth's atmosphere, starting from amino acids. They came up with the infinitessimal probability of one in $10^{40,000}$ – one in ten with forty thousand zeroes after it – and concluded that life could not possibly have arisen by chance. Hoyle famously compared the odds against the spontaneous formation of life with the odds of a tornado blowing through a junkyard producing a 747 jet aircraft (*The Intelligent Universe*, London 1983, p. 19). That led him to admit that life indeed needed a creator, whom he called a "super-intellect" in outer space.

Design can be seen too in the "fine-tuning" of the forces necessary for the very existence of the universe. Eric Metaxas wrote in *The Wall St Journal* December 2014: "The fine-tuning necessary for life to exist on a planet is nothing compared with the fine-tuning required for the universe to exist at all. For example, astrophysicists now know that the values of the four fundamental forces – gravity, the electromagnetic force, and the 'strong' and 'weak' nuclear forces – were determined less than one millionth of a second after the big bang. Alter any one value and the universe could not exist. For instance, if the ratio between the nuclear strong force and the electromagnetic force had been off by the tiniest fraction of the tiniest fraction – by even one part in 100 quadrillion – then no stars could have ever formed at all. Feel free to gulp. Multiply that single parameter by all the other necessary conditions, and the odds against the universe existing are so heart-stoppingly astronomical that the notion that it all 'just happened' defies common sense. It would be like tossing a coin and having it come up heads 10 quintillion times in a row. Really?"

So yes, there is evidence for design everywhere in nature. It was God who put it there.

302 Atheism and science

Now that atheists are so much in the news, claiming that intelligent people, especially scientists, no longer believe in God and that only the unenlightened do, what are we to think? How can we answer them?

First of all, atheists should know, and so should the rest of us, that most of the greatest scientists have believed in God.

Francis Bacon (1561-1626), regarded by many as the father of modern science, taught that God has provided us with two books, the book of nature and the book of the Bible, and he considered that a truly educated person should study both. Mathematician and astronomer Johannes Kepler (1571-1630) shared the same conviction, as did many of the great scientists since the Renaissance.

Among the scientists who believed in God were such luminaries as Nicolaus Copernicus, Blaise Pascal, Robert Boyle, Sir Isaac Newton, Michael Faraday, Gregor Mendel, Louis Pasteur, Lord Kelvin and Charles Darwin. Kepler wrote: "The chief aim of all investigations of the external world should be to discover the rational order which has been imposed on it by God, and which he revealed to us in the language of mathematics."

It was precisely belief in a rational God, who left us a universe that is ordered and can be studied by the human intellect, that provided the foundation for the prodigious scientific advances of the last few centuries. Sir Alfred North Whitehead (1861–1947), British philosopher and mathematician, in answer to the question of how scientific knowledge could have expanded so quickly in the years leading up to Sir Isaac Newton's *Principia Mathematica* in 1700 answered: "Modern science must come from the medieval insistence on the rationality of God."

Albert Einstein, as I wrote in an earlier column (cf. n. 301) saw the order that existed in the universe as a "miracle", "an eternal mystery", since if the universe were the result of chance there should be only chaos. Other eminent twentieth century physicists who believed in God were Max Planck, Werner Heisenberg, Erwin Schrödinger and Paul Dirac. Likewise, Francis Collins, Director of the Human Genome Project, which has succeeded in mapping all the genes in the human body, is a well-known believer.

More recently, philosopher Antony Flew gave as a reason for his conversion to belief in God after 50 years of atheism that the study of DNA has shown, "by the almost unbelievable complexity of the arrangements which are needed to produce life, that intelligence must have been involved."

This does not mean that all scientists and intelligent people believe in God. But it does mean that a large number of the most eminent scientists of all time, right down to the present, have been believers, often moved or at least reinforced in their belief by their own scientific discoveries. In short, belief in God is reasonable. It is not just for the unenlightened and ignorant.

303 Darwin, God and evolution

Reading statements from some scientists, I get the impression that the discoveries of Charles Darwin and his theory of evolution have completely done away with the need for God. Is this the case? Can't we believe in both God and evolution?

Like you, I have read statements of scientists who seem to think that Darwin's *On the Origin of Species*, published in 1859, put the final nail in God's coffin.

We could begin by asking what Charles Darwin himself thought about the matter. If we open his *On the Origin of Species*, we find on the bottom of the title page two quotations, both of which mention God. The first is from William Whewell (1794-1866), a scientist, philosopher and one of the most influential figures in nineteenth-century Britain. The quotation is from his Bridgewater Treatise, officially entitled *Astronomy and General Physics Considered With Reference to Natural Theology, published in Cambridge in 1833*. The quotation reads: "But with regard to the material world, we can at least go so far as this – we can perceive that events are brought about not by insulated interpositions of Divine power, exerted in each particular case, but by the establishment of general laws."

That is, Whewell – and obviously Darwin too – sees that God acts in the universe through the laws of nature he put there. The *Stanford Encyclopedia of Philosophy*, in its entry on Whewell says: "Understanding involves seeing a law as being not an arbitrary 'accident on the cosmic scale,' but as a necessary consequence of the ideas God used in creating the universe. Hence the more we idealize the facts, the more difficult it will be to deny God's existence. We will come to see more and more truths as the intelligible result of intentional design. This view is related to the claim Whewell had earlier made in his Bridgewater Treatise (1833), that the more we study the laws of nature the more convinced we will be in the existence of a Divine Law-giver."

The second quotation is from Francis Bacon's *Advancement of Learning*. Bacon (1561-1626) is regarded by many as the father of modern science. His quotation reads: "To conclude, therefore, let no man out of a weak conceit of sobriety, or an ill-applied moderation, think or maintain, that a man can search too far or be too well studied in the book of God's word, or in the book of God's works: divinity or philosophy; but rather let men endeavour an endless progress or proficience in both." Again, Darwin is encouraging the reader to grow in understanding of God's word and works, found in the Scriptures and in nature. Clearly, in quoting this passage Darwin himself sees no opposition between his discovery of natural selection and the existence of God.

As for Darwin himself, in the second-last paragraph of *On the Origin of Species* he writes: "Authors of the highest eminence seem to be fully satisfied with the view that each species has been independently created. To my mind it accords better with what we know of the laws impressed on matter by the Creator, that the production and extinction of the past and present inhabitants of the world should have been due to secondary causes, like those determining the birth and death of the individual. When I view all beings not as special creations, but as the lineal descendants of some few beings which lived long before the first bed of the Silurian system was deposited, they seem to me to become ennobled."

That is, while Darwin acknowledges that many eminent writers believe that each species was created directly by God, he himself believes that, following the laws written in nature by God, the different species have arisen by gradual evolution from other species created by God, and that this in fact ennobles them.

Clearly, Darwin believes in both God and evolution. Pope Benedict XVI expressed a similar view. In a conversation with priests on 24 July 2007 he rejected the idea that "those who believe in the Creator would not be able to conceive of evolution, and those who instead support evolution would have to exclude God. This antithesis is absurd because, on the one hand, there are so many scientific proofs in favour of evolution which appears to be a reality we can see and which enriches our knowledge of life and being as such" (cf. J. Flader, *Question Time 1,* q. 6).

So, in conclusion, God is not dead. We can believe in both God and evolution.

304 God and natural disasters

In conversations with my friends about recent floods, cyclones, bush fires and earthquakes, I have found myself defending God against the charge that he is not in control, or that he is not a good God or that he is punishing us for our sins. How should I respond?

We can always begin by explaining that these natural disasters have been part of human history from the beginning. They are simply consequences of the natural structure of the planet that God made. Added to this is original sin, which is described in the book of Genesis as having an effect even on nature, with thorns and thistles making life harder for man (cf. *Gen* 3:18). St Paul describes nature as "subjected to futility" and "groaning in travail" (cf. *Rom* 8:20-22).

These disasters are sometimes called "acts of God", as if God brought them about in order to punish us. We should never think like this, even though some people are quite happy to accept that natural disasters are a just punishment for the sinful ways of their society. Certainly we have to make up for our sins at some stage of our life, either here or in Purgatory, but it is simplistic to attribute a natural disaster to God as a punishment. There are instances in the Scriptures of God sending disasters to punish the people, especially in the Old Testament, but these are always exceptional. They include the flood at the time of Noah (cf. *Gen* 6:5-7:24) and the destruction of Sodom and Gomorrah (cf. *Gen* 19:24-25).

But is God not in control of nature? God is always in control. He made the universe out of nothing and he holds it in being at every instant. His fatherly providence extends to the birds of the air and the lilies of the field (cf. *Mt* 6:26, 28), even to the hairs on our head (cf. *Mt* 10:30). Then why does he allow these disasters and other evils? The *Catechism of the Catholic Church* answers that "with infinite wisdom and goodness God freely willed to create a world 'in a state of journeying' towards its ultimate perfection. In God's plan this process of becoming involves the appearance of certain beings and the disappearance of others, the existence of the more perfect alongside the less perfect, both constructive and destructive forces of nature" (*CCC* 310).

Looking at it in another way, God is a true father who does not want to control every aspect of the life of his children. He allows us to fall and hurt ourselves, to suffer in various ways. Suffering has been part of human existence since the original sin of our first parents. God allows natural disasters to happen because, in his infinite wisdom, he knows that they can serve his purpose of bringing souls to eternal life. Out of evil God brings good: "We know that in everything God works for good with those who love him" (*Rom* 8:28).

Indeed, much good comes out of the immense suffering involved in natural disasters. People are led to realise how fragile their life is, how uncertain their days on earth, and they are often moved to repent of their sins and draw closer to God in trustful prayer. Also, when they see that many families have lost loved ones and property, they are moved to overlook the petty grievances they harboured in their own families and to cling more tightly to each other.

In natural disasters, people are moved to pray more and to attend Mass for those who are suffering, and this contributes immensely to their own sanctification. Then too, thousands of people put themselves out as volunteers to help in the aftermath of a tragedy, and many more donate money, clothes, blankets or food. These disasters bring out the very best in everyone and they unite nations and communities in solidarity with each other. And of course God is always there beside those who suffer, comforting them (cf. *Mt* 11:28) and taking some to eternal life with him.

But God's part in the drama of suffering will always remain a mystery, beyond our ability to comprehend fully. In the words of the Catechism, "We firmly believe that God is master of the world and of its history. But the ways of his providence are often unknown to us. Only at the end, when our partial knowledge ceases, when we see God 'face to face', will we fully know the ways by which – even through the dramas of evil and sin – God has guided his creation to that definitive Sabbath rest for which he created heaven and earth" (*CCC* 314).

305 The fall of the angels

Why did some of the angels fall and become devils when they were created in heaven and were so close to God? Also, why didn't they have the opportunity to repent and be saved as we do?

To situate the questions in context we recall that our first parents were tempted by the devil in the form of a serpent (cf. *Gen* 3:1-7). We know that the devil is a fallen angel, created originally with all the powers and happiness of the other angels, but who for some reason rejected God and remained separated from him forever in hell. The *Catechism of the Catholic Church* says of the serpent: "Scripture and the Church's Tradition see in this being a fallen angel, called 'Satan' or the 'devil.' The Church teaches that Satan was at first a good angel, made by God: 'The devil and the other demons were indeed created naturally good by God, but they became evil by their own doing'" (Lateran Council IV (1215), DS 800; *CCC* 391).

You mention that the devils – or angels at the beginning – were created in heaven and very close to God. Many people think this but it is clear that the angels, while very blessed and close to God, were not in heaven. When a soul is in heaven it is drawn irresistibly to the goodness and love of God and it cannot reject him. It is impossible for any soul in heaven to sin.

The angels at the beginning were given many endowments from God. In the natural sphere they were pure spirits with a very keen mind and a strong free will. By their nature, angels are superior to all other creatures, including humans. In the supernatural sphere they, like Adam and Eve, were given the state of grace, which is a sharing in the divine life and the divine nature. They were indeed very close to God, even though they were not in heaven. They knew God and were able to love him with a knowledge and love more perfect than ours. And of course they were called to eternal life with God in heaven.

Then why did some of the angels reject God? The answer can only be pride. Some of the Fathers of the Church apply to the devil God's words to a wayward Israel: "For long ago you broke your yoke and burst your bonds; and you said, 'I will not serve'" (*Jer* 2:20). Even though created with such a superior nature, some of the angels did not want to serve anyone, not even the God who had made them and blessed them so much. John Milton, in his *Paradise Lost*, has the devil say: "Better to reign in hell, than serve in heaven" (I, 263).

The Catechism teaches: "This 'fall' consists in the free choice of these created spirits, who radically and irrevocably *rejected* God and his reign. We find a reflection of that rebellion in the tempter's words to our first parents: 'You will be like God'" (*Gen* 3:5; *CCC* 392). The devils too wanted to be like God and were cast forever into hell. St Peter writes: "God did not spare the angels when they sinned, but cast them into hell and committed them to pits of deepest darkness to be kept until the judgment" (*2 Pet* 2:4). Our Lord himself, speaking of those who in the last judgment will be damned, says: "Depart from me, you cursed, into the eternal fire prepared for the devil and his angels" (*Mt* 25:41). Those who don't believe in hell should remind themselves of these words. The devil believes in hell! He exists and is in hell, so there must be a hell, at least for the devils.

But why weren't the devils given a second chance, or many chances, as we are? The answer lies in the superior understanding of the angels' mind. They understood perfectly from the outset the consequences of their choice, were they to reject God. They knew they had only one opportunity and that their choice was irrevocable. The Catechism says, quoting St John Damascene: "It is the *irrevocable* character of their choice, and not a defect in the infinite divine mercy, that makes the angels' sin unforgivable. 'There is no repentance for the angels after their fall, just as there is no repentance for men after death'" (*De Fide orth.* 2, 4; *CCC* 393).

In conclusion, we should strive to be ever more humble and happy to serve God, who himself came to serve and not to be served (cf. *Mt* 20:28).

306 The devil

Recently our family saw a frightening film involving an exorcism and my son has been disturbed ever since. He wants to know what sorts of things the devil can do and what he can do to feel more protected.

The first thing to be aware of is that the devil is real. He is not just a way of speaking about the presence of evil in the world. He is a fallen angel who is allowed by God to tempt us.

We see the activity of the devil at the very beginning of the Bible, where he appears in the form of a serpent and tempts Adam and Eve. He appears throughout the Old Testament, amongst other passages in the Book of Job, where he is allowed to inflict various forms of suffering on Job, including the loss of his children and property and even his health (cf. *Job* 1:6-2:7). The devil is mentioned numerous times in the New Testament as well, including his tempting Jesus at the end of his fasting in the desert (cf. *Mt* 4:1-11). And of course Jesus casts devils out of numerous people.

So we should be under no illusions. The devil is real. The *Catechism of the Catholic Church,* commenting on the phrase in the Our Father "deliver us from evil" says: "In this petition, evil is not an abstraction, but refers to a person, Satan, the Evil One, the angel who opposes God. The devil (*dia-bolos*) is the one who 'throws himself across' God's plan and his work of salvation accomplished in Christ" (*CCC* 2851).

Pope Francis spoke about the devil in his homily on 11 October 2013. With reference to the Gospel passage where Jesus casts out a devil and someone claims that he did it by the power of Beelzebul (cf. *Lk* 11:15-26), the Pope said: "Jesus casts out demons and then someone offers explanations to diminish the power of the Lord... There are some priests who, when they read this Gospel passage, this and others, say: But, Jesus healed a person with a mental illness... It is true that at that time, they could confuse epilepsy with demonic possession; but it is also true that there was the devil! And we do not have the right to simplify the matter, as if to say: All of these (people) were not possessed; they were mentally ill. No! The presence of the devil is on the first page of the Bible, and the Bible ends as well with the presence of the devil, with the victory of God over the devil."

What forms of diabolical activity are there? The most common form is temptation to sin. We see it in the temptations of Adam and Eve and of Christ. While we cannot say that every temptation is the direct work of the devil, it is true that the devil "goes about like a roaring lion, seeking whom he may devour" (*1 Pet* 5:8). And since he is "a liar and the father of lies" (*Jn* 8:44), his temptations are often very cunning and difficult to see for what they are. Only when we give in to them do we discover the deceit. One of his greatest victories is to convince so many people that he doesn't exist!

A more serious form of demonic activity is what is often called diabolical oppression, or obsession. Here the person experiences a very strong urge to do something damaging to their spiritual or physical health, like drinking alcohol to excess, using drugs, looking at pornography, indulging in sexual fantasies or acts... Other forms of oppression include strong and lasting feelings of anger, bitterness, jealousy, hatred, desire of revenge, etc.

The most serious form of diabolical activity is possession. Here the person has done something to let Satan into their life and the devil controls at least their lower powers. St Mark describes the case of the Gerasene man possessed by many devils, who had superhuman strength so that no one could bind him, even with chains, and who was always crying out and bruising himself with stones (cf. *Mk* 5:1-13). These cases can be particularly frightening and often an exorcism is the only way to free the person.

In the face of this diabolical activity, we should not be afraid. After all, Christ overcame the power of Satan by his death on the Cross. The devil cannot harm us if we do not welcome him into our life. We can say the prayer to the Guardian Angel and the Prayer to St Michael the Archangel and entrust ourselves to the protection of Our Lady, Queen of the Angels and Help of Christians. And of course we should be careful not to let young children see films that might disturb them.

307 Pope Francis and the devil

Pope Francis is regarded by some as a theological "liberal", yet I understand he has spoken out publicly about the devil, something not often done by "liberals". What has he said?

Pope Francis, who by the way is not a theological "liberal", has spoken numerous times about the devil. The day after his election on 13 March 2013 he said, "When one does not profess Jesus Christ – I recall the phrase of Leon Bloy – 'Whoever does not pray to God, prays to the devil.'"

The following day he said, "Let us never give in to pessimism, to that bitterness that the devil tempts us with every day." Pope Francis is indeed the eternal optimist, constantly inviting the Church to live out the joy that Christ wants us to have: "These things I have spoken to you, that my joy may be in you, and that your joy may be full" (cf.

Jn 15:11). But he knows that whereas Christ wants us to be happy, and we will be happy when we are close to God – "Rejoice in the Lord always" (*Phil* 4:4) – the devil wants to take us away from God and he tempts us to sadness, to pessimism.

Then in his homily for Palm Sunday that year, referring to problems that can appear insurmountable, the Pope said: "In this moment the enemy, the devil, comes, often disguised as an angel, and slyly speaks his word to us. Do not listen to him!"

Perhaps the most significant reference to the devil in the first months of his pontificate came on 5 July 2013, when he consecrated the Vatican City State to St Michael the Archangel. He was joined by his predecessor, Emeritus Pope Benedict XVI, for the ceremony in the Vatican gardens, where he blessed a statue of St Michael the Archangel. In his address he said: "Michael – which means 'Who is like God' – is the champion of the primacy of God, of his transcendence and power. Michael struggles to restore divine justice and defends the People of God from his enemies, above all from the enemy *par excellence*, the devil. And St Michael wins because in him there is the God who acts. This sculpture reminds us then that evil is overcome, the accuser is unmasked, his head crushed, because salvation was accomplished once and for all in the blood of Christ. Though the devil always tries to disfigure the face of the Archangel and that of humanity, God is stronger, it is his victory and his salvation that is offered to all men. We are not alone on the journey or in the trials of life; we are accompanied and supported by the angels of God, who offer, so to speak, their wings to help us overcome so many dangers, in order to fly high compared to those realities that can weigh down our lives or drag us down. In consecrating Vatican City State to St Michael the Archangel, I ask him to defend us from the evil one and banish him."

Then in the homily in his morning Mass on 11 October 2013 Pope Francis again referred to the devil: "Jesus came to destroy the devil, to give us the freedom from the enslavement the devil has over us. And this is not exaggerating. On this point, there are no nuances. There is a battle and a battle where salvation is at play, eternal salvation; eternal salvation of us all. There is criterion for watchfulness. We must always be on guard, on guard against deceit, against the seduction of evil." Pope Francis called on the faithful to guard their hearts, feelings and the presence of the Holy Spirit and not to "let go, feeling secure, believing that all is going well". He added that "if you do not guard yourself, he who is stronger than you will come. But if someone stronger comes and overcomes, he takes away the weapons in which one trusted, and he shall divide the spoil. Vigilance!"

So it is clear that Pope Francis regards the devil as a real enemy both of the Church and of individual souls. His appeal to watchfulness echoes that of St Peter: "Be sober, be watchful. Your adversary the devil prowls around like a roaring lion, seeking someone to devour" (*1 Pet* 5:8). We do well to heed this advice.

Sacred Scripture

308 The unity of the Scriptures

I know we Catholics accept the Old Testament along with the New Testament and we read it in Mass, but I tend to look on it as somehow outdated and not very relevant to Christianity. Is there really any relationship between the two Testaments?

We should not look on the Old Testament as merely the Scripture of the Jews, as if it had nothing to do with Christ and the New Testament. It has everything to do with Christ and so is extremely relevant for us Christians. Along with the New Testament it really forms one book.

To begin with, we should remember that both the Old and the New Testaments have one and the same author, God himself. The Second Vatican Council teaches that both Testaments "have God as their author, and have been handed on as such to the Church herself" (*Dei Verbum*, 11).

Naturally, the books had different human authors – Moses, David, Solomon, Matthew, Luke, Paul, etc. – but the individual writers put down in writing only what God wanted them to write. The Second Vatican Council explains it like this: "To compose the sacred books, God chose certain men who, all the while he employed them in this task, made full use of their powers and faculties so that, though he acted in them and by them, it was as true authors that they consigned to writing whatever he wanted written, and no more" (*DV* 11). We see here how God used the faculties of the various writers in such a way that, while they were true authors, God himself remained the principal author of the whole of Scripture.

But the unity between the two Testaments goes beyond their divine authorship. There is a unity in the very content of all the Scriptures that transcends the variety of writers and the times in which they were written. The principal source of this unity is the fact that the whole Old Testament, while relating historical facts and passing on the teachings of the Jews, is ultimately about Jesus.

For example, Our Lord himself went back to the Old Testament to explain to the two disciples of Emmaus how these writings were really about him: "And beginning with Moses and all the prophets, he interpreted to them in all the Scriptures the things concerning himself" (*Lk* 24:27). Later that same day in the Upper Room, in the presence of these two disciples and the other apostles, he again did this, adding the psalms: "'These are my words which I spoke to you, while I was still with you, that everything written about me in the law of Moses and the prophets and the psalms must be fulfilled.' Then he opened their minds to understand the Scriptures, and said to them, 'Thus it is written, that the Christ should suffer and on the third day rise from the dead...'" (*Lk* 24:44-46).

Jesus had also said to the Jews, "You search the Scriptures, because you think that in them you have eternal life; and it is they that bear witness to me" (*Jn* 5:39). The Scriptures, of course, are the writings of the Old Testament.

The *Roman Catechism,* issued after the Council of Trent, sums it up: "And indeed the Prophets, whose minds were illuminated with light from above, foretold the birth of the Son of God, the wondrous works which he wrought while on earth, his doctrine, character, life, death, Resurrection, and the other mysterious circumstances regarding him, and all these they announced to the people as graphically as if they were passing before their eyes. With the exception that one has reference to the future and the other to the past, we can discover no difference between the predictions of the Prophets and the preaching of the Apostles, between the faith of the ancient Patriarchs and that of Christians" (Part I, Art. II, n. 2).

In 1920 Pope Benedict XV wrote in his Encyclical *Spiritus Paraclitus*: "Toward Christ, as toward their centre, all the pages of both Testaments converge." And Pope Benedict XVI said that the Scriptures of both Testaments "are seen in their entirety as the one word of God addressed to us. This makes it clear that the person of Christ gives unity to all the 'Scriptures' in relation to the one 'Word'" (Apost. Exh. *Verbum Domini*, 39).

St Augustine writes of the unity of the two Testaments in the familiar words: "The New Testament lies hidden in the Old and the Old Testament is unveiled in the New" (*Quaest. In Hept.* 2, 73).

Perhaps the most succinct statement of the unity of the whole Bible comes from Hugh of St Victor: "All divine Scripture is one book, and this one book is Christ, speaks of Christ and finds its fulfilment in Christ" (*De Arca Noe*, 2, 8). So yes, the Old Testament is very relevant to us Christians.

309 The interpretation of Scripture

Occasionally in our Bible study group we disagree on the interpretation of certain passages of Scripture, even though we are all Catholics. Does the Church have an official interpretation of the Bible, or at least of the difficult passages? If so, where would we find it?

The interpretation of the Bible has been a vexing question since the beginning of the Church. There have always been disagreements about the interpretation of certain passages, some of them quite legitimate. But some passages admit of only one interpretation that is consistent with the teaching of the Church.

In the early centuries the Fathers of the Church and other writers began to write extensive commentaries on the Scriptures. While there were naturally some differences of opinion about the meaning of certain passages, overall there was widespread agreement. These commentaries came to form part of what today we call the living Tradition of the Church. On one hand they reflected what the early

Church as a whole already believed and practised, and at the same time they helped to form the thinking and practice of the Church. Just as the Holy Spirit inspired the writing of the Scriptures, so the same Spirit was working to guide the formation of this living Tradition.

In this way the interpretation of the Fathers came to be accepted by the later Magisterium of the Church as a sure norm of authentic interpretation. For example, the Council of Trent prohibited interpreting the Scriptures "contrary to the unanimous agreement of the Fathers" (*DS* 786), and Pope Leo XIII wrote in his encyclical *Providentissimus Deus* (1893): "The Fathers have supreme authority whenever they all explain in one and the same way any passage in the Bible as pertaining to the teaching of faith or morals" (*DS* 1944).

Since the Scriptures were written within the Church, they can only be interpreted correctly within the faith of the Church. Thus Pope Benedict XVI wrote in his Apostolic Exhortation *Verbum Domini* (2010): "Saint Jerome recalls that we can never read Scripture simply on our own. We come up against too many closed doors and we slip too easily into error. The Bible was written by the People of God for the People of God, under the inspiration of the Holy Spirit. Only in this communion with the People of God can we truly enter as a 'we' into the heart of the truth that God himself wishes to convey to us" (n. 30).

Since the Church has based her teaching on the Scriptures and on the early Tradition that interpreted the Scriptures, any interpretation today should always be consistent with the teachings of the Church and never contrary to those teachings. Where do we find these teachings? A very accessible source is the *Index of Citations* at the back of the *Catechism of the Catholic Church*. The Index lists the thousands of scriptural passages cited in the Catechism, from *Genesis* to *Revelation*, with all the paragraphs in the Catechism which quote those passages. In them we see how the Church bases her teaching solidly on Scripture and in so doing gives an authentic interpretation and application of those texts. Any interpretation we are inclined to make of a given text can thus be compared with the Church's own teaching to see if it is consistent.

In addition to the teachings found in the Catechism, which was first published in English in 1994, the more recent writings and addresses of Pope John Paul II and his successors have made frequent use of Scripture, thus offering a further interpretation of those texts.

Apart from her general teaching based on Scripture, the Church may also give an authentic interpretation of a particular text in answer to a question or controversy, although this is less frequent. For example, the Council of Trent defined that the words of Christ "This is my body" affirmed the Real Presence of Christ in the Eucharist (cf. *DS* 874) and that the words of *James* 5:14 ff. promulgate the sacrament of the Anointing of the Sick (cf. *DS* 908).

The Church sometimes gives authentic interpretations of passages of Scripture through the Pontifical Biblical Commission, established by Pope Leo XIII in 1902. Over the years, the Commission has published 36 statements, often to answer questions of interpretation.

In short, we should always ensure that our interpretation is consistent with Church teaching. In some cases it is possible that different interpretations may be equally consistent with those teachings and hence equally valid.

310 Who wrote Genesis?

In a recent Bible study group someone asked who wrote the book of Genesis and when? Someone thought Moses wrote it but she unsure. Can you help us?

Rather than ask who wrote Genesis, we should ask who wrote all five first books of the Bible, known as the Pentateuch, since it seems they have a common origin and form a unity. Those books are Genesis, Exodus, Leviticus, Numbers and Deuteronomy.

The *Navarre Bible* on the Pentateuch says there was a strong tradition that it was indeed Moses who wrote the books. For one thing, they were called the "Law of Moses" in the Bible itself. For example, the book of Joshua says, "as it is written in the book of the law of Moses," and it goes on to say that Joshua "wrote upon the stones a copy of the law of Moses, which he had written" (*Josh* 8:31-32; cf. *Josh* 23:6; *Neh* 8:1-8).

This was the tradition at the time of Our Lord too. Philip says to Nathanael, "We have found him of whom Moses in the law and also the prophets wrote…" (*Jn* 1:45). St Paul too seems to accept Moses as the author of the Pentateuch: "Moses writes that the man who practises the righteousness which is based on the law shall live by it" (*Rom* 10:5; cf. *Lev* 18:5). We see here the great authority the five books of the Pentateuch had at that time as the word of God written by Moses.

Nonetheless, from very early times biblical writers were aware that the Pentateuch as we now know it dates from the time of the return from exile in Babylon in the sixth century BC. For example, St Jerome explains that the account of Moses' death (cf. *Deut* 34:1-12) and phrases such as "to this day" used in the book of Genesis (cf. *Gen* 26:33; 35:20) were written by Ezra when he copied out the Law of Moses after returning from Babylon (cf. *De Perpetua Virginitate B. Mariae*, 7).

In more recent times, beginning in the eighteenth century, the sources of the Pentateuch have been the subject of much research. It seems clear that the final edition of the books used materials from many different periods, some of them very old, which were rearranged and rewritten by the inspired writers. They reveal a core teaching which was particularly meaningful to the Jews after their experience of the exile – that Israel is God's chosen people and that they have received the gift of the Law from God and they must be faithful to it if they are to remain as a people and dwell in the promised land.

According to the Navarre commentary, we have no reliable information as to what form this material took prior to its being incorporated into the final version of the Pentateuch, or what the history of this material was. But there is good reason to suppose that ancient traditions about the patriarchs, Moses and the years in the desert, and the conquest of the promised land under Joshua were all collected and expanded in various ways at periods of greater religious and cultural activity among the Jewish people.

Scripture scholars identify at least four different traditions that fed into the final version of the Pentateuch. A first tradition seems to come from the northern kingdom, which fell to the Assyrians in the ninth century BC. Since God is referred to by the name Elohim in this tradition, it is called the Elohist tradition and is identified by the letter E.

A second tradition comes in the seventh century BC under Kings Hezekiah and Josiah, when there were profound religious changes which helped towards a new understanding of the past and brought a literary revival, with the writing of the books of Joshua, Judges, Samuel and Kings. This account is described as the Deuteronomic (D) because it included part of Deuteronomy as an introduction to the history narrated in those books.

A third tradition, known as the Yahwist and identified by the letter J from the German *Jahwist*, involved narrative cycles of the great events from the origin of the world to the entry into the promised land.

And a fourth tradition, known as the Priestly (P) seems to have originated during the Babylonian exile in the sixth century BC, when the priests kept up the people's faith by reminding them of the traditions of their ancestors.

So the authorship of the Pentateuch is not at all clear, even though it is often attributed to Moses. What matters is that we show great respect for the inspired origin of these important books, even if we are not sure exactly who wrote them and when.

311 Is Genesis a myth?

I have occasionally heard it said, even from teachers, that the first chapters of Genesis are just a myth or legend. I always thought we were supposed to regard the account of the creation of the world and of Adam and Eve as real. Who is right?

This is indeed a frequently asked question. Common sense and a little understanding of science already tell us that Genesis cannot be just a myth. After all, the world had to begin somehow – it was not always there with the marvellous order and harmony we see in it. Scientists, mathematicians and philosophers are coming to the conclusion that the universe had a beginning in time – that it could not always have existed (cf. R. Spitzer, *New Proofs for the Existence of God*, Eerdmanns 2010).

And human beings had to begin somewhere too. Somewhere, somehow there had to be a first pair of human beings from whom all of us are descended, since the human family is clearly one (cf. J. Flader, *Question Time 1*, q. 4). So, is Genesis just a myth? No it isn't. The Pontifical Biblical Commission, established by Pope Leo XIII in 1902, has issued several statements on the matter. On 30 June 1909, the Commission issued a long statement replying to various questions on the historical character of the first three chapters Genesis. In answer to the first question it stated that the various exegetical systems defended under the guise of science to exclude the literal historical sense of those chapters do not rest on a solid foundation. That is, in principle one cannot reject the literal historical sense.

The Commission went on to answer "in the negative" to the question of whether it may be taught that "the aforesaid three chapters of Genesis contain not accounts of actual events, accounts, that is, which correspond to objective reality and historical truth, but either fables derived from the mythologies and cosmogonies of ancient peoples and accommodated by the sacred writer to monotheistic doctrine after the expurgation of any polytheistic error; or allegories and symbols without any foundation in objective reality proposed under the form of history to inculcate religious and philosophical truths; or finally legends in part historical and in part fictitious freely composed with a view to instruction and edification." So out go the fables, symbols and legends.

It answered "in the negative" too to the question of whether the literal historical sense may be called in doubt in particular as regards facts "which touch the foundations of the Christian religion", including "the creation of all things by God in the beginning of time; the special creation of man; the formation of the first woman from the first man; the unity of the human race; the original felicity of our first parents in the state of justice, integrity, and immortality; the command given by God to man to test his obedience; the transgression of the divine command at the instigation of the devil under the form of a serpent; the degradation of our first parents from that primeval state of innocence; and the promise of a future Redeemer."

Nonetheless, the Commission stated that "each and every word and phrase" need not be understood in the literal sense when it is obvious that a "metaphorical or anthropological" sense is intended, and that certain passages may be interpreted in an "allegorical and prophetic sense."

Likewise, as regards the six days of creation, the Hebrew word for day, *Yom*, "may be taken either in the literal sense for the natural day or in an applied sense for a certain space of time."

A later declaration of the Commission on the historicity of the first eleven chapters of Genesis came in the form of a letter to Cardinal Suhard of Paris dated 16 January 1948. It began by saying that the question of the literary forms of these chapters is obscure and complex, and that it is agreed that they are not "history in the classical and modern sense". Rather, "they relate in simple and figurative language, adapted to the understanding of mankind at a lower stage of development, the fundamental truths underlying the divine scheme of salvation, as well as a popular description of the origins of the human race and of the chosen people."

Returning to your question, while there is some uncertainty regarding the exact interpretation of the text and of its literary genres, the first chapters of Genesis do fall into the general category of history, and therefore they cannot on any account be called "myth" or "legend".

312 Apocryphal books of the Bible

I have often heard people speak of the "apocrypha" or "apocryphal books" of the Bible. What exactly are they?

The word "apocrypha" is a plural Greek word meaning "hidden away". It is used in different ways by different people.

For example, Protestant Christians use the term to refer to books of the Bible which they do not regard as divinely inspired, but which are accepted by the Catholic Church as part of the canon, or list, of inspired books. These are mainly books of the Old Testament, but there are some New Testament books which Protestants regard as apocryphal as well.

Catholics, on the other hand, use the term to refer to ancient works not included in Catholic Bibles nor in the Jewish scriptures, works such as the Book of Enoch, the Testament of the Twelve Patriarchs, the Assumption of Moses and the Fourth Book of Ezra. Catholics also regard some writings from New Testament times as apocryphal, among them such spurious works as the Gospels of Peter and Thomas, the Acts of Andrew and the Apocalypse of Mary.

There is an interesting history to the differences regarding which books of the Old Testament are to be regarded as the inspired word of God. The differences involve not only Catholics and Protestants, but also Jews. At the time of Our Lord, the Jews had no precisely defined canon of inspired writings. There were some books which were accepted by all, namely those written in Hebrew before the second century before Christ. These included the first five books of the Bible, known as the Pentateuch, the books of Joshua, Judges, Samuel, Kings, Psalms, the prophets, and many others.

But there were other books of more recent origin, mostly from the second and first centuries before Christ, which were held in high esteem but were not yet officially accepted as part of the scriptures. Some had been written in Hebrew and Aramaic, and others in Greek. They included the books of Tobit, Judith, Wisdom, Sirach (Ecclesiasticus), Baruch, 1 and 2 Maccabees and parts of Esther and Daniel. In the Catholic tradition they are called "deuterocanonical" to distinguish them from the "protocanonical" books of the original Jewish canon. Protestants would call them apocryphal.

These more recent works were included in a Greek translation of the Old Testament known as the Septuagint, a Latin word meaning 70, because it was begun by 72 educated Jews in Alexandria during the reign of Ptolemy II in the third century BC. This version was used primarily by Greek-speaking Jews outside Palestine. It was not universally accepted by Palestinian Jews of the Pharisaic tradition. As regards its use in the Church, as the number of Greek-speaking Christians increased, the Greek Septuagint scriptures came into general use and they were used in the apostolic preaching.

Towards the end of the first century AD, the Jews met at Jamnia to decide on their canon, moved in part by the growing controversies with Christians, who used the Septuagint version. They decided to accept only the earlier books written up to the time of Ezra. Although the decision was not binding on the Church, it did lead some Christian writers to have doubts about the extra books which had come into general use. Among them was St Jerome, who nonetheless included them in his Latin translation of the Bible, known as the Vulgate.

At the end of the fourth century and the beginning of the fifth, councils were held at Hippo and Carthage in North Africa which accepted the longer Septuagint canon. Finally, in 1546 the Council of Trent issued a decree declaring that all the books contained in the Latin Vulgate Bible were to be accepted as sacred and canonical.

In the sixteenth century Protestants also took issue with some New Testament writings which had been accepted by the Catholic Church since the fourth century. They included Hebrews, James, 2 Peter, 3 John, Jude and Revelation. There were various reasons for questioning these books, among them the fact that some of them clearly supported the Catholic position where it differed from the Protestant. The King James version includes all the books of the Catholic New Testament but not the deuterocanonical books of the Old Testament.

313 Who wrote the Gospel of Matthew?

I am a confused Scripture teacher. Having taught that Matthew the Apostle wrote the first Gospel, I find in a new Bible that "It is generally accepted by scholars today that the author of the first Gospel was not the Apostle Matthew ... but a second generation Christian..." Who is right? And was the Gospel written in Greek around 85 AD as this Bible says?

Your question reminds me of those "consolation" questions Groucho Marx used to ask on his quiz show when the contestant failed to answer the prescribed questions. He would ask, for example, "Who was buried in Grant's tomb?" or "Who wrote Beethoven's Ninth Symphony?" Who wrote Matthew's Gospel? Sounds familiar. Also, we have to be careful not to let the opinions of "scholars" or theologians become a "parallel magisterium", which is given the same authority as the official teachings of the Church. But returning to your question, there is ample evidence that it was indeed the apostle Matthew who wrote the first Gospel, that he wrote in Aramaic, not Greek, and that he wrote it much earlier than 85 AD.

As regards the authorship, Christian tradition unanimously attributes the first Gospel to Matthew. Virtually all the ancient manuscripts that preserve the title of the work have some form of the words "according to Matthew". Among the Fathers of the Church and other writers, St Irenaeus, Origen, St John Chrysostom, St Jerome and St Augustine all say that Matthew wrote the Gospel.

On 19 June 1911 the Pontifical Biblical Commission (PBC), with the approval of Pope St Pius X, affirmed that Matthew was indeed the author of the first Gospel: "In view of the universal and constant agreement of the Church, as shown by the testimony of the Fathers, the inscription of Gospel codices, most ancient versions of the Sacred Books and lists handed down by the Holy Fathers, ecclesiastical writers, Popes and Councils, and finally by liturgical usage in the Eastern and Western Church, it may and should be held that Matthew, an Apostle of Christ, is really the author of the Gospel that goes by his name" (n. I).

As regards the language, according to the historian Eusebius (*Church History* III.39.16), the early Christian Papias said that Matthew composed the sayings of Jesus in the Hebrew language. Eusebius (*Church History* V.10.3) also says that in India Pantaenus found the Gospel according to Matthew written in the Hebrew language, where St Bartholomew had left it. And he says (*Church History* VI.25.3-4) that Origen in his first book on the Gospel of Matthew states that he had learned from tradition that the first Gospel was written by Matthew, who composed it in Hebrew for the converts from Judaism. St Jerome too repeatedly declared that Matthew wrote his Gospel in Hebrew (*Ad Damasum,* xx, *Ad Hedib.* iv), as did St Cyril of Jerusalem, St Gregory of Nazianzus, St Epiphanius, St John Chrysostom, St Augustine and others. When they say Hebrew it is understood to mean the Hebrew spoken in Israel at the time of Christ, which we know today as Aramaic. In spite of the certainty that Matthew wrote in

Aramaic, there are unfortunately no surviving copies of that version, and only the Greek translation remains. In this regard the PBC, in the same declaration, affirmed: "The belief that Matthew preceded the other Evangelists in writing, and that the first Gospel was written in the native language of the Jews then in Palestine, is to be considered as based on Tradition" (n. II).

As for when Matthew wrote his Gospel, it is most likely that he did so in the 50s or 60s of the first century. There are two main reasons for saying this. First, Matthew records Jesus' prophecy that Jerusalem would fall, with the burning of the city (cf. *Mt* 22:7) and the destruction of the Temple (cf. *Mt* 24:2). Jerusalem and the Temple were destroyed in the year 70, but there is no mention of it in the Gospel. Also, Matthew refers seven times to the opposition of the Sadducees to Christ and the disciples, but the Sadducees ceased to be a force with the destruction of Jerusalem by the Romans in the year 70. In this regard the PBC declared: "The preparation of this original text was not deferred until after the destruction of Jerusalem, so that the prophecies it contains about this might be written after the event; nor is the alleged uncertain and much disputed testimony of Irenaeus (*Advers. haeres.*, lib. III, cap. I, n. 2), convincing enough to do away with the opinion most conformed to Tradition, that their preparation was finished even before the coming of Paul to Rome" (n. III).

So yes, Matthew wrote his Gospel and he did so in Aramaic long before the year 85.

314 The historicity of the Gospels

I have heard people say that what we read in the Gospels isn't always true, for example that Jesus didn't necessarily do all the miracles the Gospels say he did. Frankly, this disturbs me. Is it true?

Let us begin by establishing a few basic truths about the Bible. The first one is that the Bible is the inspired word of God. It is not a human work written by some wise, or not so wise, men many years ago to pass on their ideas about Jesus, or Moses or Adam for that matter.

The Second Vatican Council, in the Dogmatic Constitution on Divine Revelation *Dei Verbum*, teaches: "The divinely revealed realities, which are contained and presented in the text of sacred Scripture, have been written down under the inspiration of the Holy Spirit. For Holy Mother Church relying on the faith of the apostolic age, accepts as sacred and canonical the books of the Old and the New Testaments, whole and entire, with all their parts, on the grounds that, written under the inspiration of the Holy Spirit (cf. *Jn* 20:31; *2 Tim* 3:16; *2 Pet* 1:19-21; 3:15-16), they have God as their author, and have been handed on as such to the Church herself" (*DV* 11).

Secondly, if God is the author, the Bible cannot contain errors. God is Truth. He can neither deceive nor be deceived. He would certainly not have allowed the Church to accept the books of the Bible as a norm of faith if these books contained errors. The Second Vatican Council says as much: "Since, therefore, all that the inspired authors, or sacred writers, affirm should be regarded as affirmed by the Holy Spirit, we must acknowledge that the books of Scripture, firmly, faithfully and without error, teach that truth which God, for the sake of our salvation, wished to see confided to the sacred Scriptures" (*DV* 11). In 2010 Pope Benedict cited this text in his Apostolic Exhortation *Verbum Domini* (n. 19).

Many centuries before, the Fathers of the Church had been just as clear. St Jerome, for example, wrote: "The Scripture cannot lie" (*In Jer.* 31, 55). And St John Chrysostom: "When you see someone who, moved by his own reasoning, dares to contradict Holy Scripture, treat him like a crazy man" (*In Gen. 1 hom.*, 10, 6). Naturally, in interpreting the Scriptures it is first necessary to determine the mind of the sacred writer and to study the different literary forms or genres they used. In this regard the Council teaches: "In determining the intention of the sacred writers, attention must be paid, *inter alia*, to literary forms for the fact is that truth is differently presented and expressed in the various types of historical writing, in prophetical and poetical texts, and in other forms of literary expression" (*DV* 12).

It is clear that some parts of the Bible use forms such as allegory, poetry, prayer, etc., and therefore they do not pretend to be history, which narrates events which actually happened. As regards the Gospels, some have maintained that rather than being strictly history, they reflect the faith of the early Christian community or the imagination of the writer.

To address this issue the Pontifical Biblical Commission, with the approval of Pope Paul VI, issued an Instruction on "The Historicity of the Gospels" on 21 April 1964. The Instruction stated, among other things, "The work of exegetes is all the more necessary today because many writings in circulation question the truth of the events and sayings reported in the Gospels." It goes on to say that "the Gospels were written under the inspiration of the Holy Spirit, who preserved their authors from every error."

A year later, the Second Vatican Council in the Dogmatic Constitution *Dei Verbum* stated categorically: "Holy Mother Church has firmly and with absolute constancy maintained and continues to maintain, that the four Gospels just named, whose historicity she unhesitatingly affirms, faithfully hand on what Jesus, the Son of God, while he lived among men, really did and taught for their eternal salvation, until the day when he was taken up" (*DV* 19). These teachings shore up our faith in everything reported in the Gospels. They confirm that Jesus did in fact do and say everything he is reported to have said and done.

And on the basis of this teaching we can judge those who today presume to challenge some of the facts related in the Gospels: that Jesus didn't really do this or that miracle, that he wasn't really born in a stable, that he didn't really rise from the dead, etc.

Jesus Christ

315 Jesus' humanity

I remember reading in a Catholic publication that Jesus was not born in the usual manner but miraculously passed through Mary's body. Was that so?

The answer depends on what was meant by "miraculously passed through Mary's body". In one sense it is true and in another false.

I will begin with the false explanation. This would suppose that Mary did not actually conceive Jesus in her womb and carry him for nine months, but rather suddenly found herself carrying a child. This was the belief of early Gnostics like Valentin and Apelles, who taught that Jesus had descended from heaven and passed through Mary without receiving anything from her, "just as the water flows through a canal" (Epiphanius, *Haer.* 31, 4). This is clearly false. It calls into question the very humanity of Jesus. We say that Jesus is "true God and true man" because he was conceived by Mary his mother, he received his body from her and he was carried in her womb for nine months until he was ready to be born on Christmas day. He is truly man.

Refuting the Gnostic ideas, St Athanasius wrote: "Gabriel announced the good news to Mary with all clarity: he did not say simply: 'what is born in you', in case it might be thought that the body had been introduced into her from outside; he said: 'what is born of you', so that it would be accepted that what she gave birth to, came from her in the natural way" (*Lett. to Epictetus,* 5-9). Two of the Gospels give the genealogy of Christ to show that he was true man, with an ancestry like that of any other. Matthew traces Jesus' family tree beginning with Abraham (cf. *Mt* 1:1-16) and Luke begins with Jesus and traces his ancestry back to Adam (cf. *Lk* 3:23-38).

The other explanation presupposes that Jesus was conceived in his mother's womb and grew there in the natural way, but when he came to be born he passed out of Mary's body in a miraculous way. This is true. I dealt with it in an earlier column on Mary's perpetual virginity (cf. J. Flader, *Question Time 1*, q. 34). What was miraculous was that Mary, who was a virgin, gave birth to Jesus without rupturing her bodily integrity. The *Catechism of the Catholic Church* explains it like this, quoting the Second Vatican Council's Dogmatic Constitution *Lumen Gentium*: "The deepening of faith in the virginal motherhood led the Church to confess Mary's real and perpetual virginity even in the act of giving birth to the Son of God made man. In fact, Christ's birth 'did not diminish his mother's virginal integrity but sanctified it'" (*LG* 57; *CCC* 499). The Fathers of the Church compared this mystery to the rays of the sun passing through glass without breaking it, Christ emerging from the sealed tomb without removing the stone, etc.

The reality of Christ's true humanity is of fundamental importance for our faith. The Catechism gives four reasons why the Word, the second person of the Blessed Trinity, became man.

The first is "in order to save us by reconciling us with God, who 'loved us and sent his Son to be the expiation for our sins'" (*1 Jn* 4:10; *CCC* 457). The Fathers of the Church teach, in different ways, that only by assuming human nature into his divine person could Jesus redeem us in our humanity. He only redeemed what he assumed. St Paul says as much, emphasising Christ's humanity: "For there is one God, and there is one mediator between God and men, the man Christ Jesus, who gave himself as a ransom for all" (*1 Tim* 2:5). In his letter to the Romans, he relates Adam's sin to Christ's redemptive obedience: "For as by one man's disobedience many were made sinners, so by one man's obedience many will be made righteous" (*Rom* 5:19).

The second reason why the word became flesh is "so that all might know God's love: 'In this the love of God was made manifest among us, that God sent his only Son into the world, so that we might live through him'" (*1 Jn* 4:9; *CCC* 458). Because Jesus was truly man, he could reveal in a tangible way how much God loves us. Through him the love of God was made visible.

The third reason is "to be our model of holiness" (*CCC* 459). Jesus is perfect man and so he can teach us by example how we ought to live in order to be the saints God wants us to be. In Jesus sanctity is not just a concept; it is a person. "Learn from me", he can rightfully say (*Mt* 11:29).

And finally "The Word became flesh to make us 'partakers of the divine nature'" (*2 Pet* 1:4). By assuming our humanity into his divine person, Jesus made us sharers in his own divinity.

For all these reasons we give thanks to Almighty God for the gift of his Son Jesus, true God and true man, on that first Christmas.

316 The birth of Christ

I have three questions on the birth of Christ. Why do we say he was born in a stable when the Bible doesn't make any mention of this? What are swaddling clothes? And what exactly was the sign announced by the angel of a child wrapped in swaddling clothes lying in a manger?

The birth of Christ has a number of extraordinary aspects and your questions touch on some of these. The first is that the Son of God, the King of Kings, was born in such humble surroundings. Surely God in the flesh should have been born in a palace, a castle, or at least a dignified inn. And he should have been laid in a bed or a cot, not in a manger, a feeding trough for animals.

But God's ways are not man's ways, and God clearly wanted it to be that way in order to teach us something. From the humble circumstances of Christ's birth we learn, in the words of the *Catechism of the Catholic Church*, that "To become a child in relation to God is the condition for entering the kingdom. For this, we must humble ourselves and become little" (*CCC* 526). And from the poverty of the stable we learn that the possession of material wealth, with all its associated comforts, is not as important as the possession of God. Mary and Joseph, while poor in the material sense, were truly rich in having the very Son of God, the King of Kings, in their family.

Returning to your questions, why does Christian tradition, and even the Catechism, say that "Jesus was born in a humble stable" (*CCC* 525) when nowhere in the Scriptures do we find any explicit mention of it? Indeed, St Matthew limits himself to saying that "Jesus was born in Bethlehem of Judea" and, significantly, when he tells of the arrival of the magi he says that "going into the house they saw the child with Mary his mother" (*Mt* 2:1, 10). The reference to a house can be explained by the possibility that after the birth in a stable, Mary and Joseph were finally able to find a house in which they lived at least until the presentation of Jesus in the Temple of Jerusalem forty days after his birth. St Luke doesn't mention a stable either but he does say that after Jesus' birth Mary wrapped him in swaddling cloths "and laid him in a manger, because there was no place for them in the inn" (*Lk* 2:7). Since a manger is a feeding trough for animals it has always been assumed that Jesus was born in some sort of stable.

Pope Benedict XVI, in his book *Jesus of Nazareth – The Infancy Narratives*, comments on the significance of the manger: "The manger is the place where animals find their food. But now, lying in the manger, is he who called himself the true bread come down from heaven, the true nourishment that we need in order to be fully ourselves. This is the food that gives us true life, eternal life. Thus the manger becomes a reference to the table of God, to which we are invited so as to receive the bread of God" (p. 68). We might add that the name Bethlehem means precisely "house of bread".

But why do we associate the birth of Christ with the actual presence of animals, in particular an ox and an ass? Pope Benedict, acknowledging that the Gospel makes no mention of animals, writes: "But prayerful reflection, reading Old and New Testaments in the light of one another, filled this lacuna at a very early stage by pointing to *Is* 1:3: 'The ox knows its owner, and the ass its master's crib; but Israel does not know, my people does not understand" (*ibid.*, p. 69).

And what are swaddling clothes? In ancient times, as often seen in icons of the nativity scene, the newborn child was customarily wrapped round and round with a narrow band of cloth like a mummy. It was thought this would help the limbs to grow straight. Pope Benedict comments: "The child stiffly wrapped in bandages is seen as prefiguring the hour of his death: from the outset, he is the sacrificial victim... The manger, then, was seen as a kind of altar" (*ibid.*, p. 68). The swaddling cloths can be seen too as a reference to Christ's kingship and his descent from King Solomon, the son of King David. Solomon, in the book of Wisdom, writes: "I was nursed with care in swaddling cloths. For no king has had a different beginning of existence; there is for all mankind one entrance into life, and a common departure" (*Wis* 7:4-6).

Finally, why did the angel say to the shepherds, "And this will be a sign for you: you will find a baby wrapped in swaddling cloths and lying in a manger" (*Lk* 2:12). Certainly a baby lying in a manger would be a sign, since this was most uncommon. But since the angel mentioned the swaddling cloths specifically, this too may have been part of the sign.

So there is much symbolism and much to be learned from these simple aspects of Christ's birth in Bethlehem.

317 When was Christ born?

My daughter recently came home from school saying that her teacher said Christ was probably born several years BC, which would mean he was born several years "before Christ". I thought we counted the years from the date of his birth. Who is right?

Actually, your daughter's teacher is more right than you and the calendar are. But let me explain. St Luke says that when Quirinius was governor of Syria the Emperor Caesar Augustus called a census of the whole world and it was this census that made Mary and Joseph journey to Bethlehem where Christ was born (cf. *Lk* 2:1-2).

Pope Benedict XVI, in his book *Jesus of Nazareth – the Infancy Narratives*, before entering into the date of the census offers a very interesting commentary on the relationship between Augustus and Christ. He says that there is an inscription at Priene from the year 9 BC which says that the day of the Emperor's birth "gave the whole world a new aspect. It would have fallen into ruin had not a widespread well-being shone forth through him, the one now born ... Providence, which has ordered all things, filled this man with virtue that he might benefit mankind, sending him as a Saviour *(soter)* both for us and our descendants... The birthday of the god was the beginning of the good tidings that he brought for the world. From his birth, a new reckoning of time must begin" (p. 59).

It is not difficult to see that what was said of the Roman Emperor applies even more appropriately to Jesus. After all, it was Christ, much more than Augustus, who gave the whole world a new aspect, who was filled with virtue that benefitted mankind, who was a true Saviour, whose birth was the beginning of truly good tidings and which should usher in a new reckoning of time, as in fact it did. What is more, in the year 27 BC, three years after Augustus became emperor, the Roman Senate awarded him the title *Augustus*, meaning "worthy of adoration", a title which applies most appropriately to Jesus, the Son of God.

As to the date of the census, Pope Benedict comments that since it took place at the time of King Herod the Great, who died in the year 4 BC, it must have been at least in that year or before. Moreover, since Herod ordered the killing of all male babies beneath the age of two (cf. *Mt* 2:16), Christ could have been born as early as 5 or 6 BC.

Pope Benedict says that there is considerable debate regarding the actual year of the census. The Jewish historian Flavius Josephus says the census took place in the year 6 AD, under the governor Quirinius. He says that Quirinius was only active in Syria and Judea from that year on, although this claim is uncertain. In any case, Quirinius was already in the Emperor's service in Syria around 9 BC. Some scholars point out that the census was a long process, conducted in two distinct phases and spread out over several years, so this could explain the discrepancy. Indeed, St Luke says that "this was the first enrolment" (*Lk* 2:2).

Another attempt at ascertaining the year of Christ's birth starts from the bright star that the magi followed to Jerusalem and then on to Bethlehem (cf. *Mt* 2:1-2). While some writers, including St John Chrysostom (cf. *In Matt. Hom.*, VI, 2), maintain that the star was not something visible to the eye but rather a light in the soul of the magi, others search for the date of an unusually bright celestial phenomenon that would have drawn the magi. Johannes Kepler, who died in 1630, calculated that in the year 7-6 BC there was a conjunction of the planets Jupiter, Saturn and Mars which would have looked like a bright star and could have moved the magi to make their journey to Bethlehem. Likewise, there seems to be a reference in Chinese chronological tables to a bright star that appeared in 4 BC and was visible for a long time. All in all, much uncertainty remains, with most scholars placing the birth of Christ between 6 and 4 BC, with some widening it to between 7 and 2 BC.

The question then remains as to how the calendar used by the whole world today can be so mistaken. This is related to the further question of when it was that the whole world began to use this calendar. It was the monk Dionysius Exiguus, who died in about 550 AD, who gave the year for the birth of Christ on which the calendar is based. Around the year 525 he said Christ had been born on December 25 in the year 1. Naturally, he could easily have been mistaken by a few years when 500 years had passed from the birth of Christ.

So it is a very interesting history and perhaps we shall never know exactly in which year Christ was born.

318 Where was Jesus born?

My aunt and uncle recently returned from the Holy Land and showed us pictures of the Church of the Nativity in Bethlehem. Can we be sure that this is the place where Jesus was born?

As with all matters of this sort, especially those going back more than 2000 years, there will always be a degree of uncertainty, but there is a long-standing tradition that the Church of the Basilica stands over the place where Jesus was born.

We know by the Gospels of Matthew (cf *Mt* 2:1) and Luke (cf. *Lk* 2:4-7) that Jesus was born in Bethlehem of Judea. The Emperor Caesar Augustus had called for a census of the whole world and each person was to be enrolled in the place of his ancestors. Since Joseph was of the house and family of King David, who grew up in Bethlehem (cf. *1 Sam* 16:1), Joseph went there with Mary and it was there that she gave birth to Jesus.

The prophets of the Old Testament had foretold that the Messiah would be born in Bethlehem. We recall the prophecy of Micah: "But you, O Bethlehem Ephrathah, who are little to be among the clans of Judah, from you shall come forth for me one who is to be ruler in Israel, whose origin is from of old, from ancient days" (*Mic* 5:2). For this reason, when the magi asked King Herod where the king of the Jews had been born, the King consulted the leaders of the Jews and they quoted the passage from Micah that he would be born in Bethlehem (cf. *Mt* 2:1-6). It is fascinating that in order to fulfil this prophecy God used a Roman Emperor to call a census at that very time, so that Jesus would be born not in Nazareth, where Mary and Joseph lived, but in Bethlehem.

Returning to your question, what evidence is there that the present Church of the Nativity is on the actual site where Jesus was born? According to several Fathers of the Church, Jesus was born in a cave near Bethlehem. St Justin Martyr, who died in 165 AD, wrote in his *Dialogue with Trypho*: "Joseph took up his quarters in a certain cave near the village; and while they were there Mary brought forth the Christ and placed him in a manger, and here the magi who came from Arabia found him" (Ch. 78).

Later Origen of Alexandria, who died around 254, wrote: "In Bethlehem the cave is pointed out where he was born, and the manger in the cave where he was wrapped in swaddling cloths. And the rumor is in those places, and among foreigners of the Faith, that indeed Jesus was born in this cave who is worshipped and reverenced by the Christians" (*Contra Celsum, 1, 51*).

The present-day Church of the Nativity is believed to be situated over this cave. In the year 135 the Emperor Hadrian is said to have built a temple to Adonis, the Greek god of beauty and desire, on the site of Christ's birth in order to wipe out the memory of this event. In 327 the Emperor Constantine and his mother St Helena commissioned a church over the site of the cave. It was part of a project following the Council of Nicaea in 325 to build churches on the major sites of the life of Christ. The Church of the Holy Sepulchre in Jerusalem (cf. J. Flader, *Question Time 2,* q. 273) and the Church of the Annunciation in Nazareth were also built at this time.

The Constantinian Church of the Nativity was destroyed by fire during a dispute between Jews and Samaritans in the sixth century, but in 565 the Emperor Justinian I replaced it with a new basilica in the same architectural style as the original one. Since then this Church of the Nativity has had numerous additions but it is still on the original site. In a subterranean part of the Church there is a silver fourteen-pointed star embedded in the marble floor marking the traditional site of the birth of Jesus.

The Church of the Nativity is considered to be the oldest continuously operating Christian church in the world. On 29 June 2012 it was declared a World Heritage Site by the United Nations Educational, Scientific and Cultural Organisation (UNESCO). It is within the Palestinian territories, and we pray for a lasting peace between Jews and Palestinians so that these two peoples can live in harmony and so that pilgrims can visit this important site in safety.

319 The circumcision of Christ

As I recall, years ago we celebrated on New Year's Day the feast of the circumcision of Christ. Now we celebrate on that day the feast of Mary, Mother of God. Can you tell me why we celebrated the circumcision and when and why the change was made?

As you say, on January 1 we used to celebrate the feast of the circumcision of Our Lord. This was an appropriate day for the liturgical celebration of this event because a week after the birth every male Jewish child was circumcised and a name was given him. St Luke describes it: "And at the end of eight days, when he was circumcised, he was called Jesus, the name given by the angel before he was conceived in the womb" (*Lk* 2:21).

The circumcision of Christ has an interesting origin and symbolism. It dates back to the time of Abraham, around 1900 BC. The book of Genesis records that when Abraham was ninety-nine years old, God made a covenant with him, promising to multiply his offspring and to give them the land of Canaan for an everlasting possession. At the same time he changed his name from Abram to Abraham (cf. *Gen* 17:1-8). God told him: "This is my covenant, which you shall keep, between me and you and your descendants after you: Every male among you shall be circumcised. You shall be circumcised in the flesh of your foreskins, and it shall be a sign of the covenant between me and you. He that is eight days old among you shall be circumcised... So shall my covenant be in your flesh an everlasting covenant" (*Gen* 17:10-13).

Ever since, as a sign of the covenant, every male child was circumcised on the eighth day after his birth, and this became the means of incorporation into the people of the covenant, just as Baptism is for Christians today. St Paul himself would boast of having been "circumcised on the eighth day, of the people of Israel, of the tribe of Benjamin, a Hebrew born of Hebrews" (*Phil* 3:5). Circumcision distinguished the Jews from the Gentiles, who were peoples of the uncircumcision.

Our Lord's circumcision thus manifests that he is truly man, born of a woman into the Jewish nation, whom he had come to redeem. God had chosen his people of the Old Testament to prepare the way for the Incarnation of his Son, who would be their Messiah, their anointed one, who would free them from their sins and establish a new and definitive covenant with them.

Christ's circumcision also has great symbolic value. It was in his circumcision that he first shed his blood, foreshadowing the piercing of his side by a soldier as he hung on the cross (cf. *Jn* 19:34). It prefigured the water of Baptism through which Christians enter the new Covenant. St Paul writes: "In him also you were circumcised with a circumcision made without hands, by putting off the body of flesh in the circumcision of Christ; and you were buried with him in baptism" (*Col* 2:11-12).

When Christ was circumcised, he was given the name Jesus, which the angel had announced both to Joseph (cf. *Mt* 1:2) and to Mary (cf. *Lk* 1:31). The name Jesus means saviour and so the angel had told Joseph that the child was to be named Jesus "for he will save his people from their sins" (*Mt* 1:21).

The feast of the Circumcision was celebrated on the eighth day after Christmas, and therefore on January 1, from the very early centuries. Christmas began to be celebrated on December 25 from at least the fourth century (cf. J. Flader, *Question Time 1,* q. 141). Since January 1 was the beginning of a new calendar year, the Christian feast had to compete with the pagan festivities celebrated on that day, as it does today. The feast of the Circumcision was celebrated in the Gallican rite from the sixth century and in the Byzantine calendars in the eighth and ninth centuries. The Octave of Christmas was celebrated at the same time, especially in Rome from the seventh century.

Even though the feast was of the Circumcision, the texts of the Mass and Divine Office came to include many references to Our Lady. Until 1960 the Roman calendar celebrated on January 1 the Circumcision and the Octave of the Nativity. In the revised calendar of 1960 January 1 was called simply the Octave of the Nativity. Finally, in the Roman calendar of 1969 the feast became the Solemnity of Mary, the Mother of God, but it is also referred to as the Octave of the Nativity. It is fitting that we celebrate Mary's divine maternity on the octave of Christmas, when we celebrate the birth of the Son of God. The feast of the Holy Name of Jesus is celebrated on January 3.

320 Jesus' "brothers and sisters"

I recently saw a documentary on television in which the presenter, speaking as a matter of fact, said that Our Lady had five children. I know that the Bible speaks of Jesus' "brothers and sisters". Why do we Catholics believe that Jesus was Mary's only child?

As you say, there are several passages in the New Testament that refer to Jesus' brothers and sisters, or simply his brothers or brethren. Let us look at them, so that we cannot be accused of closing our eyes and ignoring them.

St Matthew relates that when Jesus was teaching in the synagogue in "his own country", the people said: "Is this not the carpenter's son? Is not his mother called Mary? And are not his brethren James and Joseph and Simon and Judas? And are not all his sisters with us?" (*Mt* 13:53, 55-56; cf. *Mk* 6:1, 3). It is clear that the people referred to are not merely the brothers or sisters of Jesus in the broad sense in which all his disciples were his brethren, but rather relatives in a more strict sense.

Later, on relating the crucifixion scene, Matthew says that there were many women there, among whom, in addition to Our Lady, was "Mary the mother of James and Joseph" (*Mt* 27:56). It is clear from this that James and Joseph were not Jesus' brothers, but rather the sons of another woman named Mary.

St John sheds further light on the question. Narrating the scene of the crucifixion he says that standing by the cross of Jesus were "his mother, and his mother's sister, Mary the wife of Clopas, and Mary Magdalene" (*Jn* 19:25). It is highly likely that this Mary, the wife of Clopas, is the same Mary who is the mother of James and Joseph. As John tells us, she is also the sister of Mary, the mother of Jesus. This explains why James and Joseph were known as "brothers" or "brethren" of Jesus. They were in fact his cousins or at least close relatives.

While some English translations refer to James and Joseph as Jesus' "brothers", rather than "brethren", it is clear from these passages that they were not his brothers, but rather his cousins. The word "brethren" used by the Revised Standard Version Catholic Edition is thus more appropriate. By the same token, the word "sister" used to describe Mary, the wife of Clopas, in relation to Our Lady may not refer to a blood sister but rather to a sister in the broader sense of kinswoman or relative. In that case, James and Joseph would not have been Jesus' cousins but rather other close relatives. As for Simon and Jude, mentioned by Matthew as being brethren of Jesus, they too would have been relatives. Similarly, the references to Jesus' "sisters" must be understood in this sense.

Summing up, the *Catechism of the Catholic Church* says: "The Church has always understood these passages as not referring to other children of the Virgin Mary. In fact James and Joseph, 'brothers of Jesus', are the sons of another Mary, a disciple of Christ, whom St Matthew significantly calls 'the other Mary' (cf. *Mt* 27:56; 28:1). They are close relations of Jesus, according to an Old Testament expression" (cf. *Gen* 13:8; 14:16; *CCC* 500).

Apart from the scriptural arguments we have just seen, the most powerful reason why the Church teaches that Jesus had no brothers or sisters is sacred Tradition. Many of the early Christians knew Mary and Joseph and Jesus, and they knew and passed on to others that Mary did not have any other children. So from the beginning, the Church believed and taught that Mary was a virgin not only in giving birth to Jesus but also afterwards for the rest of her life. She had no carnal relations with Joseph at any stage and hence no more children. This was fitting, since as many spiritual writers have maintained, it would have been unbecoming for the immaculate womb of Mary, which was the dwelling place of the incarnate Son of God for nine months, to have later borne other children.

Among the Fathers of the Church, the perpetual virginity of Mary was taught by St Ambrose, St Jerome, St Augustine, St Epiphanius and St Basil, to name a few. The latter wrote: "The friends of Christ do not tolerate hearing that the Mother of God ever ceased to be a virgin" (*Hom. in S. Christi generationem*, 5). Following this tradition, the fifth Ecumenical Council, held in Constantinople in 553 AD, gave Mary the title "perpetual virgin", in Greek *Aeiparthenos*. It is a dogma of faith.

321 The "hour" of Jesus

At Cana Jesus tells his mother that his hour has not yet come, and nonetheless he works his first miracle at her intercession. What exactly did he mean by his "hour"?

The "hour" of Jesus appears frequently in the Gospel of John, the first time in the passage you cite at the wedding feast of Cana. When Mary tells Jesus that the wine has run out he answers: "My hour has not yet come" (*Jn* 2:4). Clearly his "hour" does not refer to the manifestation of his divinity in general, since he will manifest it moments later when he works his first miracle, changing water into wine.

The Greek word used for hour in most of these passages is *ora*, which is properly translated as *hour*. Another word Jesus uses is *kairos*, meaning more exactly *time.* For example, Jesus tells his disciples "Go to the feast yourselves; I am not going up to this feast, for my time has not yet fully come" (*Jn* 7:8). Even though he uses a different word, it is clear that his meaning is very similar to that when he spoke to his mother at Cana. Later in that same chapter, St John himself says: "So they sought to arrest him; but no one laid hands on him, because his hour had not yet come" (*Jn* 7:30). The same idea of no one arresting him because his hour had not yet come appears again in the next chapter (cf. *Jn* 8:20).

As his final Passover approaches and after his triumphal entry into Jerusalem on Palm Sunday, Jesus reveals something of the content of his hour when he tells his disciples: "The hour has come for the Son of man to be glorified" (*Jn* 12:23). A few lines later he clarifies it even further: "Now is my soul troubled. And what shall I say? 'Father, save me from this hour'? No, for this purpose I have come to this hour. Father, glorify your name" (*Jn* 12:27-28). So his hour involves his own glorification but at the same time some element of suffering.

Pope John Paul II comments on this passage: "With these words

Jesus reveals the inner drama that is oppressing his soul in view of his approaching sacrifice. He has the possibility of asking the Father that this terrible trial might pass. On the other hand, he does not wish to flee from this painful destiny: 'For this purpose I have come'. He has come to offer the sacrifice that will bring salvation to humanity" (Address, 14 Jan. 1998).

The aspect of suffering is further borne out when Jesus compares his own hour to that of a woman in labour: "When a woman is in labour, she has pain, because her hour has come; but when she is delivered of the child, she no longer remembers the anguish, for joy that a child is born into the world" (*Jn* 16:21). The hour of Jesus too involves pain but also new life. In his long priestly prayer in the Last Supper, Jesus repeats the idea of giving life. He says to the Father: "Father, the hour has come; glorify your Son that the Son may glorify you, since you have given him power over all flesh, to give eternal life to all whom you have given him" (*Jn* 17:1).

What do we glean from all this? That Jesus' hour involves his glorification brought about by his painful death on the cross and his Resurrection, through which he gives eternal life to all mankind. It is the culmination, the fulfilment of the whole purpose of his becoming man: to redeem us by his death and Resurrection. "For this purpose I have come to this hour."

But, paradoxically, Jesus' hour is also the hour of his enemies. He says to the chief priests and captains of the temple when they come to arrest him in the Garden of Gethsemane: "This is your hour, and the power of darkness" (*Lk* 22:53). In this hour, which is so crucial for mankind, the forces of darkness, of evil, of Satan rally together to do battle with God and somehow try to thwart his plan. The *Catechism of the Catholic Church* describes it dramatically: "It is precisely in the Passion, when the mercy of Christ is about to vanquish it, that sin most clearly manifests its violence and its many forms: unbelief, murderous hatred, shunning and mockery by the leaders and the people, Pilate's cowardice and the cruelty of the soldiers, Judas' betrayal – so bitter to Jesus, Peter's denial and the disciples' flight. However, at the very hour of darkness, the hour of the prince of this world, the sacrifice of Christ secretly becomes the source from which the forgiveness of our sins will pour forth inexhaustibly" (*CCC* 1851).

We give thanks to Jesus for going through with his hour to free us from our sins.

322 Veronica and the face of Jesus

I have always been intrigued by the sixth Station of the Cross, Veronica wiping the face of Jesus, which is not found in the Bible. What is the basis for it?

The sixth Station of the traditional fourteen Stations of the Cross involves a woman named Veronica wiping the face of Jesus with a cloth or veil as he carried the cross to Calvary, leaving the image of his face imprinted on the cloth. This is certainly not a matter whose historical authenticity can be verified by documentary evidence, but it does involve a strong tradition of many centuries.

The name Veronica is a Latin rendering of the Greek name Berenice or Beronike, meaning bearer of victory. But popular tradition has attributed its origin to the Latin word *vera,* meaning true, and the Greek word *eikona,* meaning image or icon. Hence the name would mean *true image,* or *true icon,* and it would refer rather to the veil than to the woman who offered the veil to Christ.

Eusebius of Caesarea in his *Historia Ecclesiastica* (vii, 18) gives the name Veronica to the woman whom Christ healed of a flow of blood (*cf. Mt* 9:20), although the tradition in the West identified that woman with Martha of Bethany. The name Veronica appears in a fourth century apocryphal work known as the *Acta Pilati,* or Acts of Pilate.

Several medieval texts mention the name Veronica as associated with the cloth. Among them is an old missal of Augsburg which has a Mass of "Saint Veronica, or the Face of the Lord". Matthew of Westminster speaks of an "effigy of the face of the Lord which is called a Veronica". Gradually people began to mistake this name for the name of a woman. The story of Veronica has become one of the most popular in Christian tradition.

One story has it that Veronica took the veil with the image of Christ's face to Rome, where she used it to cure the illness of Emperor Tiberius, who reigned from 14 to 37 AD. Veronica is supposed to have been in Rome at the time of Saints Peter and Paul and to have died there, bequeathing the image to Pope Clement and his successors.

Saint Veronica was mentioned in the reported visions of Sister Marie of St Peter, a Carmelite nun who lived in Tours, France, and started the devotion to the Holy Face of Jesus. In 1844 Sister Marie reported that in a vision she saw St Veronica wiping away the spittle and mud from the face of Jesus with her veil. She said Jesus told her that he desired devotion to his Holy Face to be fostered in reparation for sacrilege and blasphemy. The devotion to the Holy Face of Jesus was approved by Pope Leo XIII in 1885. Similarly, Blessed Anne Catherine Emmerich, in her account of revelations of the Passion of Our Lord, describes the Veronica episode and identifies the true name of the woman as Seraphia (Ch. 34).

In any case a veil remained in Rome where it was exposed to public veneration. There is historical evidence of the veil in Rome in 1011, when a scribe was identified as keeper of the cloth. Then in 1199 two pilgrims wrote separate accounts of seeing the veil while in Rome. In 1207 the cloth was publicly paraded and displayed by Pope Innocent III, who granted indulgences to anyone who prayed before it. Pope Boniface VIII had it taken to St Peter's Basilica in 1297 and it was displayed during the first Jubilee Year in 1300. For the next two hundred years it was regarded as the most precious of all Christian relics. Today in St Peter's basilica there is a beautiful statue of Veronica holding the cloth.

But where is the veil today? Perhaps the most likely candidate is the Capuchin monastery in the little Italian village of Manoppello. The veil there measures 17 by 24 centimetres and has reddish-brown marks of a bearded, long-haired man with open eyes. It is strikingly similar to the face on the shroud of Turin. It is known to have been in a chapel in St Peter's Basilica until 1608, when it was placed in the Vatican archives. According to the monastery's records, the wife of a soldier sold the veil to a nobleman of Manoppello in 1608 to get her husband out of jail and in 1618 it was placed between two plates of glass and encased in a walnut frame, where it has remained ever since.

Other similar veils, which may be the original or a copy, are venerated in St Peter's Basilica, Genoa, Vienna, Alicante and Jaen in Spain. While we cannot say with certainty that any of these veils was used to wipe the face of Jesus, we always do well to contemplate the face of Christ, as Pope John Paul II often invited us to do.

Our Lady and St Joseph

323 The betrothal of Mary and Joseph

When we say that Mary was "betrothed" to Joseph, what exactly do we mean? Is betrothal the same as engagement today?

Betrothal, as you suggest, was similar to our modern engagement in that it was an agreement between two persons about their future marriage but there were important differences.

In Jewish law and custom at the time of Our Lady and St Joseph, betrothal was much stronger than engagement is today, in that the two persons were regarded as already being legally married although not yet living together. For example, in the book of Deuteronomy a betrothed woman is already considered a wife, to the point where if she slept with another man they were both to be stoned to death, the man "because he violated his neighbour's wife" (*Deut* 22:23-24).

At that time, there were three steps leading up to marriage. *Shiddukin* was the agreement to consider becoming betrothed, *Erusim* (or *kiddushin*, meaning *sanctification*) was the official betrothal, and *Nissu'in* or *Chupah* the actual wedding ceremony. Henry Skryzynski, in his book *The Jewess Mary, Mother of Jesus* (Chevalier, Sydney 1994) describes in detail the marriage customs Our Lady and St Joseph observed. The book is based solidly on Jewish sources and much of what follows is taken from that book (pp. 174-184).

At the time of Our Lady and St Joseph, marriages were usually arranged by the two families, not by the couple themselves. Since it was the custom, or even the rule, that the man should seek out the woman, it would have been Joseph's parents who took the initiative in approaching Joachim and Anne, the parents of Mary. Once the two families agreed and the *Shiddukin* had been concluded, Mary and Joseph were allowed to meet and get to know each other, always in the company of one of their relatives. In any case, since Nazareth was a small town, Mary and Joseph would most likely have known each other beforehand, especially since their parents knew each other.

It was the custom to marry someone from one's own tribe and social class. Joseph was from the tribe of Judah, descended from David through Rehoboam, the son of King Solomon, as we learn from the genealogy given by Matthew (cf. *Mt* 1:7-16). So it is likely that Our Lady was also from that tribe. Some argue that Our Lady may have been from the tribe of Levi since she was related to Elizabeth, who was "of the daughters of Aaron" (*Lk* 1:5) and was married to Zachary, a priest and therefore also of the tribe of Levi, to which Aaron and Moses belonged. In any case both Mary and Joseph had illustrious ancestors. But they were from a modest social class, Joseph being a craftsman or carpenter.

What is more, they would have been close to one another in age. While artists have often depicted Joseph as an old man, perhaps to highlight his chastity in protecting Mary's virginity, it is most unlikely that Joseph was much older than Our Lady. Mary would have been at least twelve and a half, and Joseph probably eighteen to twenty, for this was considered the right age to marry. Skryzynski quotes a Jewish saying that "God curses him who is not married by twenty" (p. 181).

Once Mary agreed to marry Joseph, arrangements were made for the official betrothal, the *Erusim*. For this, Joseph would go to the house of Mary's parents, hand Mary a ring or a small coin and say, "Behold, be you betrothed to me". Then Joseph and his family would give presents to Mary's father, as Abraham had done when he betrothed his son Isaac to Rebekah (cf. *Gen* 24:53).

Mary's father Joachim would prepare a feast, attended by members of both families, and he would bless Mary, that she have many sons. At this time, the heads of both families signed a document known as the *Shitre Erusim*, binding both parties to marry. Among other matters, it stipulated the penalty to be paid if one party defaulted as well as the amount of Mary's dowry.

From this moment on, Mary was officially betrothed to Joseph and at law she was considered his wife, even though she continued living with her parents. For example, she could be released from her bond only by her death or by Joseph divorcing her. For this reason, when Joseph discovered that Mary was carrying a child, he considered divorcing her informally (cf. *Mt* 1:19). Following an old custom, Mary, being a virgin, would not marry Joseph until twelve months had passed. During this time, they would get to know each other more, Mary would prepare her dowry and Joseph would build their house.

324 St Joseph's dilemma

I have often wondered about St Joseph's reaction when he discovered that Our Lady was carrying a child which was not his. What were his options and why did he decide to send Mary away quietly? Could he not have accepted the child as his and proceed with the marriage?

St Matthew relates the events to which you refer: "When his mother Mary had been betrothed to Joseph, before they came together she was found to be with child of the Holy Spirit; and her husband Joseph, being a just man and unwilling to put her to shame, resolved to send her away quietly" (*Mt* 1:18-19).

First of all, it is important to understand the marriage customs of the time. Mary and Joseph were betrothed, meaning they were considered legally married. After the betrothal it was the custom for the bride to continue living with her family for about a year, after which her husband would take her to his home. St Matthew tells us that Our Lady and St Joseph had not yet come to live together, so it was within that first year that Mary came to be with child. Joseph would have become aware of this mystery sometime after Mary returned from helping her kinswoman Elizabeth in the three months leading up to the birth of John the Baptist (cf. *Lk* 1:39-56).

What were his thoughts? While we cannot know for certain because it has not been revealed, we can only imagine that Joseph would have been completely bewildered. On one hand it was obvious that Mary was with child and the child was not his. On the other hand he would not have thought for an instant that Mary had had relations with another man. He knew her too well to think that. She was so pure, so innocent, so holy. Not for nothing does the Second Vatican Council call her "model of the virtues" (*LG* 65). All in all, still not understanding, Joseph would have believed that it was somehow more possible for Mary to have conceived the child without a man than for her to have committed a sin.

We might wonder why Our Lady did not tell Joseph about the origin of the child she was carrying, or why Joseph did not simply ask her. We can only conclude that Mary somehow understood that it was not her role to reveal to Joseph the great mystery of the Incarnation, and that Joseph respected Mary's silence and did not consider it appropriate to ask her.

We can imagine the immense suffering that both of them would have undergone at this time. Joseph suffered, wondering how Our Lady could possibly have conceived this child and also wrestling with what course of action to take. And Our Lady suffered seeing that Joseph was obviously disturbed and bewildered.

What were Joseph's options? One was to accept the child as his own and proceed with the ceremony of the wedding. He could have done this, but he obviously decided against it, perhaps because it would have put him publicly in a false position. People would have assumed that he was the father of the child and he knew he was not.

Another option, which he would not have contemplated for an instant, was to denounce Our Lady for having conceived a child with another man during their betrothal. Since she was already legally his wife, this meant that she would have been considered an adulteress, and the punishment for adultery was stoning to death (cf. *Deut* 22:20-24).

A third option was to divorce her publicly, to give her a writ of dismissal. This was provided for in Jewish law, not only during the betrothal but even after the marriage had been celebrated (cf. *Deut* 24:1-4). But, given the fact that Mary was carrying a child and they had not yet come to live together, it would have dishonoured her in the eyes of all who knew her.

The option Joseph decided upon, not without immense sadness given his great love for Mary, was simply not to proceed with the marriage. "Joseph, being a just man and unwilling to put her to shame, resolved to send her away quietly" (*Mt* 1:19). In this case, Our Lady would not be rejected but rather abandoned by her husband, and it would be Joseph, not Mary, who would be the subject of shame. By this solution, Joseph was accepting that he was still bound by his commitment to Our Lady even though he would not proceed with the marriage. Theologians such as John Saward, René Laurentin and Ignace de la Potterie, basing themselves on St Thomas Aquinas and St Bernard of Clairvaux, give an explanation of Joseph's actions that makes great sense. They say that Joseph was so overwhelmed by the holiness of Mary and by the great mystery of the child of God she was carrying in her womb that he felt unworthy to be her spouse, and decided to release her of any obligation to marry him.

While this was clearly the best of the options in that it protected Mary's reputation, it was still one which wrung Joseph's heart. Not to be able to spend the rest of his life with the woman he loved and who loved him was something which would have been sheer agony for him. We can thus understand his overwhelming relief when the angel appeared to him in a dream and said, "Joseph, son of David, do not fear to take Mary your wife, for that which is conceived in her is of the

Holy Spirit" (*Mt* 1:20-21). Overjoyed, Joseph "did as the angel of the Lord commanded him; he took his wife, but knew her not until she had borne a son; and he called his name Jesus" (*Mt* 1:24-25). By publicly giving him the name Jesus, Joseph was making himself legally the father of Jesus.

Not for nothing does St Matthew call Joseph "a just man". He is a saint for all to imitate, a model of holiness and of so many virtues.

325 St Joseph's flowering staff

Why is it that St Joseph is often depicted holding a flowering staff?

The tradition of depicting St Joseph with a flowering staff, often with a lily, comes from sources that are not historically certain, even though the tradition has received widespread acceptance in Christian art. Probably the earliest such source is the *Protoevangelium of James*, an apocryphal writing of the second century. It is from this work, by the way, that we have the names of Our Lady's parents, Joachim and Anne, and the account of how Anne conceived Mary late in life after many years without being able to bear a child.

According to this work, Joachim and Anne took Our Lady to the temple in Jerusalem when she was three years old to have her raised and educated there along with other girls. When Mary was twelve, the age at which she could no longer remain there, the council of priests asked the high priest Zacharias to pray for guidance as to what was to be done with her. He prayed in the Holy of Holies and an angel revealed to him that Mary should be married to the man whose staff would show some special sign.

They then gathered all the widowers in Judea, each with his staff. The high priest took the staffs into the temple where he prayed, and then went to give them back to the men. None of the staffs showed any special sign until he gave Joseph his staff, from which a dove emerged and came to rest on Joseph's head. The high priest then realised that Joseph had been chosen by God to be Mary's husband.

Another account comes in the Coptic Synaxarium, a calendar of saints' days, for the third day of the month of Kiahk. When Our Lady had been twelve years in the temple of Jerusalem, having entered at three, the priests took counsel to decide who would protect her, taking into account that she was consecrated to God. They called twelve righteous men from the house of David of the tribe of Judah, among them Joseph, and took their staffs and placed them in the sanctuary of the temple. A dove flew down and rested on Joseph's staff and so he was the one chosen by God.

A third version comes in the private revelations of Blessed Anne Catherine Emmerich, a German mystic who died in 1824 and was beatified by Pope John Paul II in 2004. She too says that Mary as a young girl was living in the temple along with other virgins under the care of pious women. When she was fourteen they informed her that she must leave the temple to be married. She answered that she was consecrated to God alone and had no inclination to marry. She went off to pray and heard a voice which consoled her, making it clear that she was to marry.

An elderly priest was carried into the Holy of Holies, where he lit the sacrifice of incense and read some prayers from a roll of parchment. He was in ecstasy and his finger alighted on a passage from the prophet Isaiah which read: "A branch shall arise from the root of Jesse and a flower shall spring from this root" (*Is* 9:1). All the men of the family of David who were unmarried were then called to Jerusalem where they were presented to the Blessed Virgin. The high priest gave each man a branch, which he held during the prayer and sacrifice, after which the branches were placed on an altar before the Holy of Holies to see if any of them flowered. When none of them did the men were told that none of them was to be Mary's husband.

The priests then went back to the register of families and found a record of six brothers from Bethlehem, one of whom, by the name of Joseph, had been absent for a long time. They managed to locate him living near Samaria working for a master carpenter and brought him to Jerusalem. They gave him a branch to hold during the prayers and sacrifice and it blossomed with a white flower like a lily. At the same time a bright light, like the Holy Spirit, descended upon him. The priests knew then that Joseph was the one chosen by God to be the husband of Our Lady. In the presence of her mother, Mary humbly accepted Joseph as her spouse.

Although we cannot be certain about the historical accuracy of these accounts, they do shed light on the tradition of depicting St Joseph with a flowering staff.

326 St Joseph's chastity

I know that Our Lady was always a virgin and that she did not have carnal relations with St Joseph. But what I find hard to understand is how St Joseph could have managed to live complete chastity all the years of his marriage with Our Lady. It seems almost impossible.

I think that anyone who reflects on this matter asks the same question. We know by faith that Mary was always a virgin but we still find it hard to understand how Mary and Joseph could have lived the whole of their married life together in complete continence.

Our Lady was always a virgin, not only before giving birth to Jesus but afterwards as well. She is the "ever virgin" Mary, and her perpetual virginity is a dogma of faith (cf. J. Flader, *Question Time 1,* q. 34). This means that she and St Joseph never had marital relations. They lived in complete continence throughout their married life together. This would have been for as long as 30 years. Since there is no mention of St Joseph in the Gospels when Jesus begins his public life around the age of 30, it seems he had died by then. If, as appears likely, St

Joseph was around 18 or 20 when they married, they could have lived in this way until St Joseph was around 50. How did they manage to live chastity so well?

First, we know that St Joseph had been chosen by God from all eternity for his role, and part of his preparation would have been the granting by God of all the necessary virtues. Just as Our Lady is "model of the virtues", as the Second Vatican Council called her (*LG* 65), so St Joseph, humanly speaking, would have been naturally very virtuous. It is inconceivable that God would have chosen as the legal father of Jesus someone who was, for example, lazy, self-centred, proud, untidy, foul mouthed, gluttonous or lacking in sobriety. Rather, as in the case of Mary, God would have filled St Joseph with virtues in preparation for his important role. Among these virtues was chastity, or self-control in the desires of the flesh. It would have been these virtues in great measure that attracted Our Lady to St Joseph as a future spouse.

Second, God would have given St Joseph all the special graces he needed for his role. God grants everyone all the graces they require for their particular role in life – as parent, teacher, community leader, religious, priest, bishop, pope,… – and we can be certain that he filled St Joseph with all the necessary graces. The words of Our Lord to St Paul remind us of this: "My grace is sufficient for you" (*2 Cor* 12:9). We see this, for example, in St Joseph's complete docility when, on four occasions, God manifests his will to him through an angel in a dream (cf. *Mt* 1:20; 2:13, 2:19, 2:22). St Joseph's immediate response suggests that he had received very special graces. Similarly, God would have given St Joseph special graces to live chastity with Our Lady.

Third, Our Lady's own exceptional virtue, especially her modesty, would have assisted St Joseph immensely. We can understand this very easily. There are some women whose behaviour, dress, conversation, etc., are sensual and seductive, and in their presence men are naturally tempted to unchaste thoughts and desires. But there are others who exude modesty, naturalness, purity in everything. Such was Mary. She was "mother most pure, mother most chaste, mother inviolate, mother undefiled", as we say in the Litany of Loreto. She would have helped anyone who knew her to control their thoughts and desires. We should remember that Our Lady was very beautiful, perhaps the most beautiful woman God ever created. To live with her for thirty years in complete continence can only be explained if Mary was the chaste and modest woman she was.

Fourth, because St Joseph loved Our Lady so much – after all, he preferred to live with her in continence rather than not be married to her at all – he was respectful of all her wishes and decisions. He only wanted her good, what God wanted for her and what she wanted for herself and for Jesus. This required living in complete continence with her, but his immense love enabled him to do this.

Finally, both St Joseph and Our Lady had a great love for God, and this moved them to do God's will in everything, including living in complete continence.

While St Joseph and Our Lady were unique, we can learn much from them in our own struggle to live chastity.

The Church

327 Early Christian symbols

I have inherited a lapel pin with the letters "IHS" on it. I've seen this on priests' vestments and would like to know what it stands for.

In addition to "IHS" there are a number of other symbols which we see commonly and which go back to the early Church. I will take advantage of your question to look here at several of them and then, in another column, I will explain the meaning of other early Christian symbols, some of which are still used today.

IHS is one of the more commonly used Christian monograms. It comes from the first three letters of the name Jesus in Greek: ΙΗΣ. The full name, as written in capitals, is ΙΗΣΟΥΣ. Since the Greek letter Eta, which corresponds to the English "E", when written as a capital is our English "H", some may think this is an "H" where in fact it is the Greek "E". The symbol appears rarely in the Roman catacombs, although it is found in the catacomb of Priscilla in a square chamber known as the Cappella Greca, or Greek Chapel. This catacomb, on the Via Salaria, was used for Christian burials from the late second century through the fourth century.

The IHS was popularised in the fifteenth century by the Franciscan St Bernardine of Siena (d. 1444) as a symbol of peace. In 1541 St Ignatius of Loyola adopted it with three nails below and surrounded by the sun as the seal of the newly founded Society of Jesus. Contrary to popular opinion, the monogram originally stood neither for "Jesus Saviour of Men" (*Iesus Hominum Salvator*) nor for the English "In His Service". Another explanation, which at least has a degree of credibility for its antiquity, is that the letters are an acronym for *In Hoc Signo* from the vision of the Emperor Constantine where he saw the Chi-Rho sign in the heavens with the words *In hoc signo vinces* (In this sign you will conquer). But the most likely explanation is clearly that it stands for "Jesus", and for this reason St Ignatius used it in the seal of the Society of Jesus.

Another early Christian symbol is the Chi-Rho, written as a "P", the Greek letter Rho, with an "X", the Greek letter Chi, superimposed on it. Chi and Rho are the first two letters in the name of Christ in Greek: ΧΡΙΣΤΟΣ (*Christos*). The monogram was used often by the early Christians and it appears frequently in the catacombs. Then in the year 312 AD, the emperor Constantine, not yet a Christian, was about to lead his army in a decisive battle against his rival Maxentius at the Milvian Bridge outside Rome. The winner would command the whole Roman empire. Constantine prayed to the "supreme God" for help and, according to the story, at mid-day he saw a cross of light superimposed on the sun, with the Greek words Τούτω Νίκα, "Conquer by this" (sign). It was later rendered in Latin as *In hoc signo vinces* (In this sign you will conquer). Not only Constantine but the whole army saw the spectacle. That night Christ appeared to Constantine in a dream and told him to make a replica of the sign he had seen, which would be a sure defence in the battle that was to be fought the following day. The emperor ordered the sign to be emblazoned on the shields of his soldiers and they won the battle.

Eusebius of Caesarea (d. 339), the great Christian bishop and historian, writes of the *labarum*, or military standard later used by Constantine: "Now it was made in the following manner. A long spear, overlaid with gold, formed the figure of the cross by means of a transverse bar laid over it. On the top of the whole was fixed a wreath of gold and precious stones; and within this, the symbol of the Saviour's name, two letters indicating the name of Christ by means of its initial characters, the letter P being intersected by X in its centre..." (*Life of Constantine*, 1.31).

From the earliest times the Chi-Rho was often represented with the Greek letters Alpha and Omega (Λ and lower case ω or upper case

Ω) depicted on the left and right within the crossbars of the Chi. They are the first and last letters of the Greek alphabet. They too represent Christ, who says in the book of Revelation, "I am the Alpha and the Omega, the first and the last, the beginning and the end" (*Rev* 22:13). These two letters are often used today in various ways on priestly vestments, altars, chalices, stained glass windows, etc.

So we see how some of the Christian symbols we use today go back to the very first centuries.

328 More early Christian symbols

On the cover of the new English missal are the letters IC XC and NI KA between the bars of a Greek cross. Can you tell me what they mean? Also, what is the meaning of INRI at the top of a crucifix?

Your questions give me the opportunity to explain a number of early Christian symbols which give rise to many questions.

The letters IC XC and NI KA appear on many Greek and Russian icons of Christ and crucifixes. The letters are similar in both the Greek and Slavonic alphabets. IC XC are the abbreviated form of the name Jesus Christ, IC being the first and last letters of Jesus, *Iησους*, and XC the first and last letters of Christ, *Χριστός*. The C is the Greek sigma (Σ), which is sometimes written as an S and sometimes as a crescent moon C. NIKA is a Greek word meaning "conquers". Thus ICXC NIKA is the abbreviated form of "Jesus Christ conquers". When used on a crucifix it has special significance, since Christ conquered sin and Satan precisely through the cross.

The letters INRI at the top of most crucifixes are Latin. They are the first letters of the Latin words *Iesus Nazarenus, Rex Iudaeorum*, Jesus of Nazareth, King of the Jews. We recall how Pilate ordered these words to be placed on the cross over Jesus' head, indicating the charge against him, to be written in Latin, Greek and Hebrew (cf *Jn*

19:19-20). A portion of this plaque can be seen today in the Church of the Holy Cross in Jerusalem, in Rome.

Another early Christian symbol for Christ which is still used today is the fish. What does a fish have to do with Our Lord? Again we go back to the Greek. The Greek name for fish is *ichthus*, or in Greek letters *IXΘYC*. Each of these five letters is the first letter of the words *Iesous Christos Theou Yios Soter,* Jesus Christ God's Son Saviour. Thus very early on, including in the catacombs, a fish was used as a symbol of Christ.

One of the earliest Christian symbols was the anchor. It was often represented with a ring at the top, a cross bar beneath it, and a curved bar at the bottom. With the cross bar it was an obvious symbol of the cross of Christ and it was sometimes represented with one or two fish, another symbol of Christ. The anchor was used instead of the cross, which is found rarely on Christian monuments during the persecution of the Church in the first four centuries.

Given its use in navigation, the anchor was also a symbol of safety or hope amidst the storms of life, especially hope in eternal life. Since Christian hope lies in Christ, it was also a symbol of him. This symbolism has a scriptural basis in the letter to the Hebrews: "... we who have fled for refuge might have strong encouragement to seize the hope set before us. We have this as a sure and steadfast anchor of the soul, a hope that enters into the inner shrine behind the curtain, where Jesus has gone as a forerunner on our behalf..." (*Heb* 6:18-20).

As a symbol of hope in eternal life the anchor was often represented with such expressions as *pax tecum, pax tibi,* or *in pace* (peace with you, peace to you, in peace), indicating the belief that the person buried there was already enjoying heavenly peace. The anchor appears very early in Christian iconography, with one in the catacomb of St Domitilla dating to the end of the first century, and some seventy in the catacomb of Priscilla alone, all before the fourth century. By the fourth century it had disappeared.

A Christian symbol found in the catacombs but which we hardly see today is the peacock. Based on the ancient legend that the flesh of the peacock did not decay, it was a symbol of immortality. It is also associated with the resurrection of Christ, because the peacock sheds its feathers every year and grows new brighter ones. Sometimes the peacock was portrayed drinking from a vase, symbolising the Christian drinking the waters of eternal life. The multitude of "eyes" on the feathers of the beautiful tail could be seen as the eyes of the all-seeing God.

The dove was another common symbol on early Christian tombs, where it was seen as a symbol of the peace and happiness of the soul in heaven. Sometimes it was represented with an olive branch in its beak. This stems from the story of Noah, where when dry land finally appeared after the flood, the dove returned with an olive branch, a symbol of the firm ground of heaven (*Gen* 8:11). Occasionally in early Christian art the dove was also a symbol of the Holy Spirit, as it came to be later and is very common today. We recall that when Christ was baptised the Holy Spirit came down on him in the form of a dove (cf. *Mt* 4:16).

329 Resignation of a Pope

Like everyone else, I was surprised by the sudden resignation of Pope Benedict, whom we had all come to love. This raises many questions. Is this provided for in law? To whom does the Pope submit his resignation? And can the Cardinals elect someone who is not a Cardinal?

We were all surprised by the sudden resignation of Pope Benedict in February 2013. He did so much good for the Church in his almost eight years as Pope, and we were looking forward to many more years.

It is not surprising that as he approached his eighty-sixth birthday, and in declining health and energy, he felt the burden of carrying the weight of the entire Church on his shoulders, with more than a billion faithful in his care and a very demanding daily workload. It is therefore understandable that Pope Benedict felt that he could not do justice to the position and he chose to relinquish it to a younger person. If one looks at the secular world, there is virtually no one anywhere near his age who is still the head of a large organisation, let alone an organisation as large as the Catholic Church.

It is clear that Pope Benedict had considered the possibility of resigning some years before. In 2010 he told the German journalist Peter Seewald that "if a Pope clearly realises that he is no longer physically, psychologically, and spiritually capable of handling the duties of office, then he has a right and, under some circumstances, also an obligation to resign."

To put the resignation in perspective, the *Code of Canon Law* requires all bishops to submit their resignation to the Pope on reaching their seventy-fifth birthday, obviously because at that age it is increasingly difficult for anyone to discharge the duties of his office. Also, and perhaps just as relevant, is the provision that a bishop who, because of illness or some other grave reason, has become unsuited for the fulfilment of his office, is earnestly requested to offer his resignation (cf. Can. 401, §§1 and 2; Can. 411). The same criterion applies to parish priests, who are to submit their resignation to the diocesan bishop on turning seventy-five (cf. Can. 538, §3). In the case of both bishops and parish priests, their resignation need not be accepted by the higher authority (cf. Can. 401, Can. 538, §3).

Even though the Pope is elected for life and does not need to submit his resignation, the *Code of Canon Law* mentions this possibility: "Should it happen that the Roman Pontiff resigns from his office, it is required for validity that the resignation be freely made and properly manifested, but it is not necessary that it be accepted by anyone" (Can. 332, §2). The last phrase about the resignation not needing to be accepted simply acknowledges the fact that, since the Pope has no lawful superior in the Church, there is no higher authority to whom he can submit his resignation and who can accept or refuse it. In this case, Pope Benedict announced his resignation in a meeting of Cardinals. Once the Pope has freely and publicly manifested his intention to resign, his resignation takes effect automatically at the time he determines.

We are of course not used to a Pope resigning, the last one to do so being over 600 years ago, but it is possible that now that Pope Benedict has resigned, other Popes may choose to do the same when they feel that they are no longer capable of carrying out the duties of the office satisfactorily.

Can the Cardinals elect as Pope someone who is not a Cardinal? While in modern times this has not happened, there is no reason why it could not happen, since there is no requirement in Canon Law that the person elected Pope be a Cardinal. There is nonetheless a longstanding tradition to this effect, going back to the Roman Synod of 769, which decided that the Pope was to be elected from among the Cardinal bishops, priests and deacons of Rome and the surrounding dioceses (cf. J. Flader, *Question Time 2,* q. 173). Even today, all the Cardinals of the world are assigned to a Roman parish so they would all fulfil this condition.

The *Code of Canon Law* envisions the possibility that the one chosen to be Pope is not even a bishop, in which case he is to be ordained a bishop immediately (cf. Can. 332 §1). It should be remembered that those to be named Cardinals need not be bishops, in which case they are to be ordained bishops (cf. Can. 351, §1). So there may be a Cardinal in the conclave who is not yet a bishop and he could be elected Pope.

How about the election of someone who is not in the conclave? This too is possible, especially if the one elected is a Cardinal who was not able to attend the conclave due to illness or for some other grave reason. Indeed, the norms for papal elections promulgated by Pope

John Paul II in 1996 envision the possibility that the newly elected Pope does not reside in Vatican City and also that he is not already a bishop (cf. *Universi Dominici Gregis*, 90).

In any case, it is all up to the Holy Spirit and so in every conclave, where the Cardinals gather to elect the next Pope, we pray very much for the Cardinal electors and for the next Pope, whoever he may be.

330 The election of a Pope

I have been talking with friends about the election of the new Pope and we have some questions. Who decides when the conclave will begin? Can the elected person refuse to accept? And at what moment does he become Pope: with the election or with his inauguration?

Many people have been asking questions like yours, so it is good to be able to answer them. The answers, by the way, are based on Pope John Paul II's Apostolic Constitution *Universi Dominici Gregis*, issued in 1996 and amended in some matters by Pope Benedict XVI.

When the Apostolic See becomes vacant by either the death or the resignation of the Pope, the government of the Church, including the election of the new Pope, is entrusted to the College of Cardinals (n. 2). The more important matters are dealt with in what are called General Congregations, which all the Cardinals who are not legitimately impeded must attend. Cardinals over the age of eighty who cannot vote in the election may attend these Congregations but they are not required to do so (n. 7). The General Congregation is to meet every day until the conclave begins (n. 11). Matters of lesser importance are handled by a Particular Congregation, consisting of only four Cardinals (n. 8).

Pope John Paul II determined that the conclave is not to begin before fifteen days after the See becomes vacant, to allow all the Cardinals to be present. But in any case the conclave must begin by the twentieth day (n. 37). On 25 February 2013, Pope Benedict XVI issued an Apostolic Letter *Normas nonnullas* allowing an election to begin before fifteen days have elapsed, provided all the Cardinal electors are present. It is understood that any Cardinals eligible to take part in the election who have indicated, for a good reason, that they will not be attending do not need to be present. It is up to the General Congregation to decide on which day the election will begin.

Can the person elected Pope decline the election? Given the enormous burden of responsibility before God and the Church that being Pope entails, it would be perfectly understandable if the person elected were reluctant to assume the office. It is known that some of the Popes have felt this reluctance, among them Pope Benedict XVI. But at the same time the person elected would have enough supernatural outlook to acknowledge that his election is an expression of the will of God, and for this reason he would normally accept the election.

In this regard Pope John Paul II's Apostolic Constitution reads: "I also ask the one who is elected not to refuse, for fear of its weight, the office to which he has been called, but to submit humbly to the design of the divine will. God who imposes the burden will sustain him with his hand, so that he will be able to bear it. In conferring the heavy task upon him, God will also help him to accomplish it and, in giving him the dignity, he will grant him the strength not to be overwhelmed by the weight of his office" (n. 86). Naturally, this does not bind the one elected to accept the office. He can still refuse, but it would be most unlikely for him to do so.

And as regards when the person elected becomes Pope, the answer is immediately. Pope John Paul II declared: "After his acceptance, the person elected, if he has already received episcopal ordination, is immediately Bishop of the Church of Rome, true Pope and Head of the College of Bishops. He thus acquires and can exercise full and supreme power over the universal Church" (n. 88). His inauguration will take place some days later but from the moment he accepts the election he already has all the powers of the Pope and he can exercise those powers. What is more, within an appropriate time after his inauguration the Pope is to take possession of the Patriarchal Archbasilica of the Lateran (cf. n. 92). The Lateran Basilica, consecrated in 324 AD, is the Pope's cathedral church as Bishop of Rome.

Finally, when the Apostolic See is vacant the prayer for the Pope in Mass is not said, but the whole Church "spiritually united with Mary, the Mother of Jesus, should persevere with one heart in prayer; thus the election of the new Pope will not be something unconnected with the People of God and concerning the College of electors alone, but will be in a certain sense an act of the whole Church" (n. 84).

331 What happens in a conclave?

Now that Pope Benedict has resigned and the cardinals will elect a new Pope, I have always been intrigued by exactly what happens in a conclave and how it works. Can you enlighten me?

The document that determines what happens when the Apostolic See becomes vacant and a new Pope is to be elected is the Apostolic Constitution *Universi Dominici Gregis,* issued by Pope John Paul II on 22 February 1996. By the way, the word *conclave,* meaning literally "with key", refers to the gathering of the Cardinal electors in the Vatican to elect a new Pope, where they are so to speak "locked away."

Which Cardinals may vote for a new Pope? The Constitution determines that only those beneath the age of eighty when the See becomes vacant may vote, and there should be no more than 120 of these. The voting itself is done in the Sistine Chapel, which is presided over by Michelangelo's well-known fresco of the Last Judgment. It is a sombre reminder that the Cardinals will one day be held to account for all their actions, in this case for their choice of a shepherd for the universal Church.

Whereas in earlier conclaves the Cardinals resided in the area of the Sistine Chapel itself throughout the days of the conclave, they now live in the more comfortable Domus Sanctae Marthae, or House of St Martha, built in 1996 on the edge of Vatican City. All other guests must leave during the conclave so that the Cardinal electors have complete privacy. Even the shutters on the windows are locked for this purpose and the Cardinals have no contact with the outside world. The Cardinals are taken back and forth to the Sistine Chapel by bus during the conclave, although some Cardinals in the last conclave preferred to walk, scrutinised by Vatican security staff.

Like the Cardinals themselves, the cooking and cleaning staff and the others who assist the Cardinals take an oath of silence, promising "absolute and perpetual secrecy" regarding anything related to the election. They also "promise and swear to refrain from using any audio or video equipment capable of recording anything which takes place during the period of the election within Vatican City" (n. 48).

On the morning the conclave begins, the Cardinal electors take part in a solemn Mass *for the election of the Pope* in St Peter's Basilica. That afternoon they chant the *Veni Creator*, a hymn to the Holy Spirit, in the Pauline Chapel of the Apostolic Palace and then process to the Sistine Chapel, which has been checked beforehand to ensure that no audiovisual equipment has been secretly installed to record or transmit the proceedings. There they take the oath to observe all the prescriptions of the Apostolic Constitution *Universi dominici Gregis*, including that of perpetual secrecy regarding the election, and they attend a meditation preached by an ecclesiastic.

That afternoon, one ballot may be held. On the following days there are two ballots in the morning and two in the afternoon until someone is elected by a two-thirds majority. Before depositing their written ballots in the box placed on the altar each Cardinal says aloud, "I call as my witness Christ the Lord who will be my judge, that my vote is given to the one who before God I think should be elected"

(n. 66). After the ballots have been counted and recorded they are burned.

If after three days no one has been elected, there is a pause for prayer and informal discussion for no more than one day, and then the voting resumes for another seven ballots, when there is another pause, and so on successively until someone is elected (cf. n. 75). If no one is elected after four such series of ballots, in subsequent ballots the Cardinals vote on only the two names who received the largest number of votes in the previous ballot until one of them has a two thirds majority, as Pope Benedict XVI determined in a *Motu proprio* in 2007. At this point they send white smoke up the chimney to announce to the world that a new Pope has been elected.

The newly elected Pope is then asked whether he accepts the election and by what name he wishes to be called. The other Cardinals come up and make an act of homage and obedience to him, and together they make an act of thanksgiving. After this the new Pope goes to the balcony of St Peter's Basilica, where the senior Cardinal Deacon announces to the people that the election has taken place and he proclaims the name of the new Pope, who gives the Apostolic Blessing.

Until then, "the universal Church, spiritually united with Mary, the Mother of Jesus, should persevere with one heart in prayer" (n. 84) for the Cardinals who are to elect the Pope and for the new Pope himself.

332 Abuses in a papal election

In recent days we have read about possible deals among the Cardinals regarding the election of the new pope; for example, that they will choose someone from a particular country provided he agrees to choose as Secretary of State someone from another country. Is this possible?

Once again, journalists can sometimes present as fact what are only rumours, or even exaggerate matters and give them a twist they never had in reality. As you say, there have been news reports of Cardinals talking about electing a Cardinal from a particular non-European country provided he agrees to choose as his Secretary of State someone from a particular European country. Likewise, there were reports of Cardinals agreeing to commit the newly elected Pope, whoever he may be, to agree never to resign.

All such reports should be regarded as without foundation. While some Cardinals may indeed think in this way, Pope John Paul II's Apostolic Constitution *Universi Dominici Gregis* which sets out the norms to be observed when the Apostolic See becomes vacant, positively forbids any such agreements. The Constitution states clearly: "I likewise forbid the Cardinals before the election to enter into any stipulations, committing themselves of common accord to a certain course of action should one of them be elevated to the Pontificate. These promises too, should any in fact be made, even under oath, I also declare null and void" (n. 82). Thus, if for any reason a Cardinal should agree to do something once elected, such a promise would be null and void and he would be under no obligation to fulfil it. That being the case, all Cardinals would be aware of the foolishness of entering into such an agreement in the first place.

The next paragraph of the Constitution is in a similar vein, forbidding taking human motives into consideration in the election of a Pope: "With the same insistence shown by my Predecessors, I earnestly exhort the Cardinal electors not to allow themselves to be guided, in choosing the Pope, by friendship or aversion, or to be influenced by favour or personal relationships towards anyone, or to be constrained by the interference of persons in authority or by pressure groups, by the suggestions of the mass media, or by force, fear or the pursuit of popularity. Rather, having before their eyes solely the glory of God and the good of the Church, and having prayed for divine assistance, they shall give their vote to the person, even outside the College of Cardinals, who in their judgment is most suited to govern the universal Church in a fruitful and beneficial way" (n. 83).

What is paramount in the choice of a Pope, as this paragraph makes clear, is the glory of God and the good of the Church. The Cardinals, before entering the conclave, pray for divine assistance in the Mass "for the election of a Pope" in St Peter's Basilica in the morning, and in the chanting of the *Veni Creator Spiritus* while they process into the Sistine Chapel in the afternoon.

Even on putting their ballot into the box on the altar in the Sistine Chapel, each Cardinal says aloud, by way of an oath, "I call as my witness Christ the Lord who will be my judge, that my vote is given to the one who before God I think should be elected" (n. 66). He then places the ballot on a plate, with which he drops it into the box, bows to the altar and returns to his place. It should be remembered that the altar in the Sistine Chapel is just in front of Michelangelo's large fresco of the Last Judgment, a powerful reminder of the seriousness of what is involved in the election of a Pope and of the fact that each Cardinal will render an account to God for his actions.

As paragraph 83 makes clear, the Cardinals do not need to choose one of their own number as Pope. Rather, "they shall give their vote to the person, even outside the College of Cardinals, who in their judgment is most suited to govern the universal Church in a fruitful and beneficial way."

As regards rumours of possible deals and commitments, they can only be speculation, since the Cardinals and all others involved in the meetings before the conclave, known as General Congregations, "are forbidden to reveal to any other person, directly or indirectly, information ... about matters discussed or decided concerning the election of the Pope in the meetings of Cardinals, both before and during the time of the election" (n. 59).

333 The Year of Faith of Pope Paul VI

Talking about the upcoming Year of Faith, my uncle said that this is not the first such year in his lifetime, but that Pope Paul VI had proclaimed a Year of Faith in the 1960s. What was the occasion for that one?

Your uncle is correct. Pope Paul VI called for a Year of Faith to be celebrated from the feast of Saints Peter and Paul, 29 June 1967, to the same feast the following year. He announced the Year in the Apostolic Exhortation *Petrum et Paulum Apostolos*, which was addressed to the bishops and was dated 22 February 1967, the feast of the Chair of St Peter.

Pope Benedict XVI, in his Apostolic Letter *Porta Fidei*, announcing the Year of Faith of 2012, refers to the earlier one. He mentions that Pope Paul VI had proclaimed that Year of Faith to commemorate the nineteenth centenary of the martyrdom of Saints Peter and Paul. He says that Pope Paul "thought that in this way the whole Church could reappropriate 'exact knowledge of the faith, so as to reinvigorate it, purify it, confirm it, and confess it'" (*PPA*, 198; *PF* 4).

It should be remembered that the Second Vatican Council had concluded in December 1965 so it was just over a year later that Pope Paul announced the Year of Faith. At that time there was considerable confusion and questioning of the most basic teachings of the Church, on matters of Scripture, dogma, morals and the sacraments. Even before the Council ended Pope Paul wrote the encyclical *Mysterium Fidei* (3 September 1965) to reaffirm the Church's constant teaching on the Real Presence of Christ in the Eucharist in the face of new and erroneous interpretations of that teaching.

There is no question but that Pope Paul wanted the Year of Faith to help the whole Church to reaffirm its belief in the faith of always.

Pope Benedict says as much in *Porta Fidei*: "In some respects, my venerable predecessor saw this Year as a 'consequence and a necessity of the post-conciliar period' (Paul Paul VI, General Audience, 14 June 1967), fully conscious of the grave difficulties of the time, especially with regard to the profession of the true faith and its correct interpretation" (*PF* 5).

In fact, Pope Paul VI went to great lengths in his Apostolic Exhortation to explain the grave situation obtaining at the time. I offer here my own translation, since the Vatican website has the text only in Italian and Latin, without paragraph numbers: "And when the religious sense among the men and women of our time has diminished, depriving the faith of its natural foundation, new exegetical or theological opinions, often borrowed from bold but blind secular philosophies, are here and there insinuated into the field of Catholic doctrine, putting in doubt or deforming the objective sense of truths authoritatively taught by the Church. And with the pretext of adapting religious thought to the mentality of the modern world, they ignore the guidance of the ecclesiastical Magisterium, they give a radically *historicist* slant to theological speculation, they dare to empty the testimony of Sacred Scripture of its historical and sacred character, and they attempt to introduce into the People of God a so-called *post-conciliar* mentality, which disregards in the Council the firm coherence of its broad and magnificent doctrinal and legislative developments with the treasure of thought and practice of the Church, only to undermine the spirit of traditional fidelity and to spread the illusion of giving to Christian thought a new arbitrary and sterile interpretation. What would remain of the content of our faith and of the theological virtue which professes it, if these efforts, detached from the help of the ecclesiastical Magisterium, were to prevail?"

Pope Paul went on to call the Church to a sincere and operative profession of the faith of always, the faith of Jesus Christ and of the apostles Peter and Paul. At the end of the Year of Faith, Pope Paul VI gave the Church the *Credo of the People of God*, a long and detailed statement of the Church's constant belief (cf. J. Flader, *Question Time 2*, q. 152).

As the new Year of Faith begins, commemorating the fiftieth anniversary of the commencement of the Second Vatican Council and the twentieth anniversary of the publication of the *Catechism of the Catholic Church*, we can strive to go deeper in our own understanding of the Church's teaching and to reaffirm our faith in it.

334 Catholics and evangelical groups

I am aware of a growing number of Catholics who have gone over to evangelical groups, and am very disturbed by this. Why does this happen and is there anything that can be done about it?

The phenomenon you describe is indeed disturbing. It is happening in other parts of the world on an even greater scale, particularly in South America, Africa and the Philippines.

Why do people who have been baptised and brought up in the Catholic Church, with the fullness of truth and of the means of salvation given by Jesus Christ, leave this Church and go over to other Christian groups? Obviously each person will have their own story and their own reasons and the best would be to ask them personally. But I believe there are some common factors.

One is that Catholics, and others, are attracted to a Sunday service that they find more lively, with rousing singing and powerful preaching. For some, this seems to satisfy their spiritual needs more. Another is that these evangelical groups often have a great spirit of fellowship, and are very welcoming to everyone who approaches them. Sometimes they knock on doors and draw people into their groups through their friendship and caring attitude. Some of these groups are charismatic, and people can be attracted by being prayed over, by healing services and other manifestations of the Spirit.

Then too, these evangelicals often know the Bible better than many Catholics and they draw in Catholics by quoting scripture passages that seem to undermine Catholic teaching, or simply by inviting them to Bible study sessions. There are undoubtedly many more reasons for Catholics gravitating to these groups, but I think these are some of the main ones.

Is there anything that can be done? The question and the answer have two aspects: what can be done to lessen the exodus of Catholics, and what can be done to bring them back?

As regards the first, there are a number of measures that can be taken. First, and perhaps most importantly, we must do a better job of forming Catholics in the faith, especially our children. It is clear that a Catholic who truly knows and loves the beauty of Catholic truth and life is not going to abandon it for another group. This has been one of the chief reasons for the haemorrhaging of Catholics from the Church in many countries.

In addition to better instruction in Catholic truth, it is also important to help our people grow in a true life of piety, in a deep personal relationship with Jesus Christ. It is not enough just "to say our prayers." Again, if someone has this relationship, they are much less prone to be attracted to a group which seems to have it. We can also foster more study of the Bible in the Church. Thanks to God there have been more and more Catholics studying the Bible in recent years, but still more can be done.

As regards our Catholic parishes and communities, we can often do a better job of being more welcoming, of creating a greater spirit of fellowship. Some parishes and groups are very good at this, and it is a big help in attracting non-Catholics and keeping the Catholics involved. There is no reason why other Christians should be better at this than Catholics.

And as for the conduct of our worship, we can often do better. Good singing certainly enhances the attractiveness of the Mass, as does good preaching, along with more reverence in the way Mass is celebrated, both by the priest and by the other ministers who assist him. We are blessed in the Church by having a Mass which is the sacrifice of the New Covenant and which has been celebrated in much the same way since the earliest centuries, with readings from Scripture, the Eucharistic prayer and the reception of the true Body and Blood of Christ in Communion. Evangelical groups do not have this. While they have what is perhaps a more lively celebration, it is not the sacrifice which Christ left to his Church, and in this aspect they are sorely lacking.

Finally, we should encourage our young people to get involved in youth groups and organisations that help them grow in their faith, so that they become truly committed Catholics.

And as regards how to bring Catholics back, our insistent prayer for them is always the most important, united with our gentle, understanding conversation, in which we listen to them and quietly help them to see how much they have left behind, always assuring them of our love and respect.

335 Rosicrucians

A friend of mine has been invited to a meeting of the Rosicrucians. He says they are some sort of quasi-religious group. Can you tell me anything about them?

The name Rosicrucian comes from the surname of its purported founder, Christian Rosenkreuz (meaning "rose cross"), a German nobleman and former monk (1378-1484), who is supposed to have founded the Rosicrucian Fraternity, or brotherhood, in 1408. It seems that while travelling through the Middle East he became acquainted with a form of Arabian magic and founded the fraternity as an anti-Catholic Christian group tinged with theosophy, his ideal of a religion.

The group's teaching was based on "esoteric truths of the ancient past", unknown to the average person, which gave insight into nature, the physical universe and the spiritual realm. In this sense it was a medieval form of Gnosticism, which also proposed to know truths not accessible to the general public. Thus their members considered themselves an intellectual elite.

When Rosenkreuz was unable to find followers among the prominent figures of Europe, he is supposed to have gathered together a small circle of friends and disciples and founded the fraternity named after him. During his lifetime the fraternity was said to have had no more than some eight members, each a medical doctor and a bachelor committed to remain single. They took an oath to heal the sick without charge, to maintain a secret fellowship and to find a replacement for themselves before they died. They were to apply themselves zealously and in all secrecy to the study of nature in its hidden forces, and to make their discoveries and inventions known to the other members of the order and to be of benefit to humanity.

Whether or not Rosenkreuz actually existed, the organisation remained largely unknown until around 1610, when it began circulating in manuscript form a manifesto entitled "Fama Fraternitatis R.C.", "Fame (or tradition) of the Fraternity of the Rose Cross". The work came to be published as a pamphlet in 1614. Beginning with the fourth edition in 1615 another tract entitled "Confessio Fraternitatis" or "Profession of the Fraternity" was added to the "Fama". It set out the nature and aims of the fraternity, promoting the "universal reformation of mankind". The "Fama" invited all the scholars and rulers of Europe to support the cause and eventually seek to join it.

The writings were hostile to the Catholic Church. The rose cross was chosen as the symbol of the order, both because of the name of the founder and because the rose and cross were ancient symbols of the occult. It appears that the author of the "Fama" was the Lutheran theologian John Valentin Andrea (1586-1654) from Württemberg or a close associate of his. In any case Andrea composed a book about the Rosicrucians which was published in 1616 and has many similarities with the "Fama".

The manifestos caused excitement throughout Europe by declaring the existence of a secret brotherhood of alchemists and sages who were preparing to transform the arts, sciences, religion, and political and intellectual landscape of Europe. Given the fascination of the age for the esoteric, magic and the occult, between 1614 and 1620 some four hundred manuscripts and books were published which discussed the Rosicrucian documents.

After 1750 Rosicrucianism was propagated by the Freemasons, especially in England and Scotland. In the hierarchy of the many degrees in Scottish Freemasonry, the eighteenth degree was called the Knight of the Rose Cross. There was clearly a mutual influence between the Rosicrucians and the Masons.

Since the late nineteenth century especially in England, Scotland and the United States, numerous Rosicrucian groups have been formed with different names and aims. The largest appears to be the Ancient Mystical Order Rosae Crucis (AMORC) founded in the United States in 1915.

Today the Rosicrucians claim to be a world-wide fraternal organisation devoted to the study and application of the natural laws that govern the universe to enable everyone to live in harmony with the creative, cosmic forces for the attainment of health, happiness and peace. Given the anti-Catholic origins and the aims and methods of the organisation, Catholics would not and should not be interested in it. After all, we have the fullness of truth in Jesus Christ.

The Last Things

336 Can atheists go to heaven?

I recently heard someone say that atheists can go to heaven. This surprised me no end. Is it true?

In principle atheists can go to heaven, but there are a number of issues to consider. As the advertisement for a special offer often says, "Conditions apply."

The first issue is what we mean by atheist. The word atheist means simply one who does not believe in God and it distinguishes the person from a theist, who does believe in God. But within the broad category of atheist there are many different attitudes and backgrounds. It is impossible to lump them all together as if they were all one. It might even be safe to say that there are as many types of atheism as there are atheists. Each one is unique.

Over the years atheists have come to divide themselves into many different types: explicit and implicit, positive and negative, strong and weak, theoretical and practical, etc. The last distinction is perhaps one of the most helpful. In simple terms a theoretical atheist is one who has taken a positive stand against the existence of God – he or she denies that God exists – whereas the practical atheist does not believe in God but has not explicitly rejected such belief. He or she lives as if there were no God. Often this state of mind is found in people who have not been taught about God. They have simply not heard of him or they have ignored him. They are indifferent to the question of God.

Another factor which is very important is what the atheist believes deep down, as distinct from what they proclaim to others. I suspect there are many atheists who proudly and defiantly proclaim there is no God, or that they don't believe in God, but who secretly wonder about God and have a residual belief in a higher power "out there" to whom they would turn in a time of crisis. This is very relevant to their eternal salvation.

Then too the issue of time is important. The person who today proclaims herself or himself to be an ardent atheist may have a big conversion tomorrow. A notable recent example is Professor Antony Flew, a British philosopher who, after 50 years of professed atheism, including writing books on the subject, came to believe in God through scientific discoveries. He relates his conversion in the book *There is a God,* published in 2007. With these considerations in mind, we return to your question, can atheists go to heaven?

We can begin with the practical atheists, especially those who simply do not know about God and who therefore live their lives without him. The Second Vatican Council, in the Dogmatic Constitution on the Church *Lumen Gentium* spoke of them expressly. The statement came in a paragraph considering the relationship of the Church to many different groups of people – other Christians, Jews, Muslims, those who do not know Christ – and it finished with those who do not know God.

The Council declared: "Nor shall divine providence deny the assistance necessary for salvation to those who, without any fault of theirs, have not yet arrived at an explicit knowledge of God, and who, not without grace, strive to lead a good life. Whatever good or truth is found amongst them is considered by the Church to be a preparation for the Gospel and given by him who enlightens all men that they may at length have life" (*LG* 16). As the Council makes clear, these people must be in this position through no fault of their own and they must strive to lead a good life. This includes being sorry for their sins. They can be saved.

As regards theoretical atheists who say they do not believe in God or that there is no God, their eternal salvation is more difficult. It is hard to see how they could spend eternity in a loving relationship with the God they have rejected during their life.

In the end, what is necessary for anyone to enter heaven, including a professed atheist, is for the person to repent of their sins and accept God's merciful love (cf. *CCC* 1033). An atheist, especially one with a faint belief that there might be a God, could still do this and be saved. We can hope and pray that even the most convinced atheist today may be able to repent and believe in God before they die. Since only God knows the state of their soul when they die, we should make no judgment about their eternal salvation. We should always pray for them.

337 Is there time in heaven?

One thing that has always intrigued me is whether there is time, in the sense of before and after, in the "eternal" life of heaven. Can you answer this?

First, we should ask what we mean by time. Time is associated with change and is measured in terms of change, so that wherever there is change of any sort there is time. The simplest example is an hour glass, where the sand falls through a narrow opening from the upper part to the lower part, always taking the same amount of time to do so. Similarly, we measure our days by the earth revolving around its own axis and our years by the earth revolving around the sun.

God, as we know, exists outside of time in eternity, where everything is present to him at once. The classic definition of eternity comes from Boethius, who defined it as "the instantaneously whole and perfect possession of unending life" (*De consolatione*, v). That God is outside of time is a great mystery for us. We cannot fathom how the God who created the universe billions of years ago and now watches over it in its constant changing is himself unchanging, outside of time. In God the whole of history is somehow present simultaneously. It is as if someone unrolled a film that recorded the whole of history and God saw it, from beginning to end, in one glance.

So if we and the universe are in time and God is in eternity, in which of these modes of existence are those in heaven, both angels and men? St Thomas Aquinas in his *Summa Theologiae* speaks of a third mode called the aeon, also known as the aevum or aeveternity. An aeon, he says, is defined as "the measure of immaterial substances", so that it applies to angels in the first place but also to the souls in heaven. As he puts it, the aeon "lies somewhere between eternity and time" (*STh* I, q. 10, art. 5). It is the unchangeable existence of immaterial substances which have a beginning but no end.

But in the case of angels and souls in heaven there is, surprisingly, both unchangeability and change. St Thomas says that angels "combine unchangeable existence with changeability of choice at the natural level, and with changeability of thoughts, affections and, in their own fashion, places." That is, while their very existence is unchangeable, their activity changes. Therefore St Thomas says that "time has a before and after, the aeon has no before and after in itself but can be accompanied by it, whilst eternity neither possesses a before and after nor can co-exist with it" (*ibid.*).

As a result, angels and the souls in heaven share in some way in all three modes of existence. In the words of St Thomas, "Inasmuch as their thoughts and affections display successiveness, immaterial creatures are measured by time... But as regards their natural existence they are measured by the aeon; and inasmuch as they contemplate God's glory they share in eternity" (*ibid.*).

We can understand this. Traditionally the Church has taught that the essential happiness of heaven consists in a "communion of life and love with the Trinity" (*CCC* 1024), where the soul shares in God's eternity and there is no before and after. But there is also the accidental happiness of being in the company of Our Lady, the angels, the saints and all our loved ones. As new souls enter heaven, those already there rejoice and this implies change and hence time. Likewise, God can allow the souls in heaven to be aware of what is happening with their loved ones on earth, and this too implies time.

Pope Benedict XVI writes of this eternal life in his encyclical *Spe salvi*: "'Eternal', in fact, suggests to us the idea of something interminable, and this frightens us; 'life' makes us think of the life that we know and love and do not want to lose, even though very often it brings more toil than satisfaction, so that while on the one hand we desire it, on the other hand we do not want it. To imagine ourselves outside the temporality that imprisons us and in some way to sense that eternity is not an unending succession of days in the calendar, but something more like the supreme moment of satisfaction, in which totality embraces us and we embrace totality—this we can only attempt. It would be like plunging into the ocean of infinite love, a moment in which time—the before and after—no longer exists. We can only attempt to grasp the idea that such a moment is life in the full sense, a plunging ever anew into the vastness of being, in which we are simply overwhelmed with joy" (n. 12).

338 Do pets go to heaven?

Recently our pet cat died and my daughter asked me whether it would go to heaven so that she can be reunited with it one day. I didn't know what to tell her.

This is indeed a frequently asked question, especially by children. In a way it reveals a somewhat naïve approach to the whole question of eternal life. The answer must begin by distinguishing two phases of life after death: the phase before the end of the world, and the phase of the "new heaven and new earth" following the final judgment at the end of the world.

In the first phase the souls of those who die in the state of grace and are perfectly purified enter heaven (cf. *Catechism of the Catholic*

Church, 1023). Only a being with an immortal, spiritual soul can go to heaven. This includes both angels and human beings. In this phase, the body does not go to heaven along with the soul, but rather remains on earth. Of course Our Lord and Our Lady are in heaven in both body and soul, and perhaps a few others, possibly including the prophet Elijah.

In view of this, it is clear that there are no other material bodies in heaven, including animals. But do animals not have an immortal soul so that they might therefore be in heaven in their souls? No, they do not. They have a soul, a principle of life, along with all other living things, including plants. But this soul is not spiritual. It is simply what is called the "form" of the matter of the body, making the body function as a single living organism. When the animal, or the plant for that matter, dies, the soul ceases to exist. There is no longer any principle of life, any form, and the matter disintegrates.

In humans, on the other hand, the soul is spiritual and has existence in its own right. By our spiritual soul we are able to think, to reason, to know immaterial concepts such as goodness or immortality, to plan for the future, etc., something even the highest animals cannot do. This spiritual soul, because it has no matter, is immortal or indestructible. When humans die, the soul lives on and goes either to Purgatory, heaven or hell.

But will our happiness in heaven not be somewhat lessened if our pets are not there with us? Not at all. The very question reveals a lack of understanding of the overwhelming joy of seeing the Blessed Trinity, Our Lady and all the angels and saints. Pope Benedict describes heaven as "like plunging into the ocean of infinite love… in which we are simply overwhelmed with joy" (Enc. *Spe salvi,* n. 12). And the Catechism says that heaven is the "fulfillment of the deepest human longings, the state of supreme, definitive happiness" (*CCC* 1024). In heaven we will be so caught up in the love of God that we will not miss anyone or anything. Even if a close relative like a son or daughter, a parent or a brother or sister of ours did not go to heaven, our own happiness would not be lessened.

When we turn to the second phase of existence, that of the "new heaven and new earth" following the general judgment (cf. J. Flader, *Question Time 1*, q. 30), there may very well be animals and plants, including pets. St Thomas Aquinas argues that there will be no animals and plants in the renewal of heaven and earth because they are corruptible (cf. *STh, Suppl.*, q. 91, art. 5). While St Thomas is always to be taken seriously, this statement is not equivalent to a dogma of faith or an official teaching of the Church.

Professor Peter Kreeft, on the contrary, argues that since God can do anything, he can raise up animals for the "new earth" in heaven: "We were meant from the beginning to have stewardship over the animals; we have not fulfilled that divine plan yet on earth; therefore it seems likely that the right relationship with animals will be part of heaven: proper 'pet-ship'" (*Everything you ever wanted to know about Heaven*, Ignatius Press 1990, pp. 45-46). In all this it is important to help our children – and ourselves! – not to be "pet-centred", but rather Christ-centred: to love our pets, yes, but to love Jesus Christ much more.

339 Is it easy to go straight to heaven?

I have always thought that it is not easy to go straight to heaven when we die, but recently a friend argued, based on the Summa Theologiae of St Thomas Aquinas, that the Anointing of the Sick removes all our temporal punishment and, in any case, there is a plenary indulgence at the moment of death for those who prayed habitually. Is this true?

We recall that in order to enter heaven the soul must be perfectly purified. The *Letter to the Hebrews* speaks of "that holiness without which no one will see the Lord" (*Heb* 12:14). And Our Lord uses the parable of the wedding garment, without which no one will be allowed into the wedding banquet of heaven (cf. *Mt* 22:1-14).

Traditionally the Church teaches that we must be purified of three realities in order to go to heaven: temporal punishment remaining for our sins, bad habits and attachments caused by sin and any lack of sorrow for venial sins. It is clear that someone with any of these on their soul is not worthy of heaven. The *Catechism of the Catholic Church* teaches: "All who die in God's grace and friendship, but still imperfectly purified, are indeed assured of their eternal salvation; but after death they undergo purification, so as to achieve the holiness necessary to enter the joy of heaven" (*CCC* 1030).

For this reason the Church has, from the beginning, prayed and offered Masses for the faithful departed, no matter how holy they were. The prayers of the funeral Mass always ask God to have mercy on the person's soul and to take them to heaven. They do not assume that the person is already in heaven. And the Church dedicates the month of November to praying especially for the souls in Purgatory, following the commemoration of All Souls on November 2. So it is clear that the Church herself does not assume that practically everyone goes straight to heaven.

What does St Thomas say about the effects of the Anointing of the Sick? He deals with the question in the Supplement to his *Summa Theologiae*, where he speaks of three consequences of sin which are healed in some way by the sacrament. The first is the guilt, or stain, of sin and this is taken away by the sacrament, at least as regards venial sins. Mortal sins must first be confessed before receiving the sacrament. The second consequence is temporal punishment, and St Thomas says that the Anointing "diminishes the debt of temporal punishment". It diminishes the debt, but it does not necessarily take it away completely. The third consequence is what St Thomas calls the "remnants of sin" and these too are diminished. By remnants he means "a certain spiritual debility in the mind" such that when it is removed "the mind is not so easily prone to sin" (cf. *STh*, Suppl., q. 30, art 1).

As is clear, St Thomas in no way suggests that all the effects of sin, especially temporal punishment, are removed so that the soul would be able to go immediately to heaven after receiving the Anointing of the Sick. Baptism does remove all the temporal punishment but the Anointing does not.

As regards the plenary indulgence granted by the Church at the moment of death, this too must be understood properly. As we know, a plenary indulgence removes all the temporal punishment owing for our sins and the Church, as you say, grants a plenary indulgence at the moment of death to all those who "are properly disposed and have been in the habit of reciting some prayers during their lifetime" (Pope Paul VI, Apost. Const. *Indulgentiarum doctrina*, n. 18). Does this mean that since most Catholics have been in the habit of praying during their life, they will receive the plenary indulgence and go straight to heaven?

Not necessarily. First, they must be "properly disposed", meaning they must be in the state of grace and they must reject all attachment to sin, even venial sin. This may be difficult to do as it requires a great love for God and with it an abhorrence of sin, even the slightest sins. But even if the plenary indulgence does take away all the temporal punishment owing for their sins, the person may still not be sorry for all their venial sins or they may still have bad habits and attachments caused by sin. Any of these would prevent their immediate entry into heaven.

So while we can hope that many people do go straight to heaven, we should take nothing for granted and should always pray and have Masses said for those who have died, no matter how good they were. It is better to offer prayers and Masses for someone who does not need them than to leave the person in Purgatory without anyone to pray for them.

340 God's mercy and hell

Could I be wasting my time or even sinning in praying for the souls in hell so that their pain may stop, for example that after a long time they would just burn away and cease to exist?

I understand perfectly your compassion for those souls but I have to say that there is no point in praying for them. The teaching of Our Lord and his Church is that the punishment of hell is everlasting. Jesus himself says, "Depart from me, you cursed, into the eternal fire prepared for the devil and his angels; for I was hungry and you gave me no food, I was thirsty and you gave me no drink... And they will go away into eternal punishment, but the righteous into eternal life" (*Mt* 25:31-46). Based on this and many other passages in which Jesus speaks of everlasting punishment, the Church has always taught the eternity of hell. For example, the *Catechism of the Catholic Church* says, "The teaching of the Church affirms the existence of hell and its eternity" (*CCC* 1035).

It is difficult to grasp the concept, let alone the reality, of a soul having to suffer for ever, with no hope of reprieve. And moreover having to suffer a punishment worse than any pain one can suffer on earth. We are inclined to ask how God in his mercy could possibly condemn anyone to such suffering. The answer is of course that God does not want any soul to have to suffer like this. Rather he "desires all men to be saved and to come to the knowledge of the truth" (*1 Tim* 2:4). And "As I live, says the Lord God, I have no pleasure in the death of the wicked, but that the wicked turn from his way and live" (*Ezek* 33:11).

It is not God that condemns the soul to hell. The person chooses it. As the Catechism explains, "To die in mortal sin without repenting and accepting God's merciful love means remaining separated from him for ever by our own free choice. This state of definitive self-exclusion from communion with God and the blessed is called 'hell'" (*CCC* 1033). In the final choice that the person makes before dying, he or she understands that that choice binds the soul forever, that there is no turning back. In a similar way, the bad angels understood clearly that if they turned against God they would be separated from him forever. It is an awesome moment in the life of a person, the moment in which they decide their eternal destiny, choosing eternal life and joy with God or eternal separation from him and suffering.

Two obvious conclusions suggest themselves. First, we should live our lives close to God at all times, struggling to grow in love for him by doing his will, receiving the sacraments frequently and repenting and turning back to him through the sacrament of Penance when we fail. In that way, we will live and die in God's love and not reject him at the end of our life.

And second, we should pray very much for all people who are presently separated from God through serious sin, especially those whom we know. While we cannot help souls who are in hell, we can help the living to repent so that they do not go to hell. This was a thought that moved the three children at Fatima very much and led them to offer up generous penances for sinners.

But, we might ask, where is the mercy of God when souls go to hell? First of all, his mercy is seen in the suffering and death of Jesus Christ on the cross for the salvation of all. As Jesus himself said, "Greater love has no man than this, that a man lay down his life for his friends" (*Jn* 15:13). God's mercy is shown too throughout our lives when he offers us all the graces we need and takes us back when we fall and ask for forgiveness. He will have forgiven us thousands of times by the time we die. That is mercy. And finally God shows his mercy even in the punishment of hell in that the souls there do not suffer all that their sins deserve. If we consider that our sins offend against the infinite love and goodness of God, we can understand that an eternity of suffering would be insufficient to make up for even one mortal sin. So God, in his mercy, allows the souls in hell to suffer much less than their sins deserve.

St Catherine of Genoa writes in *Fire of Love* (Sophia Institute Press 1996): "For the man who is dead in sin merits infinite pain for an infinite time, but God's mercy has allotted infinity to him only in time and has limited the quantity of his pain; in justice God could have given him more pain" (p. 3).

II. THE SACRAMENTS

The Liturgy

341 The Liturgical Year

I am a recent convert and have bought a missal for weekday Masses but I sometimes have difficulty knowing which Mass is being said. For example, what does it mean when it says eighth week of Ordinary Time, or year one?

Your question will be of interest to all Catholics, not only to recent converts like you. It is good that we have a basic understanding of how the calendar is structured so that we know what to expect and can live the liturgy more fully. The calendar is based around five seasons: Advent, Christmas, Lent, Easter and Ordinary Time.

The Church year begins with Advent, which is the preparation for Christmas. It is a season of hope and expectation, both of Christ's birth in history and of his second coming at the end of time. Advent begins on the fourth Sunday before Christmas and thus has four Sundays. Its length varies, depending on the day of the week on which Christmas falls, being longest when Christmas falls on a Sunday. During this season the colour of the priest's vestments and other furnishings is purple, or violet, the colour of penance.

The Christmas season begins on December 25 and ends on the feast of the Baptism of the Lord. It is a season of joy and hence the liturgical colour is white. During this season we celebrate such important feasts as the Divine Maternity of Mary on January 1, the Holy Family, and Epiphany, which commemorates the adoration of the Christ child by the magi. While the original date for Epiphany was January 6, the feast is celebrated in most countries on the Sunday closest to January 6, with the Baptism of Christ usually celebrated on the following Sunday.

After the Christmas season comes the first part of what is called Ordinary Time, or in Latin *tempus per annum*, time through the year.

Perhaps the translation of Ordinary Time is unfortunate, since no time in the worship of God is ordinary. During this time the Mass readings consider the events of Christ's life. There are thirty-four weeks in Ordinary Time, interrupted by Lent and Easter. Hence when your missal says "eighth week of Ordinary Time" or "eighth week of the year" this is what is meant. Usually the parish bulletins given out at Mass on Sundays indicate which week we are in, so you will know where to find the Mass in your missal. During this season the colour is green, the colour of life and growth as seen in plants. During this season, as indeed in all the seasons, the Church also celebrates the feast days of saints, as well as of Our Lord and Our Lady, the angels, etc. On saints' days red is used for the apostles and martyrs, and white for the other saints.

After a few weeks of Ordinary Time comes the season of Lent, in preparation for Easter. Lent begins on Ash Wednesday and has six full weeks in addition to the days between Ash Wednesday and the first Sunday of Lent. Leaving out the Sundays, which are like weekly celebrations of the joy of Easter, Lent has forty days, to commemorate Our Lord's forty days of prayer and fasting in the desert before beginning his public ministry (cf. *Mt* 4:1-2). Lent is the primordial season of penance and hence the colour is violet, or purple. During Lent the readings focus on Baptism and penance.

The Easter season begins with the Easter vigil on the eve of Easter Sunday, and it has seven full weeks, ending on Pentecost Sunday, when the Holy Spirit came down on the apostles. Easter is the most important feast of the year, celebrating Our Lord's Resurrection and our Redemption. As a season of joy, the colour is white.

After Pentecost Sunday, Ordinary Time resumes until the first Sunday of Advent, when the cycle begins all over again. The last Sunday of Ordinary Time is the feast of Christ the King.

It is important to know that the readings in Mass vary from year to year, following a three-year cycle on Sundays and a two-year cycle on weekdays. On Sundays there are three readings, including the Gospel, and all three vary each year for three years. The Sunday cycles are usually referred to as Years A, B and C. In order to know in which year we are, it is presumed that the cycles began in the year 1 AD with Year A, so that all years divisible by three are Year C.

The weekday cycles are known as Years 1 and 2, according to whether they are odd or even numbered years. The first reading in Mass varies each year following this plan, but the Gospel is the same each year. At the beginning of Ordinary Time the Gospel is from Mark, the shortest Gospel. When Mark is finished, passages of Matthew not found in Mark are read, followed by those from Luke. The Gospel of John is used especially in Easter time.

342 Applause in the liturgy

I have occasionally heard applause during Mass, for example after the homily or after a musical item, and have found it somehow strange and out of place. What should be my attitude to this?

Let me begin by saying that the Mass, or any other liturgical ceremony for that matter, is primarily directed to the worship of God. It is a time when we raise our hearts and minds to God in praise, thanksgiving and petition, and at the same time God showers his blessings and graces upon us.

The liturgy is thus a time for prayer and recollected silence and, yes, for singing out lustily in praise of God. But it is not a performance for the entertainment of those present. It is centred on God, not on the congregation. When, on the other hand, we attend a concert, a play, a sporting event or any other form of entertainment we naturally applaud from time to time, by way of showing our appreciation for the performance. This attitude and way of showing appreciation are not appropriate in the liturgy, which has an entirely different aim.

In his book *The Spirit of the Liturgy* the then Cardinal Joseph Ratzinger summed up this criterion: "Whenever applause breaks out in the liturgy because of some human achievement, it is a sure sign that the essence of liturgy has totally disappeared and been replaced by a kind of religious entertainment" (p. 198).

While it is good that the congregation should be inspired by a homily, showing their appreciation habitually by applause has a number of dangers. One is that the priest or deacon may unconsciously or consciously prepare the homily with a view to pleasing the people and eliciting applause, rather than seeking to build up the congregation in their knowledge and love of God. These two ends are very different and it would be sad if the homilist sought primarily recognition for himself.

Also, if the congregation have the custom of applauding from time to time, they can feel pressured to applaud in order not to offend the homilist, or they can judge the homily by whether others applaud or not and compare priests by the amount of applause they receive. The homilist should seek to build up the people of God, and the congregation should listen to the homily with a view to taking away something helpful for their spiritual and human life. For this reason the liturgical norms recommend a period of silence after the homily so that the people can reflect on what they have heard and assimilate it. Applause would disrupt this spirit of prayerful reflection

The same can be said about music. The purpose of music in the liturgy is to contribute to the beauty of the ceremony, and thus to enhance the glory given to God. When the music is particularly beautiful the people can naturally feel moved to applaud, as they would in a concert. But then they should hold themselves back and remember that this is not a concert but an act of worship. They can thank God in prayer for music which truly lifts up their minds to him and gives him greater glory.

Naturally, there can be exceptions. In larger Masses celebrated by the Pope, people often show their love for the Holy Father by applauding when he comes in, and they sometimes interrupt the homily with enthusiastic applause. And in some cultures, applause is far more common in general than in the Western world, and so it may appear in the liturgy as well.

Moreover, there are some ceremonies in which applause is actually suggested by the liturgical norms. This happens, for example, in the rite of ordination of a priest or deacon, after the ordaining bishop acknowledges that the person has been found worthy and is now chosen for ordination. Spontaneous applause may also come and be appropriate when a newly ordained bishop makes his way through the congregation blessing the people, or during the procession out of the church or cathedral at the conclusion of an ordination ceremony. Likewise, it is customary for the congregation to applaud a newly wed couple after they exchange their vows. But in general, the liturgy should be quiet, prayerful and uplifting. Applause should not be a normal part of it.

343 Silence in church

Recently I was in Mass with my wife when a lady in front of us began talking to someone beside her during the Offertory. It may have been important to her but I always find this exceedingly distracting and annoying. Is there anything that can be done about it?

Let me begin by considering the importance of silence, not only in Mass, but in general. Modern life tends to be noisy. People have the radio or recorded music on when they are driving, when they are working, when they are resting. And television occupies a good number of hours in many people's lives, even when the family is gathered together for a meal. It seems we feel uncomfortable when all is still, when there is silence.

Yet we all need silence. We need time to think, to reflect, to commune with God, just to be still in his presence. We need "interiority", as the *Catechism of the Catholic Church* calls it: "This requirement of *interiority* is all the more necessary as life often distracts us from any reflection, self-examination or introspection" (*CCC* 1779).

For this reason it is so important to turn off the radio, CD player or iPod from time to time. Then instead of being bombarded by sound, which leaves the mind passive and numb, we find ourselves able to think, to make plans, to talk with God, to pray. It is a different world – a world of peace and quiet. Then we wonder: why do I always have the radio on?

What a difference between our noisy, busy world and that of a monastery, where silence reigns practically, or literally, all the time! We may not be called to that life, but we can appreciate how different such a world would be. At least we could try it some of the time. It would be good for our soul and our peace of mind.

It is interesting that during the joyful season of Christmas everything about the birth of Christ in Bethlehem speaks to us of silence. The book of *Wisdom* seems to describe it: "When a deep silence covered all things and night was in the middle of its course, your all-powerful Word, O Lord, leapt from heaven's royal throne" (*Wis* 18:14-15). We sing "Silent night, holy night, all is calm, all is bright" and "How silently, how silently, the wondrous gift is given". If only we could live this spirit always!

If we need silence in our busy, everyday world, we expect to find it especially in our churches, which are the house of God. To come out of the noise of traffic, of talking and of problems into the silence of a church is truly refreshing. There we find God in the tabernacle and we can commune with him in stillness. It is like an oasis. If no Mass is being celebrated at the time, there is generally deep silence, as people pray and bring their lives and intentions before God. The prophet Habakkuk urges: "But the Lord is in his holy temple; let all the earth keep silence before him" (*Hab* 2:20).

If silence is so important in church in general, it is even more important during the celebration of the "sacred mysteries", as we call the Mass in the penitential rite. The Mass should be a time of prayer, of recollection, of actively following the prayers and readings, of preparing for holy Communion and of giving thanks for it afterwards.

Even if some are not caught up in this spirit, they should be respectful of the many others who are. This applies as well before Mass, when many arrive early in order to prepare themselves for the mysteries which are to follow, and after Mass, when many stay behind to prolong their thanksgiving. In this regard the *General Instruction of the Roman Missal* says: "Even before the celebration itself, it is commendable that silence be observed in the church, in the sacristy, in the vesting room, and in adjacent areas, so that all may dispose themselves to carry out the sacred action in a devout and fitting manner" (*GIRM* 45). This does not mean that there is no place for chatting with those we have not seen for some time. But that place is outside the church, before, or better, after Mass.

What can be done? Some churches have a sign at the entrance, reminding everyone that this is the house of God and they should observe a respectful silence. And, if necessary, the priest can remind the parishioners from time to time of the need for silence, out of reverence for God and respect for others. Let us pray that all will observe this spirit, which is so important for everyone.

344 Who can give blessings?

Occasionally I have seen lay people giving blessings to others. Is this permitted? How about deacons?

First of all, what do we mean by a blessing? The *Catechism of the*

Catholic Church says: "Among sacramentals *blessings* (of persons, meals, objects, and places) come first. Every blessing praises God and prays for his gifts. In Christ, Christians are blessed by God the Father 'with every spiritual blessing' (*Eph* 1:3). This is why the Church imparts blessings by invoking the name of Jesus, usually while making the holy sign of the cross of Christ" (*CCC* 1671).

There are two main types of blessings. The first, sometimes called "constitutive" blessings, confer a sacred character on the person, place or thing, dedicating it to the service of God. Such, for example, are the blessings of virgins and hermits, churches, altars, sacred vessels and vestments, Rosaries, crucifixes, scapulars and holy water. These are set aside for the service of God and must always be treated with great respect. The other type, sometimes called "invocative", ask for God's blessing on such things as houses, cars, meals, trips, etc., without making them sacred.

Who can give blessings? The short answer is that anyone, even lay people, can give blessings on certain occasions, but the Church restricts some blessings to bishops, others to priests and deacons, and others can be given by lay people. The general principle regarding blessings is that "the more a blessing concerns ecclesial and sacramental life, the more is its administration reserved to the ordained ministry (bishops, priests, or deacons)" (*CCC* 1669).

As for blessings reserved to bishops, the *Code of Canon Law* says: "Consecrations and dedications can be validly carried out by those who are invested with the episcopal character, and by priests who are permitted to do so by law or by legitimate grant" (Can. 1169, §1). Consecrations are the solemn rites by which persons or things are permanently made over to the service of God. For example, virgins and hermits are consecrated to God in the hands of a bishop, and the sacred chrism is consecrated, or blessed, by the bishop in the Chrism Mass in Holy Week. Dedications are the rites by which places are made over to God and become sacred places. For example, churches, chapels and altars are dedicated to God by a bishop.

Priests may carry out these rites only when they have been given express permission to do so. For example, if a priest does not have Oil of the Sick consecrated by a bishop, he may bless oil himself for a particular anointing. Apart from blessings reserved to bishops, priests can impart all other blessings (cf. Can. 1169 §2). If, however, a bishop is present, he is to give the blessing.

And a deacon "can impart only those blessings which are expressly permitted to him by law" (Can. 1169 §3). For example, deacons can give blessings at all the rites at which they preside, including the Liturgy of the Hours, Baptism, marriage, holy Communion outside Mass, and Eucharistic Benediction. In addition the Vatican's book of blessings, *De Benedictionibus*, lists twenty-one blessings that deacons may give.

As regards lay people, the *Catechism* says: "Sacramentals derive from the baptismal priesthood: every baptised person is called to be a 'blessing,' and to bless. Hence lay people may preside at certain blessings" (*CCC* 1669). There are certain ordinary blessings that all the lay faithful, including children, can carry out. These include blessing oneself with holy water upon entering or leaving a church, blessing a meal and blessing oneself at the beginning of a trip. Some other more formal blessings in *De Benedictionibus* can also be imparted by lay people, including the blessing of a family and of sons and daughters. Thirteen such blessings are listed. As regards whether lay extraordinary ministers can give blessings at Communion in Mass, see question 364 below.

In general, when a priest or deacon imparts a blessing he extends his hands over the person or thing, whereas a lay person keeps the hands folded. The blessings given by lay people do not confer a sacred character on the person or thing, but merely invoke God's protection and blessing.

The Mass

345 Jesus' blessing in the Last Supper

The Gospels say that Jesus blessed the bread before instituting the Eucharist in the Last Supper. Do we know what this blessing was?

The answer to your question is quite fascinating and it has a close relationship with the new rite of the Mass. The Gospels of Matthew and Mark both say that "Jesus took bread, and blessed, and broke it, and gave it to the disciples and said, 'Take, eat; this is my body'" (*Mt* 26:26; cf. *Mk* 14:22). It is clear that this blessing is not the institution of the Eucharist itself, which is indicated in the following words. Rather it is a traditional blessing of food.

Do we know what blessing this was? Yes we do, at least with a high degree of probability. It was customary then, as now, for Jews to bless God in meals and on other occasions with a prayer known as a Berakah, a Hebrew word meaning "blessing". The plural of the word is Berakoth. There are three main types of Berakah: blessings recited before pleasurable experiences such as eating, blessings recited when carrying out a commandment, and blessings recited in praise or gratitude. They were recited both in synagogue services and in homes and private prayer.

It is the belief of Jews that food ultimately belongs to God, the one great provider, and that before eating it one should express gratitude to God by reciting the appropriate blessing. The Berakah is an expression of both praise and thanksgiving. That is probably why Luke and Paul, in their accounts of the Last Supper do not say that Jesus blessed the bread or wine, but rather that he thanked God: he "took bread, and when he had given thanks he broke it and gave it to them, saying, 'This is my body which is given for you" (*Lk* 22:19; cf. *1 Cor* 11:24).

Likewise, Matthew and Mark do not say that Jesus blessed the chalice but only that he gave thanks over it (cf. *Mt* 26:27, *Mk* 14:23).

Another reference to Jesus blessing food comes in his meal with the disciples of Emmaus: "he took the bread and blessed and broke it, and gave it to them" (*Lk* 24:30). Most Berakoth begin with the words *Barukh Attah Adonai Eloheinu Melekh ha-Olam,* "Blessed are you, O Lord our God, King of the Universe". They then add a reference to the particular occasion of the blessing.

For example, at the time of Christ and up to the present it was customary for Jewish families or groups of friends to gather together on Friday night, the eve of the Sabbath, for the fellowship meal called the *chaburah*. This formal meal was celebrated in the home with ritual washings and prayers. The meal began with the blessing of the wine and bread using a Berakah, also known as a *Kiddush*. It said: "Blessed are you, O Lord our God, king of the universe, creator of the fruit of the vine." This was followed by the blessing of the bread: "Blessed are you, O Lord our God, king of the universe, who brings forth bread from the earth."

We immediately recognise these words as very similar to those used in the Presentation of the Gifts in the new rite of the Mass: "Blessed are you, Lord God of all creation, for through your goodness we have received the bread we offer you: fruit of the earth and work of human hands, it will become for us the bread of life."

The Berakah on Friday night also includes a reference to the meaning of the Sabbath: "Blessed are you, Lord our God, King of the Universe, who sanctified us with his commandments, and hoped for us, and with love and intent invested us with his sacred Sabbath, as a memorial to the deed of Creation. It is the first amongst the holy festivals, commemorating the exodus from Egypt. For you chose us, and sanctified us, out of all nations, and with love and intent you invested us with your Holy Sabbath. Blessed are you, Sanctifier of the

Sabbath." At the conclusion of every Berakah those present answer "Amen," meaning "it is true" or "truly".

Jesus would have heard and used these prayers often. Thus when the Gospels say that he blessed the food, or gave thanks, they undoubtedly refer to this ancient Jewish prayer, which is still used by Jews today and which is the inspiration for the prayer used in the Presentation of the Gifts in Mass.

346 The Last Supper and the Passover

I have always been intrigued by whether Jesus celebrated the Last Supper within the Passover. There seem to be contradictions in the Gospels on this. Do we know for certain?

The short answer is that we do not know for certain. As you say, there are contradictions in the different Gospels which raise interesting questions. Let us first recall what the Passover was. It was the annual celebration by the Jews, lived indeed right up to the present day, of the liberation of the Israelites from over 400 years of slavery in Egypt. On the night before they began their exodus from Egypt, they were to eat a one year-old lamb, roasted over a fire with unleavened bread and bitter herbs (cf. *Ex* 12:1-14).

Thereafter, they were to celebrate the Passover each year on the fourteenth day of the month of Nisan, in commemoration of God's power and mercy in delivering them from slavery. God had instructed them: "This day shall be a day of remembrance for you. You shall celebrate it as a festival to the LORD; throughout your generations you shall observe it as a perpetual ordinance" (*Ex* 12:14).

Each year on what was called the first day of Unleavened Bread, the Passover lambs were slaughtered in the Temple in Jerusalem, one for each family. They were then eaten in the Passover meal, or Seder, that evening. The following day was the first full day of the Passover.

As Jesus prepared to deliver mankind from slavery to sin by his death on the Cross, it would seem that he celebrated the Last Supper within the Passover. The Synoptic Gospels of Matthew, Mark and Luke all agree on this.

For example, Matthew writes: "Now on the first day of Unleavened Bread the disciples came to Jesus, saying, 'Where will you have us prepare for you to eat the Passover?' He said, 'Go into the city to such a one, and say to him, "The Teacher says, My time is at hand; I will keep the Passover at your house with my disciples"'" (*Mt* 26:17-18).

Mark's account is very similar (cf. *Mk* 14:12-16) and Luke adds: "And they went, and found it as he had told them; and they prepared the Passover. And when the hour came, he sat at table, and the apostles with him. And he said to them, 'I have earnestly desired to eat this Passover with you before I suffer'" (*Lk* 22:13-15).

On this reading, Jesus brings to fulfilment the ancient Jewish rite of the Passover by instituting the Eucharist within it. Just as the Israelites ate the first Passover meal on the night before they left Egypt, so now Jesus institutes the Eucharist on the night before he dies to free us from our sins. The Passover lamb is replaced by "the Lamb of God, who takes away the sins of the world" (*Jn* 1:29) and the unleavened bread becomes the unleavened host of the Eucharist.

The only problem comes in the Gospel of John, who begins his account of the Last Supper saying, "Now before the feast of the Passover..." (*Jn* 13:1). According to John, the Last Supper took place sometime before the Passover. Moreover, later that evening or early the following morning, when they led Jesus to the praetorium where Pilate was to judge him, John says that the leaders of the Jews "did not enter the praetorium, so that they might not be defiled, but might eat the Passover" (*Jn* 18:28).

This suggests that Good Friday, when Jesus died on the Cross, was in fact the day on which the lambs were slaughtered and later eaten in the Passover meal. It is therefore very symbolic that when the lambs were being slaughtered in the Temple, the Lamb of God was being put to death on Calvary. It also makes more sense because it is highly unlikely that the leaders of the Jews would have arrested Jesus and put him to death on the very feast of the Passover.

How are we to reconcile these seemingly irreconcilable texts? Pope Benedict XVI, in *Jesus of Nazareth – Part Two* (Ignatius Press, San Francisco 2011), suggests that while the official Jewish Passover was celebrated on the evening of Good Friday, as St John says, Jesus on Holy Thursday celebrated a farewell meal as his own "Passover" (p. 114).

Alternatively, a footnote in the RSV Second Catholic Edition (Ignatius Press, San Francisco 2006), says that "Jesus must have anticipated the Passover meal because he would be dead the following day and because the meal prefigured his death" (New Testament, p. 25). The *Catechism of the Catholic Church* agrees, saying that by "celebrating the Last Supper with his apostles in the course of the Passover meal, Jesus gave the Jewish Passover its definitive meaning" (*CCC* 1340).

347 The penitential rite and forgiveness of sins

A friend recently told me that you don't really need to go to confession since the penitential rite at the beginning of Mass forgives sins. Is this true?

This is a good question, and I suspect many people think the same way as your friend. But I also suspect that the underlying reason for the question in some people is a reluctance to go to confession and that this in turn moves them to find theological reasons to justify their position.

Let us recall what we do in the penitential rite. The rite begins with the invitation from the priest to "acknowledge our sins, and so prepare ourselves to celebrate the sacred mysteries." It is only fitting at the beginning of any sacred ceremony, especially the Mass where we are in intimate communion with God, to begin by acknowledging our unworthiness and calling to mind our sins. This expression of humility makes us at least somewhat more worthy to enter into God's presence.

This is followed by a short time of silence, where we can make a brief examination of conscience and call to mind our most recent sins or perhaps our most serious sins of the past. In this way our act of sorrow will be based on the awareness of particular sins. For this reason it is important that the celebrant leaves more than just a few perfunctory seconds for this time of silence and examination. It is not just a ritual but a real opportunity to call to mind our sins.

Then the whole congregation, including the priest, express their sorrow in one of a number of prescribed ways found in the missal. The most expressive is undoubtedly the Confiteor, or "I confess": "I confess to almighty God and to you, my brothers and sisters, that I have greatly sinned, in my thoughts and in my words, in what I have done and in what I have failed to do, through my fault, through my fault, through my most grievous fault..."

The *General Instruction of the Roman Missal* calls this a "general confession." It says that "the priest invites those present to take part in the Act of Penitence, which, after a brief pause for silence, the entire community carries out through a formula of general confession" (*GIRM* 51). By "general confession" is meant a generic confession of sins, both those of commission ("what I have done") and those of omission ("what I have failed to do"), but without mentioning any particular sins, such as lying, showing impatience, etc.

This confession should be sincere, as we express in the words: "I have greatly sinned ... through my fault, through my fault, through my most grievous fault". On saying these words we beat our breast, as the publican did in the temple. He "beat his breast, saying, 'God, be merciful to me a sinner!'" (*Lk* 18:13).

The Confiteor concludes by asking for the prayers of the saints and of the Church on earth: "... therefore I ask blessed Mary ever-Virgin, all the Angels and Saints, and you, my brothers and sisters, to pray for me to the Lord our God." When we say "you, my brothers and sisters" we are referring not just to those present in the Mass but to all our brothers and sisters throughout the world.

After the Confiteor the priest asks God to forgive everyone, including himself: "May almighty God have mercy on us, forgive us our sins, and bring us to everlasting life." Here the priest is acting not in the person of Christ the head, as he does in other parts of the Mass, but rather as leader of the congregation. He does not say "I absolve you" as he does in the sacrament of Penance, but rather asks God to absolve everyone, including himself. Whether they are absolved will depend on their sorrow.

Does this prayer forgive sins, taking into account that the priest is asking God to have mercy on us and to forgive our sins? It is certain that the very expression of sorrow in the Confiteor accompanied by true interior repentance does forgive venial sins, as does any sincere act of contrition, or many other acts, including the reception of Communion in Mass.

But the rite of itself does not forgive mortal sins. The *General Instruction of the Roman Missal* makes this clear: "The rite concludes with the priest's absolution, which, however, lacks the efficacy of the Sacrament of Penance" (*GIRM* 51). Therefore, before receiving Communion, a person in mortal sin must first receive absolution in the sacrament of Penance (cf. *Catechism of the Catholic Church* 1457).

So, as we can see, the penitential rite of the Mass is a powerful expression of sorrow, but it does not have the same efficacy as the sacrament of Penance, which we should still receive regularly, especially if we have committed mortal sins.

348 Who can give the homily?

In one of the parishes I attend on weekdays, the priest sits down while an acolyte or a lay person gives the homily after the Gospel. Is this correct? Can anyone give the homily?

The first thing to clarify is what we mean by the homily. In simple terms it is the words spoken after the Gospel, usually drawing on the readings, which explain the meaning of the text and exhort the people to put it into practice in their daily lives.

As Pope Benedict XVI pointed out in his Apostolic Exhortation *Sacramentum Caritatis*, "the homily is part of the liturgical action and is meant to foster a deeper understanding of the word of God, so that it can bear fruit in the lives of the faithful" (n. 46). So important is the homily that the *Code of Canon Law* prescribes: "At all Masses on Sundays and holydays of obligation, celebrated with a congregation, there is to be a homily and, except for a grave reason, this may not be omitted" (*CCC* 767 §2). Moreover, "It is strongly recommended that, if a sufficient number of people are present, there be a homily at weekday Masses also, especially during Advent and Lent, or on a feast day or an occasion of grief" (*CCC* 767 §3).

Who then can give the homily? The *Code of Canon Law* is very clear: "The most important form of preaching is the homily, which is part of the liturgy itself and is reserved to a priest or deacon" (*CCC* 767 §1). The Instruction *Redemptionis sacramentum*, issued by the Congregation for Divine Worship and the Discipline of the Sacraments on 25 March 2004 and basing itself on this canon of the Code, says that the homily "should ordinarily be given by the priest celebrant himself. He may entrust it to a concelebrating priest or occasionally, according to circumstances, to a deacon, but never to a lay person" (*RS* 64). Acolytes of course are included among lay persons.

The Instruction goes on to clarify that the prohibition of lay persons preaching within Mass "applies also to seminarians, students of theological disciplines, and those who have assumed the function of those known as 'pastoral assistants'; nor is there to be any exception for any other kind of lay person, or group, or community, or association" (*RS* 66).

Why is the Church so restrictive on the matter? We find the answer in Pope Benedict's Apostolic Exhortation on the Word of God *Verbum Domini*, in a section entitled "The importance of the homily": "... those who have the office of teaching by virtue of sacred ordination or have been entrusted with exercising that ministry, namely, bishops, priests and deacons, expound the word of God" (*VD* 59). That is, the homily is an exercise of the Church's office of teaching, one of the three offices exercised by Christ and entrusted by him to the Church: the offices of teaching, sanctifying and ruling.

Those in sacred orders – bishops, priests and deacons – have been prepared for this teaching role by extensive studies of sacred Scripture, theology, philosophy, etc., and accordingly the Church entrusts only to them the mission of teaching officially in its name during the liturgy. Consequently, the faithful attending the Mass can have the confidence that the person delivering the homily is well prepared for this role.

Does this mean that all bishops, priests and deacons are good preachers? Certainly not. There may very well be lay people in the congregation who could preach much better than they can. But the Church, in her motherly wisdom, has wanted to guarantee to the faithful that the person delivering the homily has at least studied the sacred sciences for a considerable period of time.

This does not preclude the priest occasionally asking a lay person to speak on some project in the parish, on the missions, etc. But this will ordinarily be done towards the end of Mass, before the Prayer after Communion or after Mass has ended. It should not take the place of the homily.

THE MASS   117

Also, in those places where there is a genuine shortage of priests, the diocesan bishop may authorise a non-ordained person to speak at a Communion service or at a "liturgy of the word", but this "may not be transformed from an exceptional measure into an ordinary practice, nor may it be understood as an authentic form of the advancement of the laity" (*RS* 161; cf. *Code of Canon Law*, Can. 766).

349 Why a new translation of the Mass?

After 40 years of using an English translation of the Mass that had simple, easy to follow English, why has the Vatican given us this new translation, which in many passages is difficult to follow and has some cumbersome phrases?

There is a long history to this translation. Although the Second Vatican Council retained Latin as the official language of the Church in the liturgy, it did allow a greater use of the vernacular. In the Dogmatic Constitution on the Sacred Liturgy, *Sacrosanctum Concilium*, the Council declared that "since the use of the mother tongue, whether in the Mass, the administration of the sacraments, or other parts of the liturgy, frequently may be of great advantage to the people, the limits of its employment may be extended" (*SC* 36).

Soon after the Council ended translations came to be prepared in the vernacular all over the world so that the faithful could participate more actively in the Mass. This fuller participation was also desired by the Council, which expressed the wish that "all the faithful should be led to that, conscious and active participation in liturgical celebrations which is demanded by the very nature of the liturgy", which "is the primary and indispensable source from which the faithful are to derive the true Christian spirit" (*SC* 14).

It will be recalled that in the Tridentine Rite, now called the Extraordinary Form of the Mass, the prayers were said by the priest in

Latin facing away from the people and they were barely audible and not intelligible to the faithful in the pews. In a sense they didn't need to be intelligible since the priest was praying to God on behalf of the people. He was talking to God, not to the people. With the change to altars facing the people and the use of the vernacular, the people could now be aware of what was being said and they could participate more consciously and actively in the Mass. This has been a great blessing.

The principle that governed the early translations was known as "dynamic equivalence". It was outlined in the Instruction *Comme le prévoit* of the Consilium for Implementing the Constitution on the Sacred Liturgy in 1969. According to this principle, translations should not be excessively concerned with the structure, form and precise expression of the Latin, but more with conveying accurately in the vernacular the original intention of the Latin. The result was the translation we have been using for some 40 years. As you say, the English was easy to follow and it flowed easily.

Over the years, a new approach to translations came to be developed and it was set out in the Instruction *Liturgiam Authenticam* of the Congregation for Divine Worship and the Discipline of the Sacraments in 2001. Among the considerations identified by the Congregation was the need to preserve the unity of the Roman Rite, which is used by the majority of Catholics. If the translations of the liturgical texts into different languages did not follow the Latin original closely enough, there could be significant differences among them and hence the unity of the liturgy could be lost, and along with it the unity of the faith which those texts express. Following the principle *lex orandi, lex credendi* (the law of praying is the law of believing) people believe as they pray, and so if their prayers are very different from those of another language group, so may be their faith. As is clear, this would endanger the unity of the Church's worship and belief.

Because the English translation, introduced some 40 years ago like that of some other language groups, was seen not to convey adequately the rich scriptural and theological content of the Latin, a new translation was seen to be necessary. Now that the new translation has been introduced, we can appreciate how much richer it is. This is obvious in such prayers as the penitential rite, the Gloria, the Eucharistic Prayers, etc., where now we see whole phrases and words that were omitted in the previous translation. In short, the new translation is a much more faithful rendering of the original Latin.

While at times the language can appear cumbersome and some of the wording strange, we will get used to it as we did with the previous translation, and we will be assured that we are once again praying with the full content of the Latin, in union with our brothers and sisters in the faith throughout the world.

350 "And with your spirit"

One of the aspects of the new translation of the Mass that I find strange is the answer "And with your spirit" after the priest says "The Lord be with you". Why do we resort to such an unusual expression, when "and also with you" is more normal English?

There is a long history to this expression, which occurs five times in the Mass: at the beginning, before the Gospel, before the Preface, in the Sign of Peace and before the Dismissal.

As older people will remember, when Mass was said in Latin the priest greeted the people with *Dominus vobiscum* and the people replied *et cum spiritu tuo*, literally "And with your spirit". When the Mass was translated into the vernacular after the Second Vatican Council, most versions translated the expression literally, English being one of the exceptions. Now we are simply joining the rest of the world in following the Latin more closely.

But what is behind this somewhat unusual expression? The greeting "The Lord be with you" goes back to Old Testament times. In the book of Ruth, Boaz says to the reapers, "The Lord be with you" and they reply "The Lord bless you". It is a very spiritual greeting, a wish that God will be with the other person. In Bavaria, Germany, people still greet one another in the street with *Grüss Gott*, literally "Greet God" or "God greets you". It is much more spiritual than a mere "Hello" or "G'day".

The expression "And with your spirit" is found in several of St Paul's letters. For example, his second letter to Timothy concludes, "The Lord be with your spirit. Grace be with you" (*2 Tim* 4:22) and his letter to the Galatians finishes, "The grace of our Lord Jesus Christ be with your spirit, brethren. Amen" (*Gal* 6:18).

It is clear that the early Christians took up and used this expression. For example, the second reading for Holy Saturday in the *Liturgy of the Hours* is from an ancient homily which describes Christ descending to the Limbo of the Fathers. There he encounters Adam, who says, "My Lord be with everyone" and Jesus replies to Adam, "And with your spirit".

The phrase "And with your spirit" refers to the soul, thus acknowledging that man is not a mere material being but one with a spiritual, immortal soul. It is a testimony to the dignity of the human person, made in the image and likeness of God. And it is a wish that God may be in the soul of the other person.

When we use this greeting in Mass we can consider that we are in union with the Church of the first centuries. We leave our place and time and enter into the timeless realm of the sacred liturgy, where we join the angels and saints in heaven worshipping God.

Although "And with your spirit" can be said to anyone, as we see in the letters of St Paul and in Christ's response to Adam, in the early centuries the Fathers of the Church applied it to the grace of the Holy Spirit present in sacred ministers by the laying on of hands.

Thus in the fourth century St John Chrysostom says in a homily, referring to Bishop Flavian of Antioch: "If the Holy Spirit were not in our Bishop when he gave the peace to all shortly before ascending to his holy sanctuary, you would not have replied to him all together, 'And with your spirit'. This is why you reply with this expression not only when he ascends to the sanctuary, nor when he preaches to you, nor when he prays for you, but when he stands at this holy altar, when he is about to offer this awesome sacrifice. You don't first partake of the offerings until he has prayed for you the grace from the Lord, and you have answered him, 'And with your spirit', reminding yourselves by this reply that he who is here does nothing of his own power, nor are the offered gifts the work of human nature, but it is the grace of the Spirit present and hovering over all things which prepared that mystic sacrifice" (*Homily on Pentecost*).

It is for this reason that since the early centuries only sacred ministers – bishops, priests and deacons – can greet the people by saying "The Lord be with you." In response to the minister's blessing, wishing the people that God be with them, they respond with a similar wish, which is at the same time a profession of faith in the special gift of the Holy Spirit received in the ordination ceremony, configuring the minister to Christ. So there is a long history, one charged with meaning, in the simple greeting "And with your spirit".

351 What does "consubstantial" mean?

Talking with some friends recently about the new translation of the Mass, one of them asked why in the Creed we now say that the Son is "consubstantial" with the Father instead of "of one being" with him. What exactly does this mean?

Admittedly, "consubstantial" is not a word we use in everyday language. Nor for that matter is "transubstantiation", which is related to it and which we apply to the Eucharist. But we must remember that the language of the liturgy, of our divine worship, need not be the language of our everyday speech. Words like "hallowed" and "trespasses", which we use in the Our Father, aren't ordinary either but we don't have any difficulty using them. They are simply the words of a very special prayer and we accept that prayers can use a special language.

But what does "consubstantial" mean, and why the change? The word goes back to the Council of Nicaea in 325, which gave us the first part of the Creed we say in Mass each Sunday. That council rejected the heresy of Arius, who maintained that the second person of the Blessed Trinity, the Son, was not equal to the Father but rather was created by the Father. In the words of Arius, he "came to be from things that were not." Arius also said that the Son of God was "from another substance" than that of the Father (Council of Nicaea I; *DS* 126). In other words, Arius maintained that the Son was not true God, but inferior to God, having been made by the Father.

What do we mean by "substance" in this case? The word is a philosophical one and refers in simple terms to something which exists by itself. For example, God, a tree, a house, a bird, all exist by themselves, on their own. They are substances, existing in their own right. In this sense, substance is distinguished from attributes, or "accidents", like colour, weight, size, etc., which do not exist on their own but only in a substance. For example, in the Eucharist we speak of transubstantiation: change of the substance from bread to the Body of Christ, while the accidents – colour, texture, taste, etc. – remain those of bread.

In God, even though there are three distinct persons – Father, Son and Holy Spirit – there are not three divine substances, or separate divine beings. If there were, there would be three Gods. There is only one divine substance, and therefore only one God. All three persons share the same divine substance, or being.

What Arius was saying was that the Son of God was "from another substance" that that of the Father. That is, the Son was a different and separate being, in fact created by the Father. Against this error the Council of Nicaea professed that the Son of God is "begotten, not made, of the same substance (*homoousios* in Greek) as the Father." The Latin translation, used in the West practically from the time of Nicaea, used the expression *consubstantialem Patri*, consubstantial with the Father.

The new translation of the Mass, in order to be as faithful to the Latin as possible, uses the equivalent English term, "consubstantial" with the Father. Even though it is not an everyday English word, it does have a very precise meaning and the translators wanted to preserve this meaning so that everywhere in the English-speaking world the Church would express its faith in the same clear and precise way.

In his Apostolic Exhortation *Verbum Domini* (2010), Pope Benedict XVI used the word to refer to two different realities. He writes: "As the Prologue of John clearly shows us, the *Logos* refers in the first place to the eternal Word, the only Son, begotten of the Father before all ages and consubstantial with him: *the word was with God, and the word was God*" (*Jn* 1:1; n. 7). That is, the Word, the Son of God, was of the same substance as the Father, consubstantial with him.

But at the same time, on becoming man, the Word took on human flesh and became of the same substance as us: "But this same Word, Saint John tells us, 'became flesh' (*Jn* 1:14); hence Jesus Christ, born of the Virgin Mary, is truly the Word of God who has become consubstantial with us" (n. 7). In summary, by using the word "consubstantial" in the Creed, the Church retains a traditional term with a very precise meaning, just as it does in retaining the word "transubstantiation".

352 "My sacrifice and yours"

Why after the presentation of the gifts in the Mass does the priest now say "Pray, brethren, that my sacrifice and yours may be acceptable to God, the almighty Father"? Isn't it the same as "that our sacrifice may be acceptable"? Why the change?

This is a very significant change, with important theological implications. The first reason for it is that it corresponds more faithfully to the Latin *meum ac vestrum sacrificium,* my sacrifice and yours.

But why does the Latin distinguish between the sacrifice of the priest and that of the congregation? And to what sacrifice is it referring? The sacrifice referred to is in the first place the sacrifice of the Mass itself; that is, the sacrifice of Christ offered to the Father on Calvary for our Redemption and made present on the altar. This is one of the many reminders in the Mass that what is being celebrated in the Eucharist is truly a sacrifice, not just a meal.

Our Lord referred to the Eucharist as a sacrifice when he instituted it in the Last Supper. As St Paul relates, he said, "This is my body which is for you" and "This chalice is the new covenant in my blood." He went on to ask the apostles to celebrate the Eucharist down the ages: "Do this in remembrance of me" (*1 Cor* 11:24-25). In order to emphasise that the Eucharist is truly a sacrifice, St Paul added, "For as often as you eat this bread and drink the chalice, you proclaim the Lord's death until he comes" (*1 Cor* 11:26). So the sacrifice of the Mass is the very sacrifice of Christ made present on the altar.

In the words of the *Catechism of the Catholic Church*, "The sacrifice of Christ and the sacrifice of the Eucharist are one single sacrifice: The victim is one and the same: the same now offers through the ministry of priests, who then offered himself on the cross; only the manner of offering is different. In this divine sacrifice which is celebrated in the Mass, the same Christ who offered himself once in a bloody manner on the altar of the cross is contained and is offered in an unbloody manner" (*CCC* 1367).

As this point from the Catechism says, "the same [Christ] now offers through the ministry of priests..." Why only through the ministry of priests? Because of the sacramental power they received through the laying on of hands in Holy Orders, priests act in the person of Christ the head of the Mystical Body when they celebrate Mass, and they are able to bring about the Real Presence of Christ in the host and the Precious Blood. They become one with Christ and thus are able to bring about this awesome mystery. No lay person can do this.

So when the priest refers to "my sacrifice" he is speaking of the sacrifice of the Mass which he brings about, acting in the very person of Christ to offer Christ as the victim to the Father. That is why in the response to the prayer "Pray, brethren" the people answer, "May the Lord accept the sacrifice *at your hands*". It is only through the priest that the sacrifice can be offered.

But this does not mean that the lay faithful are merely passive spectators. By virtue of their common priesthood, their sharing in the priesthood of Christ received in Baptism, they unite themselves with the priest by their intention in offering the Mass to the Father. For this reason the priest can also speak of "your sacrifice."

But there is still another sense in which the lay faithful join in the sacrifice. The Catechism speaks of this when it calls the Mass "the sacrifice of the Church": "The Church which is the Body of Christ participates in the offering of her Head. With him, she herself is offered whole and entire. She unites herself to his intercession with the Father for all men. In the Eucharist the sacrifice of Christ becomes also the sacrifice of the members of his Body. The lives of the faithful, their praise, sufferings, prayer and work, are united with those of Christ and with his total offering, and so acquire a new value. Christ's sacrifice present on the altar makes it possible for all generations of Christians to be united with his offering" (*CCC* 1368).

As the sacrifice of the Church, both the priest and the congregation offer themselves and the whole Church to the Father. All their concerns, their sufferings, their family, their prayer and work, can be united with the sacrifice of the Mass and so acquire a new value. So we see that there is an important distinction between the sacrifice of the priest and that of the rest of the faithful, but all offer themselves too to the Father.

353 "Lift up your hearts"

I have always been intrigued by the prayers before the Preface in the Mass, especially the "Lift up your hearts" and the new response "It is right and just". There must be something behind them that I don't understand. Can you help me?

These prayers are some of the most ancient in the Mass. They are found in the *Traditio Apostolica* of St Hippolytus, dated around 215 AD, and are used in all the Eucharistic Prayers. Thus when we say them we can unite ourselves with the Catholics of the third century, and with all those ever since.

The words of that ancient document say: "Let the deacons present the offering to [the bishop]. When he lays his hands on it, with the whole college of priests, let him say the words of thanksgiving: 'The Lord be with you'. 'And with your spirit'. 'Let us lift up our hearts'. 'They are turned to the Lord'. 'Let us give thanks to the Lord our God'. 'It is worthy and just'". We see in this dialogue almost the exact words we say today in the new translation of the Mass, which is a more literal rendering of the Latin version of St Hippolytus. What is the meaning of these prayers?

After the greeting, "The Lord be with you" and its response, the priest says in Latin *Sursum corda*, which means literally "Hearts above" or "Hearts on high." The idea is found in the Old Testament: "Let us stretch out our hearts and hands to God in heaven" (*Lam* 3:41).

In one of his sermons, St Augustine says, "Lift up your heart so that it will not rot on earth. This is the advice given by him who wishes not to destroy, but to save" (*Sermo* 60, 7). It is an exhortation similar to that of St Paul in his letter to the Colossians: "If then you have been raised with Christ, seek the things that are above, where Christ is, seated at the right hand of God. Set your minds on things that are above, not on things that are on earth" (*Col* 3:1-2).

It also echoes Our Lord's exhortation in the Sermon on the Mount to "lay up for yourselves treasures in heaven, where neither moth nor rust consumes and where thieves do not break in and steal. For where your treasure is, there will your heart be also" (*Mt* 6:20-21). Thus, as the Mass enters into its central part, the Eucharistic Prayer, we are invited to leave the world and its cares behind and lift up our minds and hearts to God.

Or, in the words of the *General Instruction of the Roman Missal*, "Now the centre and summit of the entire celebration begins, namely, the Eucharistic Prayer, that is, the prayer of thanksgiving and sanctification. The priest invites the people to lift up their hearts to the Lord in prayer and thanksgiving" (*GIRM* 78).

St Cyril of Jerusalem (315-386), says of this rite in his *Mystagogical Catechesis*, his instruction to new converts in Jerusalem around the year 352: "The priest cries out, 'Lift up your hearts!' For in this most solemn hour it is necessary for us to have our hearts raised up with God, and not fixed below on the earth and earthly things. It is as if the priest is instructing us to dismiss all physical cares and domestic anxieties, and to have our hearts in heaven with the benevolent God. Then you answer, 'We lift them up to the Lord.' In other words, you give assent to what the priest has said by the acknowledgement that you make. Let no one come here, then, who could say, 'We lift them up to the Lord,' whilst being preoccupied with physical cares" (*Cat. Myst.* 848d).

St Cyril goes on: "Then the priest says, 'Let us give thanks to the

Lord.' Certainly we ought to give thanks to God for having invited us, unworthy as we are, to so great a gift. We ought to give thanks to God for reconciling us to himself when we were his enemies. We ought to give thanks to God for having made us his adopted children by the Spirit. Then you say, 'It is right and just.' For in giving thanks, we do a worthy thing, something that is justice itself. But what God did in accounting us worthy of such benefits was not justice, but much more than just" (*Cat. Myst.* 848e).

That is, it is only right and just that we should thank God for his mercy, which went way beyond justice in redeeming us and uniting us with him, making us his adopted children. What God did for us was mercy; our thanksgiving to him is justice.

On saying this prayer we can consider all the reasons we have for praising and thanking God: creation, the incarnation, redemption, the Church, the sacraments, our faith, our life and health, our talents, our family... In summary, what is contained in this simple and ancient dialogue in the Mass is rich indeed.

354 "For all" – "For many"

In the new translation of the Mass the priest now says in the consecration of the Precious Blood that Jesus shed his blood "for many", not for "all". Didn't Christ die for everyone?

We can begin by answering your question, "Didn't Christ die for everyone?" so that we understand the scope of Redemption. The answer is that Jesus did of course die "for all". This is clear in many passages of Scripture. For example: "For the love of Christ urges us on, because we are convinced that one has died for all" (*2 Cor* 5:14); and "...he is the expiation for our sins, and not for ours only but also for the sins of the whole world" (*1 Jn* 2:2).

Then why the change to "for many"? Simply, because "for all" is an inaccurate translation of *pro multis*, for many, used in the *Missale Romanum*, which is the official missal from which translations are made. At the request of Pope Benedict XVI, in 2006 the Congregation for Divine Worship and the Discipline of the Sacraments sent a letter to the presidents of all bishops' conferences asking that in those countries where the vernacular translation was "for all", this should be changed to "for many". In this way, following the directives of the Instruction *Liturgicam authenticam*, which sets out the criteria for translations of liturgical texts into the various languages, the translation would conform to the Latin original, which is *pro multis*, literally "for many".

But why did the Latin missal say *pro multis* when it is clear that Jesus shed his blood "for all", not just "for many"? The answer goes back to the Scriptures themselves, where the Gospels, narrating the institution of the Eucharist by Christ, use the words *pro multis*, or πολλων, *pollon*, in Greek. Thus, in the Gospel of St Matthew Jesus says: "for this is my blood of the covenant, which is poured out for many for the forgiveness of sins" (*Mt* 26:28), and St Mark records identical words (cf. *Mk* 14:24). On another occasion, Jesus says: "For the Son of Man also came ... to give his life as a ransom for many" (*Mk* 10:45). This in turn is a reflection of the words used by Isaiah of the suffering servant, or Messiah: "...yet he bore the sin of many, and made intercession for the transgressors" (*Is* 53:12).

What are we to make of this distinction between "for all" and "for many"? Pope Benedict, in his second volume of *Jesus of Nazareth*, says that "many" and "all" cannot be taken to mean the same thing. The prevailing opinion of Scripture scholars today, he says, is that the word "many" in Isaiah and on the lips of Jesus does indicate a totality, but it refers to the totality of Israel, thus to a limited "all" (p. 135).

Today, it would refer to the Church and to those others who accept God's word. The letter of the Congregation for Divine Worship explains: "The expression 'for many,' while remaining open to the inclusion of each human person, is reflective also of the fact that this salvation is not brought about in some mechanistic way, without one's willing or participation; rather, the believer is invited to accept in faith the gift that is being offered and to receive the supernatural life that is given to those who participate in this mystery, living it out in their lives as well so as to be numbered among the 'many' to whom the text refers."

Theologians have explained this in terms of the *sufficiency* and the *efficacy* of Christ's death. Jesus truly "gave himself as a ransom for all" (*1 Tim* 2:6), and so his death is *sufficient* to redeem all mankind. But not all are in fact saved. His death is *efficacious* only "for many", for those who freely choose to live their lives in accordance with God's will (cf. *LG* 16).

In any case, the Congregation explains that "a text corresponding to the words *pro multis,* handed down by the Church, constitutes the formula that has been used in the Roman Rite in Latin from the earliest centuries." Moreover, "The Roman Rite in Latin has always said *pro multis* and never *pro omnibus* [for all] in the consecration of the chalice." What is more, "The anaphoras of the various Oriental Rites, whether in Greek, Syriac, Armenian, the Slavic languages, etc., contain the verbal equivalent of the Latin *pro multis* in their respective languages."

355 "The light of your face"

Can you please tell me the meaning of the unusual expression "welcome them into the light of your face" in the new translation of the second Eucharistic Prayer?

The new translation of course simply brings the English into line with the Latin, which is *in lumen vultus tui,* literally "into the light of your face." The former translation was "into the light of your presence". Those to be welcomed into the light of God's face are "our brothers and sisters who have fallen asleep in the hope of the resurrection, and all who have died in your mercy".

It should be remembered that the second Eucharistic Prayer is a new one, introduced after the Second Vatican Council. Before that, only the first Eucharistic Prayer, or Roman Canon, existed in the Latin rite. So we are dealing with a modern inclusion in the liturgy, not an ancient one. Then why this strange expression?

Since all the Eucharistic Prayers are addressed to God the Father, the expression "the light of your face" refers to the face of God the Father himself. But does God have a face? Jesus Christ, the incarnate Son of God, has a human face, which all those who knew him on earth saw and which we will see in his risen body in heaven. But God the Father and the Holy Spirit, who are pure spirit, do not have a face in the strict sense.

Yet God himself in speaking with Moses refers to his face: "'But', he said, 'you cannot see my face; for man shall not see me and live'" (*Ex* 33:20). Likewise, God says to Solomon: "If my people who are called by my name humble themselves, and pray and seek my face ... then I will hear from heaven..." (*2 Chron* 7:14). St Paul too, speaking of heaven, refers to the face of God: "For now we see in a mirror dimly, but then face to face" (*1 Cor* 13:12).

How will we see the face of God in heaven? Theologians have said that in order to do this we will be given what they call the *lumen gloriae*, the light of glory. This is understood as a special help in order to see God, who is pure spirit.

But why do we speak of the "light" of God's face? It is clear that everything about God is light. If we associate darkness with the devil, we associate light with God. Jesus himself says to Nicodemus: "And this is the judgment, that the light has come into the world, and men loved darkness rather than light, because their deeds were evil. For every one who does evil hates the light, and does not come to the light, lest his deeds should be exposed. But he who does what is true comes to the light, that it may be clearly seen that his deeds have been wrought in God" (*Jn* 3:19-21).

Indeed, Jesus calls himself the light: "I am the light of the world; he who follows me will not walk in darkness, but will have the light of life" (*Jn* 8:12). And he shows us the light of his face in the Transfiguration on Mount Tabor: "And he was transfigured before them, and his face shone like the sun" (*Mt* 17:2). Even a human being like Moses, who is a figure of Christ, reflected the light of God in his face after coming down from the mountain: "his face shone because he had been talking with God ... and they were afraid to come near him" (*Ex* 34:29-30).

We find mention of the light of God's face several times in the book of Psalms. For example: "Lift up the light of your countenance upon us, O Lord!" (*Ps* 4:6). "Blessed are the people who know the festal shout, who walk, O Lord, in the light of your countenance, who exult in your name all the day, and extol your righteousness" (*Ps* 89:15-16). "You have set our iniquities before you, our secret sins in the light of your countenance" (*Ps* 90:9).

So the expression "the light of your face" is solidly based in Scripture. One day, if we are faithful until the end, we will behold the light of God's face in heaven. Indeed, we long for it. With the psalmist we say: "Hear, O Lord, when I cry aloud, be gracious to me and answer me! You have said, 'Seek my face.' My heart says to you, 'Your face, Lord, do I seek.' Hide not your face from me" (*Ps* 27:7-9).

356 "From the rising of the sun to its setting"

Why in the new translation of the Mass, in the third Eucharistic Prayer, does the priest now say "from the rising of the sun to its setting" rather than "from East to West"?

At the beginning of the third Eucharistic Prayer the priest says, "...

you never cease to gather a people to yourself, so that from the rising of the sun to its setting a pure sacrifice may be offered to your name".

The phrase you mention is taken from the prophecy of Malachi in the Old Testament and is rich in meaning. The prophet records how God is unhappy with his people because they offer defective animals in sacrifice: "I have no pleasure in you, says the Lord of hosts, and I will not accept an offering from your hand. For from the rising of the sun to its setting my name is great among the nations, and in every place incense is offered to my name, and a pure offering; for my name is great among the nations, says the Lord of hosts" (*Mal* 1:10-11). It is a prophecy of a time to come when a perfect sacrifice, "a pure offering", would be made to God "from the rising of the sun to its setting". That is, it would be offered around the clock.

We know that the sacrifices of the Old Law could never be perfect since the victim offered was only an animal. Even when the animal was without blemish it could never take sins away. The Letter to the Hebrews compares these imperfect sacrifices with the definitive sacrifice of Christ: "For it is impossible that the blood of bulls and goats should take away sins ... But when Christ had offered for all time a single sacrifice for sins, he sat down at the right hand of God, then to wait until his enemies should be made a stool for his feet. For by a single sacrifice he has perfected for all time those who are sanctified" (*Heb* 10:4, 12-14). Indeed, the perfect sacrifice prophesied by Malachi is the sacrifice of Christ on the Cross, made present in the Mass.

The *Catechism of the Catholic Church* teaches: "The Eucharist is the memorial of Christ's Passover, the making present and the sacramental offering of his unique sacrifice, in the liturgy of the Church which is his Body" (*CCC* 1362).

Apart from the sacrifice of animals in the Temple, the Jews in the Old Testament had another sacrifice, a Communion sacrifice known as the *Todah*. It involved the slaughter of an animal, whose entrails were then placed on the altar and some parts were given to the priest, after which the family and friends ate the rest in a ritual meal, often in thanksgiving for some favour. Indeed, the name *Todah* comes from a Hebrew word meaning thanksgiving. Prayers were said in the meal, some of them in the form of psalms, among them psalms 23, 70 and 117. In addition there was an offering of unleavened bread and wine.

The ancient rabbis believed that when the Messiah would come all sacrifices except the *Todah* would cease, but the *Todah* would continue for all eternity. In fact, since the destruction of the Temple in 70 AD all other sacrifices did cease and the *Todah*, in the form of the Eucharist, the thanksgiving sacrifice with the reception of the victim in Holy Communion, has remained. The then prefect of the Congregation for the Doctrine of the Faith, Cardinal Joseph Ratzinger, later Pope Benedict XVI, wrote: "Structurally speaking, the whole of Christology, indeed the whole of Eucharistic Christology, is present in the *Todah* spirituality of the Old Testament" (*Feast of Faith*, Ignatius Press 1986, p. 57).

The very name Eucharist, like *Todah*, means thanksgiving. In the words of the Catechism, "The Eucharist is a sacrifice of thanksgiving to the Father, a blessing by which the Church expresses her gratitude to God for all his benefits, for all that he has accomplished through creation, redemption, and sanctification. Eucharist means first of all 'thanksgiving'" (*CCC* 1360).

Now that the Mass has replaced the numerous Old Testament sacrifices and there are priests all over the world, the perfect sacrifice prophesied by Malachi is indeed celebrated "from the rising of the sun to its setting". In fact, if every priest in the world celebrates one Mass each day, a very conservative estimate, every second of the day on average five Masses are beginning somewhere in the world! What is certain is that at any time of the day around the clock, there are numerous Masses being celebrated somewhere in the world. This is truly a pure offering from the rising of the sun to its setting.

357 "The Order of Bishops"

In the new translation of the Mass, reference is made in the third Eucharistic Prayer to the "Order of Bishops". What exactly does the word "order" mean?

The word "order" goes back to the early Church. The *Catechism of the Catholic Church* explains: "The word *order* in Roman antiquity designated an established civil body, especially a governing body. *Ordinatio* means incorporation into an *ordo*. In the Church there are established bodies which Tradition, not without a basis in sacred Scripture, has since ancient times called *taxeis* (Greek) or *ordines*. And so the liturgy speaks of the *ordo episcoporum,* the *ordo presbyterorum*, the *ordo diaconorum*. Other groups also receive this name of *ordo*: catechumens, virgins, spouses, widows" (*CCC* 1537).

As this text implies, the term *ordo*, or order, had a much broader meaning in the early Church than it does today, when it refers primarily to those in sacred, or holy, orders. Then it meant an established body of persons who had certain rights and duties in the early Church. Thus, for example, catechumens, or those preparing for Baptism, constituted a distinct order. They were allowed to attend the first part of the Mass, the liturgy of the Word, which until the Second Vatican Council was sometimes referred to as the "Mass of the Catechumens". Then they were ushered out for the liturgy of the Eucharist, known as the "Mass of the Faithful".

In the early Church there were three orders for groups of women: the orders of virgins, widows and deaconesses. In each case, incorporation into the order entailed the acceptance of certain duties and rights in the Church.

As regards virgins, St Paul advised all who could to remain unmarried in order to be more available for the things of God and to pursue holiness in body and spirit (cf. *1 Cor* 7:34-38). Virgins constituted a distinct group in the Church, but entry into this order did not involve the laying on of hands. In his *Apostolic Tradition* St Hippolytus says: "A virgin does not have an imposition of hands, for personal choice alone is that which makes a virgin."

In an earlier column, I wrote of the order of deaconesses (cf. J. Flader, *Question Time 2,* q. 167), who were not ordained ministers as are deacons today, but who assisted in the instruction and baptism of women, visited sick women and took Holy Communion to them, etc. Similarly, the order of widows involved certain duties, among them being very devout in their spiritual life, instructing younger women, etc.

These women's orders did not involve any primary function in the liturgy but there were at the same time orders of men which did. Apart from bishops, priests and deacons, which have always existed, these included subdeacons, porters (or door keepers), readers, acolytes and exorcists. The latter four were called "minor orders" and they were, as a rule, received as preparatory stages on the way to the priesthood. They were distinguished from the "major orders" of subdeacons, deacons, priests and bishops.

Among the roles of porters were to watch over those who entered Mass and to usher out the catechumens at the end of the "Mass of the Catechumens". Readers, or lectors, in the first centuries had the role of reading all the lessons in Mass, including the Epistle and the Gospel. Acolytes assisted the deacon in the liturgy, and exorcists prayed over people to bring about their release from various forms of demonic influence.

Pope Paul VI, in the Apostolic Letter *Ministeria quaedam*, on 15 August 1972, reformed the minor orders. The offices of reader and acolyte were retained as "ministries", and could be conferred on laymen in a ceremony to be called "institution", not "ordination". The subdiaconate, which was a "major order", was abolished in the Latin

Church, leaving the three traditional major orders of bishop, priest and deacon.

The major orders are all mentioned in the Scriptures and they have principal roles in the sacred liturgy. They are known as "holy orders" because they confer the sacrament of Holy Orders in its three degrees of episcopate, presbyterate, and diaconate through the laying on of hands by a bishop, in a ceremony properly called "ordination".

The order of bishops is thus the body of those in the Church who have received the fullness of the sacrament of Holy Orders, and who are the successors of the apostles in the Church.

358 "We dare to say"

Why in the new translation of the Mass, in the invitation to the Our Father, does the priest say "we dare to say"? Surely if Jesus has given us the prayer, we don't need to "dare" to say it.

As with the other changes, these words are a more faithful translation of the Latin, which in this case is *audemus dicere,* literally "we dare to say". But why do we need to "dare" to say a prayer which Jesus himself gave us? The answer is that we don't need to dare to say the prayer, but we do need to dare to call God "our Father".

When we consider that God is the infinite pure spirit, all powerful and all knowing, who created this vast universe out of nothing, we would tend to approach him, in the sense that we creatures can approach him at all, in a spirit of awe and reverence, even with fear and trembling. That is the way most religions have looked upon God over the centuries. They would worship God in a spirit of humility and reverence, they would try to appease him by their prayers and sacrifices, but they would not dare to call him "Father".

Jesus, the eternal Son of God who took human nature in the womb of Our Lady, turned all of that around. Through him we have been adopted as God's children and hence we can call God "Father". In the Sermon on the Mount, in addition to giving us the Our Father, Jesus referred constantly to God as our Father. For example, "But when you pray, go into your room and shut the door and pray to your Father who is in secret; and your Father who sees in secret will reward you" (*Mt* 6:6); "If you then, who are evil, know how to give good gifts to your children, how much more will your Father who is in heaven give good things to those who ask him!" (*Mt* 7:11).

St Cyprian, a third-century Father of the Church, in his long commentary on the Our Father, writes, "How merciful the Lord Jesus is towards us, how abundantly kind and good! He permits us, when praying in the sight of God, to call God our Father and to be called sons of God even as Christ is Son of God. Not one of us would dare to use that name in prayer, had not he himself allowed us to pray in that way. We must remember, then, dearest brothers, we must realise that when we call God 'Father', we ought to act like sons of God, so that as we are pleased to have God as our Father, so he will be pleased with us" (*De Dom. Orat.*, 11).

The *Catechism of the Catholic Church* explains: "In the Roman liturgy, the Eucharistic assembly is invited to pray to our heavenly Father with filial boldness; the Eastern liturgies develop and use similar expressions: 'dare in all confidence,' 'make us worthy of...' From the burning bush Moses heard a voice saying to him, 'Do not come near; put off your shoes from your feet, for the place on which you are standing is holy ground' (*Ex* 3:5). Only Jesus could cross that threshold of the divine holiness, for 'when he had made purification for sins,' he brought us into the Father's presence: 'Here am I, and the children God has given me" (*Heb* 1:3; 2:13; *CCC* 2777).

The Catechism goes on to quote a beautiful passage from St Peter Chrysologus: "Our awareness of our status as slaves would make us sink into the ground and our earthly condition would dissolve into dust, if the authority of our Father himself and the Spirit of his Son had not impelled us to this cry... 'Abba, Father!' ... When would a mortal dare call God 'Father,' if man's innermost being were not animated by power from on high?" (*Sermo* 71, 3; *CCC* 2777).

St Ambrose too is very eloquent: "O man, you did not dare to raise your face to heaven, you lowered your eyes to the earth, and suddenly you have received the grace of Christ: all your sins have been forgiven. From being a wicked servant you have become a good son... Then raise your eyes to the Father who has begotten you through Baptism, to the Father who has redeemed you through his Son, and say: 'Our Father...' But do not claim any privilege. He is the Father in a special way only of Christ, but he is the common Father of us all, because while he has begotten only Christ, he has created us. Then also say by his grace, 'Our Father', so that you may merit being his son" (*De Sacr.* 5, 4, 19).

We give thanks to God "because he has caused us to be reborn to his life by *adopting* us as his children in his only Son" (*CCC* 2782). And we live with joyful trust in God's fatherly providence, saying the Our Father with a deep sense of gratitude for having been adopted as God's own children.

359 "The supper of the Lamb"

In the new translation of the Mass, one part that has me intrigued is just before Communion, when the priest says, "Blessed are those called to the supper of the Lamb", and we answer, "Lord, I am not worthy that you should enter under my roof". Why this strange wording?

I will comment on three changes in these words, since you didn't specify which aspects you found strange. In any case, I know of other people who have also been bewildered by the new wording.

It would be helpful to begin with the words the priest says just prior to the ones you mention. When he holds up the host the priest says to the people, "Behold the Lamb of God, behold him who takes away the sins of the world." These are, of course, the words said by John the Baptist when Jesus approached him (cf. *Jn* 1:29). Jesus is the true Lamb of God, of which the paschal lamb sacrificed and eaten by the Jews on the feast of Passover was just a figure. He is the sacrificial lamb who offers his life on the cross to take away our sins and then gives himself to us in Communion.

The priest goes on to say, "Blessed are those called to the supper of the Lamb." The word Blessed, which replaces Happy, is the English translation of the Latin *Beati* and is worthy of comment. The word is well-known as the first word of the Beatitudes, which Jesus announces in the Sermon on the Mount. For example, "Blessed are the poor in spirit for theirs is the kingdom of heaven" (*Mt* 5:3). The very name "Beatitudes" derives from the Latin word *Beati*, or Blessed, used by St Jerome in the Latin Vulgate Bible. It is the word that also gives us "beatification" in English, the process whereby someone is declared "Blessed" by the Church. Also, some Eastern Patriarchs are referred to as "His Beatitude", equivalent to "His Holiness".

The usual translation of *beati* is indeed "blessed", although some versions, including the *Jerusalem Bible,* used in the Lectionary, translate the word as "happy". The word "blessed" expresses much more than "happy". It refers not just to an emotional state, as does "happy", but to an inner state of holiness, of closeness to God, of blessedness. Indeed, those called to the supper of the Lamb are truly fortunate, blessed by God.

We should remember that not all are called to receive Communion. Any non-Catholics in the congregation, with the exception of the Orthodox, are not called, nor are Catholics who are not in the state of grace or who have not lived the Eucharistic fast of one hour. Thus those who are able to receive Communion are truly blessed, both because their state of grace is already a state of holiness, and because they are invited to come forward to receive the Lamb of God in holy Communion and thus to increase their holiness.

A second change is the mention of the "supper of the Lamb", instead of "his supper". It is a more faithful translation of the Latin *ad cenam Agni*. What is the "supper of the Lamb"? It can refer to two suppers. In the first place it refers to the Communion that is about to take place. Those who receive Communion receive Christ, whole and entire, the Lamb of God who takes away the sins of the world. But it can also refer to the eternal wedding banquet of the Lamb in heaven mentioned in the Book of Revelation: "Blessed are those who are invited to the marriage supper of the Lamb" (*Rev* 19:9). Indeed, receiving Christ in Communion on earth is already an anticipation of the communion we will have with him in Heaven. Outside of heaven, there is no closer communion with Christ.

And to those who receive him in Communion Jesus promises heaven: "I am the living bread which came down from heaven; if any one eats of this bread, he will live for ever" (*Jn* 6:51). And again: "[H]e who eats my flesh and drinks my blood has eternal life, and I will raise him up at the last day" (*Jn* 6:54).

Finally, why the strange wording "Lord, I am not worthy that you should enter under my roof" instead of the more simple "Lord, I am not worthy to receive you"? Again, this is a more faithful rendering of the Latin, and a more scriptural one too. It, records the words of the centurion who had asked Jesus to heal his servant: "Lord, I am not worthy to have you come under my roof; but only say the word, and my servant will be healed" (*Mt* 8:8). We, like the centurion, express our unworthiness that Our Lord should come under our roof, into our soul, but we ask him to say the word and our soul will be healed.

Holy Communion

360 Acolytes and ministers of Communion

Do acolytes and ministers of Communion have the same functions? It seems that the functions of an acolyte have been taken over by ministers of Communion. Also, in some parishes there are ministers of Communion when it seems to me they are not really needed.

First of all, let me clarify a matter of terminology. You refer to "ministers of Communion", by which I presume you mean lay people who assist in distributing Communion. Their proper title is "extraordinary ministers of Communion" to distinguish them from priests and deacons, who are ordinary ministers of Communion. Sometimes people call them "extraordinary ministers of the Eucharist" or "Eucharistic ministers" but this is incorrect. The only minister who can bring about the sacrament of the Eucharist is a validly ordained priest, so that lay people can never be extraordinary ministers of the Eucharist.

What is the function of acolytes? In 1973 Pope Paul VI issued an Apostolic Letter *Motu proprio* entitled *Ministeria quaedam* in which he declared that the former so-called "minor orders" of acolyte, reader, exorcist and porter (doorkeeper), which were conferred in preparation for the priesthood, were to be abolished.

The functions of acolyte and reader, which could be conferred on lay men, were to be retained as "ministries". Moreover, their conferral was to be called "institution" rather than the former "ordination". Thus one is "instituted" as an acolyte. It should be noted that while only men can be formally instituted as acolytes or readers, both men and women can exercise these roles on a temporary basis, as is so often done (cf. *Code of Canon Law*, Can. 230).

The Apostolic Letter describes the functions of acolytes: "The acolyte is appointed in order to aid the deacon and to minister to the priest. It is his duty therefore to attend to the service of the altar and to assist the deacon and the priest in liturgical celebrations, especially in the celebration of Mass; he is also to distribute Communion as a special minister when the ministers spoken of in the *Code of Canon Law*, Canon 845 are not available or are prevented by ill health, age, or another pastoral ministry from performing this function, or when the number of communicants is so great that the celebration of Mass would be unduly prolonged. In the same extraordinary circumstances an acolyte may be entrusted with publicly exposing the Blessed Sacrament for adoration by the faithful and afterward replacing it, but not with blessing the people" (n. 6).

It is clear from this that acolytes have a much greater role than extraordinary ministers of Communion. They assist the deacon, if there is one, and the priest at the altar throughout the Mass, much as an altar server does. And they usually help the priest in setting things up before Mass and in taking them away afterwards. If required they also distribute Communion as extraordinary ministers. If additional assistance is needed, other lay people can be called to distribute Communion but it is clear that the acolyte should always be the first one to exercise this role.

Moreover, extraordinary ministers of Communion should be called upon only when "the priest is prevented by weakness or advanced age or some other genuine reason, or when the number of faithful coming to Communion is so great that the very celebration of Mass would be unduly prolonged. This, however, is to be understood in such a way that a brief prolongation, considering the circumstances and culture of the place, is not at all a sufficient reason" (CDW, Instr. *Redemptionis sacramentum*, n. 158). In weekday Masses in many parishes, for example, the number of communicants is such that there is no need for extraordinary ministers.

It is clear too that "the practice of those priests is reprobated who, even though present at the celebration, abstain from distributing Communion and hand this function over to laypersons" (*ibid.* n. 157). But if the priest is unable to distribute Communion himself because of weakness or old age, he may call on an extraordinary minister. Naturally this criterion applies to large concelebrated Masses when a number of priests and possibly deacons are present. In these cases there is no need for extraordinary ministers of Communion.

361 Communion for all

For a long time now I have noticed that practically everyone in Sunday Mass receives Communion. At the same time there are very few people in confessions on Saturday. Is this a good thing?

While it is always good to be able to receive Communion, I too have reservations in general about the situation you describe. Let me give some background on the matter.

Our Lord, in giving the Church the great gift of himself in the Eucharist, obviously wanted us to receive him often, and in the early Church the faithful were encouraged to receive Communion frequently. For example, in the fourth century St Ambrose wrote: "If this is daily bread, why do you receive it only once a year? Receive each and every day what will be of such benefit to you." He went on to warn, however, that the reception of Communion implied living appropriately: "And be sure to live each day in a manner that makes you worthy to receive him" (*On the Sacraments*, V, 4).

Similarly, the *Didache*, written around the end of the first century, gives the conditions for receiving Communion: "Let no one eat or drink of your Eucharist unless they have been baptised... If anyone is holy, let him come; if anyone is not so, let him repent." Thus from the beginning, the Church encouraged frequent Communion but always insisted on the need to be suitably prepared for so great a gift.

It has always been taught that no one should receive Communion in the state of mortal sin. It would be a complete lack of respect for Christ to reject him by a mortal sin and then presume to receive him in Communion without first repenting. For this reason the *Catechism of the Catholic Church* teaches: "Anyone who desires to receive Christ in Eucharistic Communion must be in the state of grace. Anyone aware of having sinned mortally must not receive Communion without having received absolution in the sacrament of penance" (*CCC* 1415). Indeed, to receive Communion in the state of mortal sin would be to commit a new mortal sin of sacrilege.

It has not always been the case that practically everyone goes up to receive Communion. In part due to the rigorist Jansenist heresy, for a long time many people believed they could receive Communion only if they had been to confession the previous day. They thought they had to be free from any stain of sin in order to receive Our Lord worthily.

This mentality is rejected in the Catechism, which teaches that Communion is a remedy for venial sin: "As bodily nourishment restores lost strength, so the Eucharist strengthens our charity, which tends to be weakened in daily life; and this living charity *wipes away venial sins*. By giving himself to us Christ revives our love and enables us to break our disordered attachments to creatures and root ourselves in him" (*CCC* 1394).

Pope Benedict XVI, in his book *Light of the World*, comments on the phenomenon of virtually everyone going up to receive Communion. In answer to a question on his practice of giving Communion on the tongue to communicants who are kneeling, he said: "In this context, where people think that everyone is just automatically supposed to receive Communion – everyone else is going up, so I will, too – I wanted to send a clear signal. I wanted it to be clear: Something quite special is going on here! *He* is here, the one before whom we fall on our knees! Pay attention! This is not just some social ritual in which we can take part if we want to" (*Light of the World*, Ignatius Press 2010, p. 159).

Those who know they are in mortal sin should therefore abstain from receiving Communion until they have been to sacramental confession. Even if they are with their family or friends, they should not receive. The very fact of not being able to receive Communion is an added incentive to avoid mortal sins and to go to confession frequently.

362 Denying Communion

I am an extraordinary minister of Communion and sometimes people come forward who I know should not be receiving it, for example people married outside the Church or in a de facto relationship. What should I do?

This is a very delicate matter. First of all, who should not be given Communion? The *Code of Canon Law* establishes: "Those upon whom the penalty of excommunication or interdict has been imposed or declared, and others who obstinately persist in manifest grave sin, are not to be admitted to Holy Communion" (Can. 915).

The phrase "who obstinately persist in manifest grave sin" includes the people you mentioned in your question; for example, people living together in a *de facto* relationship, people who have been married outside the Church often following a divorce, people who are known to be living with their gay or lesbian partner, etc. It should be remembered that, in addition, non-Catholics, with the exception of the Orthodox in certain circumstances (cf. Can. 844), cannot be admitted to Communion either.

While the person distributing Communion can never judge the subjective guilt of anyone, the fact that the person is publicly known to be living in a state which contradicts the law of God and his Church, is sufficient to judge that they are not to be admitted to Holy Communion. What is the minister of Communion to do?

On 24 June 2000, the Pontifical Council for Legislative Texts issued a Declaration clarifying that those who are divorced and remarried outside the Church do fall under the prohibition of receiving Communion mentioned in Canon 915. It also gave criterion as to how to proceed, criterion which can be applied to the other types of persons mentioned above. The Declaration mentions firstly that the prohibition of receiving Communion when one is in a state of grave sin "is derived from divine law and transcends the domain of positive ecclesiastical laws". That is, the Church merely reiterates what is already forbidden by God.

The Declaration goes on to say that in the first place it is the individual faithful themselves who have the responsibility of refraining from receiving Communion when they are not in the state of grace. They should observe what is written in Canon 916: "Anyone who is conscious of grave sin may not ... receive the Body of the Lord without previously having been to sacramental confession..."

If someone persists in going up to receive Communion despite the prohibition contained in these canons, often moved by ignorance, it then devolves especially on the priest to speak with them privately and explain why they should not do so: "Naturally, pastoral prudence would strongly suggest the avoidance of instances of public denial of Holy Communion. Pastors must strive to explain to the concerned faithful the true ecclesial sense of the norm, in such a way that they would be able to understand it or at least respect it" (*Decl.* n. 3).

If in spite of being told not to receive Communion the person continues to come forward, pastors "are to give precise instructions to the deacon or to any extraordinary minister regarding the mode of acting in concrete situations" (*Decl.* n. 3). It then falls to the priest and other ministers to deny the person the Sacrament: "In those situations, however, in which these precautionary measures have not had their effect or in which they were not possible, the minister of Communion must refuse to distribute it to those who are publicly unworthy. They are to do this with extreme charity, and are to look for the opportune moment to explain the reasons that required the refusal. They must, however, do this with firmness, conscious of the value that such signs of strength have for the good of the Church and of souls" (*Decl.* n. 3).

This is without question a very sensitive and difficult task. But it is truly necessary to safeguard the dignity of the sacrament of the Eucharist, the sanctity of marriage and respect for those many other people in the congregation who struggle to live in accordance with the Church's teachings, often at great cost, and who are scandalised when others who do not are welcomed to Communion.

363 How to receive Communion

In my parish the priest is positively discouraging people from receiving Communion on the tongue or kneeling, arguing that this is not the custom in the parish. Personally, I do not consider myself worthy to receive Communion in the hand. What should I do?

I have answered this question, or similar ones, in the past (cf. J. Flader, *Question Time 1*, q. 71), but it is obviously opportune to deal with it again. It is sad that the situation you describe continues, when the Vatican has been so clear on the matter.

To be sure, there is value in having everyone receive Communion in the same way, as a sign of unity. The Australian bishops, in the Australian edition of the *General Instruction of the Roman Missal*, approved by the Vatican in 2012, indicated in this regard: "In the dioceses of Australia standing is the most common posture for receiving Holy Communion, though individual members of the faithful may choose to receive Communion while kneeling. When approaching to receive Holy Communion, the faithful bow in reverence of the Sacrament that they are to receive" (n 160). The Interim Text for Australia of this document, published in 2007, added: "The customary manner of reception is recommended to be followed by all, so that Communion may truly be a sign of unity among those who share in the same table of the Lord" (*GIRM* 160). Notice that even in this interim text receiving Communion standing was "recommended", not "mandated".

So the faithful have a right to receive Communion kneeling as well as standing. The Vatican's Instruction *Redemptionis sacramentum* (2004) makes this clear: "Therefore it is not licit to deny Holy Communion to any of Christ's faithful solely on the grounds, for example, that the person wishes to receive the Eucharist kneeling or standing" (n. 91). Pope Benedict XVI himself in the later years of his pontificate returned to the practice of giving Communion to the faithful who were kneeling.

As regards receiving on the tongue, this traditional way remains in force, as the Sacred Congregation for Divine Worship pointed out in the Instruction *Memoriale Domini* in 1969 (cf. J. Flader, *Question Time 1*, q. 71). That Instruction, however, allowed conferences of Catholic bishops to request permission to give Communion in the hand, and today this way of receiving is allowed practically everywhere in the world. The Instruction *Redemptionis sacramentum* confirms the right of everyone to receive Communion on the tongue: "Although each of the faithful has the right to receive Holy Communion on the tongue, at his choice, if any communicant should wish to receive the Sacrament in the hand, in areas where the Bishops Conference with the *recognitio* of the Apostolic See has given permission, the sacred host is to be administered to him or her" (n. 92).

There is thus a true right of the faithful to receive Communion on the tongue, as also to receive it kneeling. No pastor can deny the exercise of this right, nor can any other minister of Communion. And no parish custom can override a universal right of each person.

What should one do if their pastor or a minister of Communion discourages them or refuses to give them Communion? Some have simply gone to a different parish. But this is often inconvenient and it is a sad state of affairs when they need to resort to this. It is especially sad at a time when we are so conscious of defending the rights of asylum seekers and other migrants, of minorities, etc., that we trample on the rights of our own faithful in the Church.

Redemptionis sacramentum calls the violation of this right a "grave matter" (n. 173) and it goes on to say how to proceed if this right is not respected: "Any Catholic, whether Priest or Deacon or lay member of Christ's faithful, has the right to lodge a complaint regarding a liturgical abuse to the diocesan Bishop or the competent Ordinary equivalent to him in law, or to the Apostolic See on account of the primacy of the Roman Pontiff. It is fitting, however, insofar as possible, that the report or complaint be submitted first to the diocesan Bishop. This is naturally to be done in truth and charity" (n. 184).

We pray that the right of the faithful to receive Communion in whichever way they choose will be respected everywhere.

364 Blessings in Communion

I am an acolyte and have been giving the customary blessing to people who come up with their arms crossed to indicate that they do not wish to receive Communion. Someone told me I should not do this. Does the Church say anything about it?

The Congregation for Divine Worship and the Discipline of the Sacraments shed some light on the matter in a letter in 2008. It was in answer to a query as to whether there were any particular guidelines regarding the practice of a minister or extraordinary minister of Communion giving a blessing at Communion time. The letter, with protocol number 930/08/L, was dated 22 November 2008 and was signed by Fr Anthony Ward, SM, Under-Secretary of the Congregation.

It began by stating that "this matter is presently under the attentive study of the Congregation," and so "for the present, this dicastery wishes to limit itself to the following observations."

The first observation is that "the liturgical blessing of the Holy Mass is properly given to each and to all at the conclusion of the Mass, just a few moments subsequent to the distribution of Holy Communion." This is of course the final blessing given by the celebrant at the end of Mass to all those present. It includes those who have not been able for whatever reason to receive Communion, so that these latter do receive a blessing in this moment.

Second, "Lay people, within the context of Holy Mass, are unable to confer blessings. These blessings, rather, are the competence of the priest (cf. *Ecclesia de Mysterio*, Notitiae 34 (15 Aug. 1997), art. 6, § 2; Canon 1169, § 2; and Roman Ritual *De Benedictionibus* (1985), n. 18)." Therefore, acolytes and other extraordinary ministers of Communion may never give a blessing.

Third, "Furthermore, the laying on of a hand or hands – which has its own sacramental significance, inappropriate here – by those distributing Holy Communion, in substitution for its reception, is to be explicitly discouraged." It is clear that this applies to anyone distributing Communion, including priests and deacons.

Fourth, "The Apostolic Exhortation *Familiaris Consortio*, n. 84, 'forbids any pastor, for whatever reason or pretext even of a pastoral nature, to perform ceremonies of any kind for divorced people who remarry'. To be feared is that any form of blessing in substitution for Communion would give the impression that the divorced and remarried have been returned, in some sense, to the status of Catholics in good standing." This is a very important consideration, which implies that the fact of giving a blessing to certain persons may be interpreted as an acknowledgement or even blessing of their way of life. This is borne out by the next observation.

Fifth, "In a similar way, for others who are not to be admitted to Holy Communion in accord with the norm of law, the Church's discipline has already made clear that they should not approach Holy Communion nor receive a blessing. This would include non-Catholics and those envisaged in Can. 915 (i.e., those under the penalty of excommunication or interdict, and others who obstinately persist in manifest grave sin)."

Therefore, it would seem that not even priests or deacons should give a blessing to non-Catholics or others whose marriage situation or way of life is not in keeping with the law of God and the Church. Naturally, a problem arises when such persons come forward and the minister is unaware of their situation.

The Congregation does not address the issue of whether a blessing may be given to Catholics, including children who have not yet made their first Communion, who for whatever reason do not wish to receive Communion and who come forward to receive a blessing. Until the Congregation issues norms on the matter, it would seem reasonable for priests and deacons to continue to give a blessing to these people. The whole matter would be simplified if only those able to receive Communion came forward, or if those who came forward with their arms crossed did not receive a blessing.

365 Taking Communion to the sick

In my parish there are a number of lay people who take Communion to the sick, but occasionally I see them take the hosts and then chat with people after Mass before going to the home of the sick. Is this proper? How should Communion be taken to the sick?

Your question affects many people, both the ministers and the families of the sick, so it is a good one to answer. There are no written norms of which I am aware apart from the actual rite of Communion for the sick, but there is a certain spirit that should govern all the actions of the minister of Communion, and it is this that I will discuss here. To facilitate the description, I will assume that the minister is a woman and that she is taking Communion to just one person.

The first thing to remember is that the minister is not just taking a host to a sick person. She is taking Jesus himself. It is an awesome privilege and it carries with it a great responsibility. It should be done with great reverence. Consider, for example, how the priest treats Our Lord in Mass. After the consecration of each species – the bread which becomes the Body and the wine which becomes the Blood of our Lord – he genuflects to show his reverence to Our Lord.

The Latin rubric describing this genuflection actually says *Genuflexus, adorat* – "Having genuflected, he adores". This is only fitting, since Jesus himself is now present on the altar. The Gospels relate how the Apostles themselves on occasion adored Our Lord. For example, just before his Ascension into heaven, "when they saw him they worshiped him" (*Mt* 28:17).

This spirit of reverence obtains throughout the rest of the Mass. When the people come up to receive Communion they make a sign of reverence beforehand, at least bowing if they are to receive Communion standing, or even kneeling to receive Our Lord. After receiving Communion they return to their seat and give thanks to Our Lord for coming into their body and soul, and many remain for some time after Mass to continue their thanksgiving. During this time they would not think of talking to anyone else. They are focussing on Our Lord.

This is the spirit with which a minister takes Communion to someone outside Mass. At the end of Mass she takes from the altar the pyx, a small round vessel containing the host, and leaves immediately for the house of the sick person. While she may smile or say hello to someone who greets her, she makes it clear that she is carrying Our Lord and so does not stop to chat with anyone.

In the car she does not turn on the radio or chat with other persons. It is best that she prays silently or says the Rosary or some other prayers with any others in the car. Their focus is on Our Lord who is the most important passenger in the car. If Jesus were actually sitting there with them they would be wholly focussed on him.

When they arrive at the house, the family members of the sick person should have prepared a table with a white cloth, a crucifix, two candles and a small bowl with a little water in it. While in a hospital setting it is generally inadvisable to use candles, in a home this presents no problem. Many families use lighted candles to decorate the dinner table or for other purposes.

The minister greets the family at the door and then proceeds to the room of the sick person. On the table she opens out a corporal, a white linen cloth used only for the Blessed Sacrament, and places the pyx on it, genuflecting reverently along with any others in the room. The others remain kneeling from this point on. The sick person of course may be in bed or sitting in a chair. She then proceeds through the rite of Communion, giving Communion to the sick person and to any others who may wish to receive it and have not already received Communion that day.

At the end, she purifies the pyx with a small purifier, making sure that any particles of the host fall into the bowl with water. She may also wash her fingers in this bowl. Since the bowl may now contain particles of the host, she may ask the sick person to drink the water, or she may do it herself, or she may pour it into a flower pot or under a bush in the garden where no one will step on it.

Only after the final prayers have been said and the sick person has had a little time to give thanks for having received Our Lord, should she engage in normal conversation. This way of acting is a great catechesis to all involved and helps them appreciate the great gift that the Eucharist is.

The Real Presence

366 Who has the Real Presence?

Recently two different Catholic friends expressed the belief that the Catholic Church is not the only one with the Real Presence in the Eucharist, citing the Church of England as another. I have always believed that only a Catholic priest could bring about the Real Presence. Who is right?

Actually, your friends are right, at least in part. But let us consider the matter more in depth. First of all, what does a priest need in order to change bread and wine into the Body and Blood of Christ? He needs valid priestly ordination and of course the right intention.

But what makes his ordination valid? After all, there can be ministers in other denominations who call themselves priests and have been ordained by a bishop, but who are not validly ordained. Valid ordination requires that the bishop who ordains the priest has himself been validly ordained by another bishop who can trace his orders back to the apostles. This is what is known as apostolic succession (cf. J. Flader, *Question Time 2*, q. 168).

The Second Vatican Council taught that "by divine institution the bishops have succeeded to the place of the apostles as shepherds of the Church" (Dogm. Const. *Lumen Gentium*, 20). As the apostles went about founding new communities, they transmitted the power of holy orders which they had received from Christ himself to other men through the laying on of hands. Through this action, which is the sacrament of Holy Orders, the newly ordained bishop or priest can bring about the Real Presence in Mass, as well as absolve sins in the sacrament of Reconciliation and confer the Anointing of the Sick. St Paul reminds Timothy of the power given him through the laying on of hands: "I remind you to rekindle the gift of God that is within you through the laying on of my hands" (2 *Tim* 1:6).

Where do we find apostolic succession today, and with it the power of bringing about the Real Presence? In the first place, we find it in the bishops of the Catholic Church, who can trace their episcopal ordination back in an unbroken line to the apostles. We also find it in the bishops of the non-Catholic Eastern Churches, customarily known as the Orthodox. Even though they are not in communion with the Holy See, they do have valid orders since they can trace their ordination back to the apostles and they have a correct understanding of the sacrament of Orders and the Eucharist. For this reason in certain circumstances Catholics can receive Communion from an Orthodox priest, with full confidence that they are receiving the Real Presence (cf. *Code of Canon Law,* Can. 844 §2).

Apostolic succession exists too in various groups that have separated from the Catholic Church in more recent times. Among them are the Old Catholics, who separated from the Church in 1870 over the First Vatican Council's declaration of papal infallibility, and the Society of St Pius X, founded by Archbishop Marcel Lefebvre in 1969. When the Archbishop ordained four bishops in 1988 without a mandate from the Holy See, all were excommunicated and the Society is no longer in communion with the Church, although their bishops and priests are validly ordained (cf. J. Flader, *Question Time 1*, q. 108). All of these groups have the Real Presence in the Eucharist.

What about the Anglicans? In 1896 Pope Leo XIII ruled in the Apostolic Letter *Apostolicae Curae* that they do not have valid orders since the form of words and the accompanying intention used in the ordination of priests and bishops at the time of King Edward VI was defective. Even though this form was corrected a century later, by that time there were no longer any validly ordained Anglican bishops remaining and so apostolic succession was broken.

Nonetheless, there are some Anglican bishops and priests today, especially among the Anglo-Catholics, who probably do have valid orders, since those bishops were ordained by Orthodox or Old Catholic bishops along with an Anglican bishop, all of whom had a proper understanding of Holy Orders and a correct intention. In many of their churches there is a tabernacle with a sanctuary lamp, and Our Lord is most probably present there. In summary, Catholic priests are not the only ones with the power to bring about the Real Presence.

367 Pope Francis and a Eucharistic miracle

Someone told me that Pope Francis had approved a Eucharistic miracle when he was Archbishop of Buenos Aires. Is this true? Can you tell me anything about the miracle?

It is true that Pope Francis, when he was Archbishop of Buenos Aires, ordered an investigation into a Eucharistic miracle that had taken place in a parish church in 1996 and he later approved veneration of the host in a chapel in the church. The facts of what took place are narrated by Ron Tesoriero in his book *Reason to Believe,* published in 2007.

On 18 August 1996 a priest in Buenos Aires was shown a host that had been left in a candle holder in the church. Because it was very dirty, rather than consume it he placed it in a bowl of water and put it in the tabernacle. Eight days later on 26 August he went to do his prayer in the Blessed Sacrament Chapel of the church, using a letter Pope John Paul II had written to the Bishop of Liège, Belgium, on the occasion of the 750th anniversary of the first celebration of the feast of Corpus Christi in that diocese (cf. J. Flader, *Question Time 2*, q. 271). On opening the tabernacle he saw that the host had turned red and a blood-like substance was coming out of it. This increased over the following weeks.

He informed the then Auxiliary Bishop Jorge Bergoglio, later Pope Francis, who asked a professional photographer to take photos of the host, first on 26 August and then again on 6 September. Later, as Archbishop of Buenos Aires, he asked a Bolivian-born professor, Dr Ricardo Castañon, to conduct an investigation into what had happened. In October 1999 Ron Tesoriero went with representatives of the Archbishop to witness Dr Castañon removing a small piece of the host and some of the liquid and transferring them to a test tube, which was then sealed and labeled for forensic analysis.

In April 2004 Ron and Mike Willesee, both Australians, went to New York with the sample to have it examined by Dr Frederick Zugibe, a heart specialist and forensic pathologist. Without knowing the origin of the sample, Dr Zugibe looked into his microscope and described what he saw. He said that he was looking at human tissue, from the heart and specifically from the left ventricle, which pumps the blood. Moreover, the heart was inflamed and there had been recent injury to it, as in cases where someone has been beaten severely around the chest.

Even more remarkably, he could see white blood cells, which indicate injury and inflammation. There were many of them and they were all intact. He said these cells can exist only if they are fed by a living body, and that the person from whom the sample was taken was alive at the moment the tissue was collected. When Mike asked him how long the white blood cells would remain vital if they were in human tissue that had been placed in water he answered: "Oh, they would dissolve within minutes and no longer exist." All this was caught on film.

Mike then asked him, "What would you say if I were to tell you that the source of this sample had been placed in ordinary tap water for a month, then stored for three years in distilled water before a piece was taken and fixed for examination?" The answer was "Absolutely unbelievable. No explanation can be given by science."

"And what would you say if I told you that the source of this specimen was a piece of wheaten bread, a Communion host?" After some hesitation as he took in this extraordinary revelation about what he had just examined, Dr Zugibe answered, "How or why a

Communion host could change its character and become living human flesh and blood is outside the ability of science to answer."

Indeed, it is. But occasionally God allows miracles to take place to strengthen our faith. One such miracle took place in Bolsena, Italy, in 1263, when a host that had just been consecrated in Mass by a priest who doubted the Real Presence began to ooze blood when the priest held it up for the veneration of the faithful. Following this miracle, Pope Urban IV instituted the feast of Corpus Christi a year later, in 1264 (cf. J. Flader, *Question Time 1*, q. 150). Pope Urban was originally from Liège, where the bishop had instituted a diocesan feast of Corpus Christi in 1246.

It is significant that on the day the host in Buenos Aires was discovered to have turned red, the priest was doing his prayer with the Pope's letter commemorating the institution of the diocesan feast of Corpus Christi 750 years before.

368 A Eucharistic miracle in Poland

I read with great interest your column on the Eucharistic miracle that Pope Francis approved when he was a bishop in Buenos Aires in 1996. Now a friend tells me there has been another miracle in Poland with similar scientific findings. Can you tell me anything about it?

The miracle took place in 2008 in the town of Sokołka, near Bialystok on the border with Belarus. Australian lawyer Ron Tesoriero, who spoke with the people involved, relates the facts in his new book *Unseen*, published in 2013.

On 12 October 2008 in the church of St Anthony of Padua, a young assistant priest, Fr Jacek Ingielewicz, accidentally dropped a consecrated host during Mass. He picked it up and, since it was soiled, placed it in a vessel of water and put it in the tabernacle. After Mass the parish priest, Fr Stanislaw Gniedziejko, asked the sacristan, Sr

Julia, to place the host and water in a glass bowl and put it in the safe in the sacristy.

A week later, on 19 October, Fr Stanislaw asked the sacristan if the host had dissolved and when Sr Julia opened the safe she discovered that there was a red stain on the host which looked like blood. She called Fr Stanislaw, who was very moved when he saw it, and informed his superior, Archbishop Edward Ozorowski. A few days later the Archbishop went with his Chancellor to see the host and on 29 October he asked Fr Stanislaw to take the host out of the water and lay it on a linen corporal, which he then placed in the tabernacle of the chapel in the priests' house.

The Archbishop appointed a special commission to investigate the matter, with the aim of determining whether anyone had interfered with the host. On 5 January 2009 he asked two pathomorphologists from the Medical University of Bialystok to conduct a scientific examination of the host. The two, Professor Sobaniec-Lotowska and Professor Sulkowski, hold chairs in different departments of the university and have published widely in their fields, having worked as specialists for over thirty years.

In the presence of the Chancellor, Fr Andrew Kakareka, and others Professor Sobaniec-Lotowska removed a small piece of the host, about a square centimetre in size. She reported that it was brittle, brownish in colour and with remains of the Communion host attached.

After analysing the material under an electron microscope the two professors reported that it consisted entirely of cardiac tissue. Various aspects of the material made them certain that it was indeed heart muscle tissue. Professor Sobaniec-Lotowska described the sample as heart muscle, "just before death. It is in agony, a moribund condition, caused by great stress. This is proved by the presentation of a very strong phenomenon of 'segmentation' or damage to myocardial fibres at the site of the intercalated discs, which does not occur after death. Such changes can be observed only in living fibres and they show evidence of rapid spasms of the heart muscle in the period just before death."

In a later interview on 13 August 2010, Professor Sobaniec-Lotowska elaborated on this finding: "The cardiac impact had been recent. The heart was alive, just before death. The sample analysed was not from a dead person. The person was alive. There was one square centimetre of heart. A fragment of muscle. If one had to remove it from a person, he would die." Pointing to a photograph of the tissue she repeated her amazement that even though it had been in water for weeks the cardiac tissue was still visible. She said that if it had been in water even for one week it would not be visible.

The professors were also amazed that there had been no autolysis, the process whereby a cell is destroyed by its own enzymes when the organism is injured or dying. In their opinion there was no scientific explanation for this phenomenon. "What is even more difficult to comprehend", Professor Sulkowski said, "is that the tissue, which appeared in the host, was closely bound to it, to the host that is, penetrating the base on which it appeared. Please believe me that even if someone intended to tamper with the sample, it would be impossible to bind the two pieces of matter in such an indissoluble way."

So once again a Communion host has been miraculously transformed into living heart tissue, readily identifiable under an electron microscope, and the tissue shows signs of great stress. Our Lord is obviously going to great lengths to confirm the truth of his Real Presence in the Eucharist.

369 The Eucharistic miracle of Lanciano

I have been fascinated by your account of the Eucharistic miracles of Buenos Aires and Poland. What is the connection, if any, between these miracles and the one of Lanciano in Italy?

The common thread in these Eucharistic miracles, as well as in the many others that have taken place throughout the centuries, is the fact that a consecrated host has changed into recognisable features of human tissue and sometimes blood.

We know that after the consecration in the Mass, when the priest pronounces the words of Christ on instituting the Eucharist, the host becomes the Body of Christ and the wine becomes his Blood. We don't see the Body or Blood, because they continue to have the characteristics of bread and wine, but we know by faith that they are there.

Occasionally, sometimes to shore up the faith of people who doubted his Real Presence, Our Lord has done a miracle to make clear that the Eucharist is truly his Body and Blood. In recent decades some of these miracles have been subjected to scientific examinations, which have resulted in extraordinary findings. Such is the case with the miracles of Buenos Aires in 1996, Poland in 2008, and even the eighth century miracle of Lanciano.

The first great Eucharistic miracle was that of Lanciano, the ancient Italian city of Anxanum. It took place in 750 AD in the church of St Legontian when a Basilian monk doubted the Real Presence of Christ in the Eucharist. After he had consecrated the Body and Blood of Our Lord, the host was suddenly changed into physical flesh and the consecrated wine into physical blood, which coagulated into five globules of different shapes and sizes. They are still on display in Lanciano, even though almost 1300 years have passed since they first appeared.

In 1971 the flesh and blood were examined scientifically by Dr Odoardo Linoli, Professor of Anatomy and Pathological Histology and of Chemistry and Clinical Microscopy at the Arezzo Hospital. He was assisted by Dr Ruggero Bertelli, retired Professor of Anatomy at the University of Siena. Their findings were truly extraordinary, and similar to the findings in the miracles of Buenos Aires and Poland. The flesh was identified under a microscope as human flesh from the left ventricle of the heart, showing clearly the myocardium, the endocardium and the vagus nerve.

What is more, Professor Linoli was amazed at the evenness of the slice of tissue he was examining. He commented that only a highly skilled hand in dissection could have obtained such an "even and continuous" slice of heart tissue. This is especially intriguing if one takes into account that the first anatomical dissections reported in the medical literature took place only after the 1300s, some six hundred years after the miracle.

The blood was of type AB, the rarest blood type, which is found more commonly in the region around the Mediterranean. In Italy between 0.5% and 1% of all people have type AB blood, whereas in Israel and the Middle East the percentage is 14-15%. The blood in the sample of flesh was also of type AB. Significantly, this is the same blood type identified in the Shroud of Turin. What is more, the proteins in the blood sample were in the same proportions as in fresh normal blood.

One of the experiments conducted on the blood sample involved liquefying it and studying its capillary properties; that is, the rate at which it climbs a narrow tube. Professor Linoli found that the capillary properties matched exactly those of human blood taken from a man that very day. The fact that the flesh and blood have been preserved for almost thirteen centuries even though exposed to the action of atmospheric and biological agents, and without any preservative, is itself a miracle.

Professor Linoli's findings were published in "Quaderni Sclavo di Diagnostica Clinica e di Laboratori" in 1971. In 1973 the Higher Council of the World Health Organisation appointed a scientific commission to investigate Professor Linoli's findings. After 500 examinations, carried out over fifteen months, the commission confirmed the earlier findings.

These miracles and the scientific evidence that supports them can help to reaffirm our faith that the Eucharist is truly the Body and Blood of Our Lord at a time when many doubt it.

Penance

370 Whose sins you shall retain

Jesus said to the apostles: "If you forgive the sins of any, they are forgiven them; if you retain the sins of any, they are retained". What are the situations which would call for retention of sins and does this have anything to do with excommunicating the person?

Just to remind ourselves, the words you quote are from Our Lord in the upper room on the evening of his Resurrection. St John relates the scene: "On the evening of that day, the first day of the week, the doors being shut where the disciples were, for fear of the Jews, Jesus came and stood among them and said to them ... 'Peace be with you. As the Father has sent me, even so I send you.' And when he had said this, he breathed on them, and said to them, 'Receive the Holy Spirit. If you forgive the sins of any, they are forgiven; if you retain the sins of any, they are retained'" (*Jn* 20:19-23). By these words Jesus gave the Church the great sacrament of mercy as the fruit of his death and Resurrection.

It is worth noting the role of the Holy Spirit in the forgiveness of sins. Not for nothing did Jesus first say, "Receive the Holy Spirit". The Holy Spirit is the paraclete, the advocate, who pleads our cause before the Father and, as the spirit of love, wants all souls to be united with God. For this reason, the priest says in the prayer before the absolution of our sins that God "sent the Holy Spirit among us for the forgiveness of sins".

Since the apostles, and their successors the priests in the ministry of reconciliation, have to judge whether they can forgive the sins or they have to retain them, it is clear that they must first hear the sins of each person in a private confession. Only in exceptional circumstances, which I can describe in another column, can the priest absolve sins without first having heard the person's confession.

What is meant by retaining sins, as distinct from forgiving them? To retain in this context means simply not to forgive the sins. Under what circumstances would the priest not forgive someone's sins? Could it be that there are some sins that are so serious that they simply cannot be forgiven? No, there are no such sins. All sins, no matter how serious or how frequent, can be forgiven, provided the person is sorry for them.

Therefore, what determines whether the penitent can be forgiven or not is whether they are sorry for their sins. There are some people who, for a variety of reasons, are not sorry and have no intention of changing their behaviour. Ordinarily these people know that because they are not sorry they cannot be forgiven either by God or by the priest, and so they do not go to confession. When someone does go to confession this usually implies that they are sorry and they wish to be forgiven. For this reason it is very rare that a person who goes to confession is not forgiven. Why might this happen?

One possibility is that the person is falling repeatedly into serious sin and is making no serious effort to avoid it. They are taking advantage of the sacrament to cleanse their soul, perhaps to be able to receive Communion, and then they go back to their habit of sin. This is an attitude which non-Catholics sometimes attribute to Catholics and we must be very careful to avoid it.

If the confessor knows that the penitent is repeatedly confessing the same sins and he suspects that they are not really trying to improve, he will usually ask some questions to clarify to what extent they are really struggling to overcome the habit of sin. He will also give practical advice on how to struggle more effectively. As long as the person shows that they are sincerely sorry and are struggling, albeit unsuccessfully, they can be forgiven.

What is necessary for absolution is the determination and effort to struggle to overcome the sinful habit, not success in the struggle (cf. J. Flader, *Question Time 2*, q. 211). A person may take years to overcome a habit of sin, or they may never fully overcome it, but as long as they are sincerely struggling, they can be forgiven. Our Lord knows our weakness and he has given us the sacraments for that reason. The sacraments are not rewards for virtue but helps for weakness.

Another situation where sins cannot be forgiven is where the person has gone to confession simply to please their mother or spouse or some other person, and they are not sorry at all nor doing anything to avoid falling again. This will usually become clear to the priest and he will explain that he cannot forgive them until they are truly sorry.

And no, retaining sins has nothing to do with excommunication, which is imposed either by the law itself or by a bishop. A priest cannot excommunicate anyone. Naturally, if the penitent does not receive absolution for a mortal sin, he or she cannot receive Communion, but this is not excommunication.

371 The importance of individual confession

Why did the Church ban the Third Rite of Reconciliation? Many friends and I used to enjoy going to it twice a year in our parish and then suddenly it stopped some ten years ago. Several of my friends have hardly been to confession since.

The Church hasn't banned the Third Rite which, by the way, consists in the general absolution of a large number of people at once without their individual confession.

The rite was first introduced during the First World War to allow priests to absolve a large number of soldiers before they went into battle when it would have been impossible to hear all their confessions individually. At the time of the Second World War the conditions were extended to other circumstances of imminent danger of death, and finally in 1972 they came to include situations such as those in mission territories where, if the priest did not absolve a large number of people at once, they would have to go for a long time without the grace of the sacraments through no fault of their own.

The norms on what has come to be called "general absolution" were incorporated into the 1983 *Code of Canon Law* in canons 961-963 and into the *Catechism of the Catholic Church* in paragraphs 1483-1484 (cf. J. Flader, *Question Time 1,* q. 80).

Up until the late 1990s the Third Rite was used in many parishes in Australia. Significant numbers of people took advantage of it, partly because they were helped by the readings from Scripture, prayers and often a homily, and because many others were attending as well, emphasising the communal, ecclesial aspect of the sacrament. But especially since there was no need to confess their sins individually to the priest, they found it much easier than going to individual confession.

Why did it suddenly stop? Perhaps the more apposite question would be why it began in the first place. It is clear that the conditions required for its use simply do not exist in Australia, particularly the condition that if the priest did not absolve a large number of penitents collectively they would have to go for a long period of time without the grace of the sacraments through no fault of their own. While the number of priests has diminished somewhat, we are still well served with priests and parishes so that the sacrament of Reconciliation is readily available all over this country.

By the late 1990s the use of general absolution was fairly widespread, especially in some dioceses. During their five-yearly *ad limina* visit to Rome in 1998, the Australian bishops discussed this matter, along with others, with Pope John Paul II and Vatican officials. At the end of their visit a long *Statement of Conclusions* was signed by representatives of the Australian bishops and of the Roman Curia. Among other matters, it encouraged the use of individual confession and, with respect to general absolution, it said: "Unfortunately, communal celebrations have not infrequently occasioned an illegitimate use of general absolution. This illegitimate use, like other abuses in the administration of the Sacrament of Penance, is to be eliminated... The bishops will exercise renewed vigilance on these matters for the future, aware that departures from the authentic tradition do great wrong to the Church and to individual Catholics" (n. 45). Naturally, while general absolution is not to be used in this country, it still remains an option in countries where the conditions for its use exist.

Those who do take regular advantage of individual confession know how much good it does them. Apart from receiving forgiveness of their sins, they have an opportunity to do a thorough examination of conscience, to tell their sins personally to God through the priest and to receive helpful spiritual direction and encouragement. With the abundant grace the sacrament gives them, they begin their spiritual struggle anew each time, with their soul free from sin and filled with hope.

Pope John Paul II, in an address to priests at the beginning of Lent in 1981, said that "confession periodically renewed, the so-called confession 'of devotion', has always accompanied the ascent to holiness in the Church." And on 13 March 1999 he told priests hearing confessions in the patriarchal basilicas of Rome: "It should not be forgotten that the so-called confession of devotion was the school which formed the great saints."

Would that more people made frequent use of this sacrament. Their growth in holiness through it would be a great blessing for themselves, for their families, for the Church and for the whole of society.

372 The benefits of confession

I go regularly to confession but I know many people, including my husband and son, who hardly go at all. How can I encourage them to go more often and what has happened that so few go these days?

If we look back over the years, it is clear that in the 1960s and early 70s many people went to confession regularly. There were a good number of priests in the parishes and often there were queues of people waiting to go to confession on Saturdays, as well as on other days.

Then, more or less coinciding with the introduction of the new Rite of Penance in the mid-1970s the numbers fell off. With the new rite there was certainly a misunderstanding of the mind of the Church, with some people suggesting that we were no longer to go to confession frequently with our "laundry list" or "shopping list" of sins. Rather, we were to wait for the big conversion after we had fallen away and so confession would be much less frequent. This of course was false. There were other factors as well, but what is certain is that the numbers of people going regularly to confession dropped significantly from the mid-1970s on.

What can we do to help people return to the sacrament? Apart from praying and offering little sacrifices for them, we can remind them that the sacrament of Penance has at least the following ten benefits.

First, and most obviously, we receive forgiveness of our sins. When we have been burdened by sin it is a great relief to hear the words of forgiveness – "I absolve you from your sins" – and to know that "what is loosed on earth is loosed in heaven" (*Mt* 18:18).

Second, we receive sanctifying grace, a sharing in God's own life, which makes us holy and pleasing to him. When we have been stained by sin, even venial sin, we come away from confession with our soul completely clean and filled with divine life. For this reason, regular confession is a great help in growing in holiness.

Third, we receive a specific sacramental grace proper to the sacrament which in this case helps us to avoid falling again into the sins we have just confessed. While we know we may fall again, we experience a greater strength after confession to avoid doing so.

Fourth, each confession brings a new beginning in the spiritual struggle. Especially when we have come with mortal sins, but also when our sins have been venial, the knowledge that we are clean and full of grace is a big help in deciding to struggle harder to avoid falling again. People who do not have this sacrament do not have this clean break, this decisive moment in which to begin again. It is a big help in the spiritual struggle.

Fifth, we are always helped by the words of advice and encouragement the priest gives us in confession. They are a brief form of spiritual direction and they assist us in our spiritual struggle.

Sixth, we grow in self-knowledge through the examination of conscience that necessarily precedes confession. We come to know ourselves better, to see our weaknesses, and this helps us to improve in those areas.

Seventh, we grow in the virtues of humility and sincerity by the fact of confessing our sins to the priest. Sometimes we may be embarrassed to confess certain sins but the very fact of telling them to another helps us grow in these important virtues.

Eighth, the penance the priest asks us to undertake makes up at least in part for the temporal punishment owing for our sins and thus shortens our time in Purgatory if indeed we need to go there at all. This too is a big help in growing in holiness.

Ninth, confession often brings about healing of the soul. If we have gone into the confessional burdened by guilt, anger, hatred, desire of revenge, sadness or even depression, we often emerge significantly healed and ready to begin again.

And tenth, as the fruit of the other benefits, we always leave the confessional with a deep sense of joy and peace of soul. It is the joy experienced by the prodigal son when, after confessing his sins to his father, he is embraced and kissed and given the best robe (cf. *Lk* 15:11-24).

With all these benefits, it is a real shame that so many of our fellow Catholics miss out. We should make use of the sacrament regularly ourselves and do all we can to help others do the same.

373 The seal of confession

If the government passes a law requiring priests to inform the police or to testify in court about any serious matters they hear in confession, what will happen? Will priests comply?

This issue has suddenly leapt into the public arena with respect to the sexual abuse issue, so it is important to be acquainted with some facts.

First, the requirement that priests never divulge to anyone what they hear in confession is known as the seal of confession. The *Catechism of the Catholic Church* says of it: "Given the delicacy and greatness of this ministry and the respect due to persons, the Church declares that every priest who hears confessions is bound under very severe penalties to keep absolute secrecy regarding the sins that his penitents have confessed to him. He can make no use of knowledge that confession gives him about penitents' lives. This secret, which admits of no exceptions, is called the 'sacramental seal', because what the penitent has made known to the priest remains 'sealed' by the sacrament" (*CCC* 1467).

The *Code of Canon Law* is equally clear: "The sacramental seal is inviolable. Accordingly, it is absolutely wrong for a confessor in any way to betray the penitent, for any reason whatsoever, whether by word or in any other fashion" (Can. 983 §1). The following Canon adds: "The confessor is wholly forbidden to use knowledge acquired in confession to the detriment of the penitent, even when all danger of disclosure is excluded" (Can. 984 §1).

What are the "severe penalties" for violating the seal? "A confessor who directly violates the sacramental seal, incurs a *latae sententiae* excommunication reserved to the Apostolic See; he who does so only indirectly is to be punished according to the gravity of the offence" (Can. 1388 §1). A *latae sententiae* penalty is one which a person incurs by the mere fact of violating the law. It does not need to be declared by a bishop. So if a priest were to violate the seal, he would be automatically and immediately excommunicated, by the law itself.

The effect of excommunication is that the priest cannot celebrate Mass, celebrate or receive any sacrament, including the sacrament of Penance, or exercise his priestly ministry until such time as he repents and does what he can to make up for the offence (cf. Can. 1331 §1). What is more, in this case the lifting of the excommunication and granting of absolution are reserved to the Holy See. Only a few extremely grave sins carry with them the penalty of excommunication reserved to the Holy See and this is one of them.

What do we make of this? That the Church regards the violation of the confessional seal as an extremely grave matter. All priests know this, and therefore they will not divulge to the police or say in court anything they have heard in the course of a confession. If they are put in jail for this, they will happily go to jail.

Why is it so serious? Because if the Church did not protect the confidentiality of what is said in confession, people would not trust their priests and they would not confess anything that might incriminate them. Just as they trust their doctor, psychologist, lawyer or counsellor to respect their confidentiality, so all the more they trust their priest. People would stop going to confession if the seal were not respected.

Moreover, paedophiles and other people with serious problems would not go to confession for fear the confessor would take the matter to the police. They would thereby deprive themselves of a very valuable aid in overcoming their sinful habit. But if a paedophile confesses this most serious sin, shouldn't the priest be able to take some action? Yes, and he will. He will strongly urge the person to take action to address his problem: to seek professional help, to resign his position, to inform the relevant people and possibly even to give himself up to the police.

The confessor may also ask the penitent to see him outside of confession and to repeat what was said, giving permission to the priest to reveal to others the content of this conversation. Then the priest may tell others – for example, the person's superior, a counsellor, even the police – that the person has this problem. But without this second conversation outside of confession, the confessor cannot disclose anything he has heard. And of course, if he sees that the paedophile is not sorry for what he has done and is not taking appropriate action to address his problem, the confessor can refuse to absolve him.

In short, the sacramental seal is extremely important for everyone, and the Church will never change its law or make exceptions to it. We can all breathe a sigh of relief.

374 Absolution without prior confession

Recently I was visiting a friend in hospital who was going to have a serious operation and hadn't been to confession for a long time. Since he was in a ward with three other people, the priest gave him absolution without having heard his confession. Is this permitted?

Your question implies that confession of sins is ordinarily necessary in order for the priest to grant absolution, and indeed it is. It follows from Our Lord's words on giving the sacrament of Penance to the apostles on the evening of his resurrection: "If you forgive the sins of any, they are forgiven; if you retain the sins of any, they are retained" (*Jn* 20:23). If the priest must judge whether he can forgive the sins or not, he must obviously hear the sins and assess the sorrow of the person in order to make that judgment.

For this reason the *Code of Canon Law* says: "Individual and integral confession and absolution constitute the sole ordinary means by which a member of the faithful who is conscious of grave sin is reconciled with God and with the Church" (Can. 960). This statement refers only to the absolution of grave, or mortal, sins, since venial sins can be forgiven by God in many ways, including a sincere act of contrition, the penitential rite at the beginning of Mass, a good Communion, etc.

In saying that individual and integral confession and absolution are the sole "ordinary" means for the forgiveness of grave sins, the canon is implying that there can be "extraordinary" circumstances in which even grave sins can be forgiven without prior individual confession. The situation you mention in your question is one of those. The same canon goes on to say: "Physical or moral impossibility alone excuses from such confession, in which case reconciliation may be attained by other means also" (Can. 960). What is meant by "physical or moral impossibility"?

Physical impossibility refers to the human impossibility of actually communicating with the confessor. This can be due to such circumstances as extreme illness, inability to speak due to a stroke or dumbness, lack of a common language with the confessor, lack of time in the face of imminent danger, etc. In addition, moral theology textbooks generally include here invincible ignorance of the serious sinfulness of something the penitent has done and the simple forgetting of a sin. In both of these cases the person is unable to confess the sin.

Moral impossibility refers to a situation in which the person could confess their sins but in the particular circumstances it would result in some grave harm for the penitent, the confessor or a third person. Examples include imminent danger to life arising from the possible transmission of a serious illness, the risk of violating the sacramental seal when others close at hand could overhear the confession, and the danger of loss of reputation to a third person if a sin cannot be confessed without revealing the name of an accomplice. Naturally the loss of reputation of the penitent in the eyes of the confessor does not excuse the person from making a complete confession. In all these cases the confessor can absolve the penitent without having heard all or any of their sins but he should advise the person to mention in a future confession any serious sins omitted.

Over the years the Church has given norms for granting absolution without prior confession in cases of imminent danger of death. These came during the First and Second World Wars to allow absolution to be given even to a large number of people at once when there was imminent danger of death due to such situations as war, a sinking ship, an airplane in danger of crashing, an earthquake, etc. In 1972 the norms were extended to situations in which there is not sufficient time to hear the confessions of a large number of people who would have to go for a long time without sacramental absolution through no fault of their own if they were not absolved collectively. These have become the norms for the Third Rite of Reconciliation (cf. Can. 961-963; J. Flader, *Question Time 1*, q. 80).

In conclusion, the Church is a mother who makes ample provision for absolving the sins of her children in special circumstances, but who nonetheless follows the teaching of her divine Founder in requiring the complete confession of all serious sins in ordinary circumstances.

375 Shedding of blood and the forgiveness of sin

In the Letter to the Hebrews it says: "Without the shedding of blood there is no forgiveness of sins." Why does blood need to be shed for sins to be forgiven? What is the connection?

The passage to which you refer is in the ninth chapter of the letter, which begins by describing the worship of God in the old covenant and goes on to say how much more perfect is the sacrifice of Christ in the new covenant. The letter was addressed to Hebrews, that is to Christians who had formerly been Jews and who knew very well the laws and customs of the old covenant. Under that law, there were many rites of atonement for sin, and these rites most often involved the sprinkling of blood.

For example, on the day of atonement, Aaron was to kill a bull as a sin offering for himself and his household, and to kill a goat as a sin offering for the people. He was then to sprinkle the blood of the animals on the mercy seat of the ark of the covenant and later on the horns of the altar (cf. *Lev* 16:11-19). In this way "he shall make atonement for the holy place, because of the uncleannesses of the sons of Israel, and because of their transgressions, all their sins" (*Lev* 16:16).

The letter to the Hebrews goes on to recall how Moses ratified the old covenant by sprinkling the blood of calves and goats on the book and on the people, saying, "This is the blood of the covenant which God commanded you" (*Heb* 9:20; cf. *Ex* 24:6-8). He went on to sprinkle the blood on the tent and on all the vessels used in worship (cf. *Heb* 9:21). After relating all of this the letter comes to the verse you mention in your question: "Indeed, under the law almost everything is purified with blood, and without the shedding of blood there is no forgiveness of sins" (*Heb* 9:22).

In saying that "almost everything is purified with blood" the letter is recalling that in the old covenant, while most rites of purification were done with blood, some used fire and water, or water only (cf. *Num* 31:22-24, *Lev* 16:26, 28). But when it was a matter of atonement for sin and not simply the purification of ritual uncleanness, the rite usually involved the sprinkling of blood. There were exceptions to this too, however. For example, when the people had sinned and were struck with the plague, Moses commanded Aaron to take incense "and carry it quickly to the congregation, and make atonement for them" (*Num* 16:46).

In any case, the old covenant rites of atonement which did involve the shedding and sprinkling of blood could not bring about the true remission of sin, but only prefigured it: "For it is impossible that the blood of bulls and goats should take away sins" (*Heb* 10:4). Therefore, God in his mercy and wisdom chose to bring about the effective remission of sin through the shedding of the blood of his Son Jesus Christ, "the Lamb of God who takes away the sin of the world" (*Jn* 1:29).

The letter to the Hebrews goes on to say that whereas the high priest entered the Holy Place each year for the rite of atonement "with blood not his own", Christ "has appeared once for all at the end of the age to put away sin by the sacrifice of himself" (*Heb* 9:25-26; 10:4). Christ "entered once for all into the Holy Place, taking not the blood of goats and calves but his own blood, thus securing an eternal redemption. For if the sprinkling of defiled persons with the blood of goats and bulls and with the ashes of a heifer sanctifies for the purification of the flesh, how much more shall the blood of Christ, who through the eternal Spirit offered himself without blemish to God, purify your conscience from dead works to serve the living God" (*Heb* 9:12-14).

In summary, the rites of atonement of the old covenant, even when they involved the shedding and sprinkling of the blood of animals, could not bring about the true remission of sins. It took the shedding of the blood of the Son of God himself, Jesus Christ, on the altar of Calvary, to bring about the effective remission of sin and the reconciliation of mankind with God.

As St Paul says, "In him we have redemption through his blood, the forgiveness of our trespasses, according to the riches of his grace which he lavished upon us" (*Eph* 1:7). Returning to your question, without the shedding of the blood of Christ there is no forgiveness of sins. We thank God for this sacrifice by which he redeemed us, and we can show our gratitude by making frequent use of the sacrament of reconciliation in order to benefit from it.

Holy Orders and Matrimony

376 Is celibacy too hard?

In the last few days some of my friends have been questioning the value of priestly celibacy after a priest revealed that he has fallen in love and been married civilly. They say it is too hard for a priest to live without love and that the requirement should be changed or we won't have enough priests. How do I answer them?

Celibacy, or virginity for the love of God, has been in the Church from the beginning. In the early centuries there were many people, both men and women, who freely chose to live their lives in complete dedication to God without marrying. Some of them were incorporated into the order of virgins.

As I explained in this column some years ago (cf. J. Flader, *Question Time 1*, q. 94), at least from the beginning of the fourth century the Latin Church has required that all priests remain celibate. Since then, God has given to his Church a never-ending stream of priests completely dedicated to him in celibacy.

Is the requirement of celibacy too hard a burden to bear? The history of celibacy, not only in the priesthood, but among the early Christian virgins and those in the religious and eremitical life throughout the ages reveals that it is not. At the present time there are over a million men and women committed to God in celibacy in the various vocations, including over 400,000 priests. They are a marvellous witness to Christ's unconditional love for his Church and to the eternal love we will have with God in heaven.

Naturally not all people can live a life of celibacy. It is always a gift that God gives to relatively few. When God calls someone to this way of life, he grants them all the graces they will need to be faithful. "My grace is sufficient for you", Our Lord assures St Paul (*2 Cor* 12:9).

Celibacy is not imposed on anyone – it is freely chosen. When a young man considers becoming a priest, he knows that celibacy is an essential aspect of the vocation, just as a young woman considering becoming a nun does. Even in the Eastern rites which allow married priests, there are a good number of men who choose celibacy. As for a shortage of priests, in the world at large there are now well over 100,000 seminarians – one for every four priests! – all embracing celibacy, and the number is constantly growing.

Fortunately, the rigorous screening process before admitting someone to the seminary or to the religious life today, plus the long period of formation before someone makes a permanent commitment, help greatly in the discernment of one's suitability for a life of celibacy.

What is more, the priest does not live without love. His vocation is a way of love, both divine and human. It is a total self-giving to the love of God, who loves us "to the end" (*Jn* 13:1). For this reason, the priest responds to Christ's love by spending time with him each day in such activities as the Mass, the Divine Office, mental prayer, the Rosary, spiritual reading, etc. In the same way, married people know they have to spend time together, to keep putting love into their relationship, if they want it to grow and mature. If they do not do this, their love will grow cold.

At the same time, the priest must protect the treasure of his vocation by being careful in how he relates to women, just as married people do in their relations with people of the opposite sex. It is simply a matter of common sense, of prudence.

Naturally, the priest may experience difficulty from time to time in living his life of celibacy. So do spouses in their marriage. But like them, he knows he must be faithful to his commitment "in good times and in bad, in sickness and in health" until the end. In those times, the knowledge that many souls depend on him will be a spur to remain faithful, and he will see the need to intensify his spiritual life and to seek the help of a fellow priest as a spiritual guide.

In addition to divine love, the priest also experiences human love – that of the people in his care. He loves them as his brothers and sisters in Christ, as his spiritual children. And their love for him, shown in kindness, gratitude and invitations to dinner or family functions, helps to enrich his priesthood with the human love we all need and desire.

If we want our priests to be faithful to the end, as the immense majority of them are, it is important to show them that we love them and value their service, and especially to pray for them.

377 Why celibacy only in the West?

Why is it that priests in the Eastern Catholic rites and Orthodox priests can be married but priests in the Latin rite cannot? How did this difference come about?

In the first centuries it is clear that priests and deacons could be married. St Peter, for example, had been married for he had a mother-in-law (cf. *Mt* 8:14-15). And St Paul writes to Timothy that deacons and priests should be men of one wife (cf. *1 Tim* 3:12; *Tit* 1:6). Nonetheless, St Paul, who was celibate himself as was Jesus, extols the value of remaining unmarried (cf. *1 Cor* 7:25-27).

Cardinal Alfons Stickler, Vatican librarian and archivist from 1985 to 1988 and author of *The Case for Clerical Celibacy* (Ignatius Press 1995), shows how even though clerics could be married in the early Church, in both East and West they were expected to refrain from sexual relations with their wife.

The first known written laws on clerical celibacy are those of the provincial Council of Elvira, held around 305 in southern Spain. The council forbade clerics dedicated to the service of the altar – bishops, priests and deacons – to have marital relations with their wives and to have children. Those who violated this norm were to be excluded from the clerical state. The law should be seen as supporting an existing custom, not as establishing a new practice, which would have given rise to a storm of protest.

Canon 3 of the Ecumenical Council of Nicaea in 325 gave the same criterion, forbidding a cleric to have living with him anyone other than a woman above suspicion, such as a mother, sister, aunt, etc. It is understood that he could have a wife but had to live in continence with her.

Several councils in Carthage at the end of the fourth century and the beginning of the fifth also affirmed clerical continence. A *Code of Canons of the African Church*, agreed upon unanimously by all the bishops in the Council of Carthage in 419 stated: "It pleases us all that bishop, priest and deacon, guardians of purity, abstain from [conjugal intercourse] with their wives, so that those who serve at the altar may keep a perfect chastity." It attributes this practice to the apostles themselves: "what the apostles taught and what antiquity itself observed, let us also endeavour to keep."

As regards the teaching of Popes, in 385 Pope Siricius wrote to the bishop of Tarragona in Spain affirming that the prohibition on priests and deacons having children goes back to the origins of the Church. Cardinal Stickler quotes numerous other statements of Popes, saints and councils all agreeing on the apostolic origins of celibacy, understood as continence in marriage for clerics.

Only after the Council of Trent in the sixteenth century did it become the common practice to ordain only young unmarried men to the priesthood. Since then, priestly celibacy has come to mean what it does today: that priests must be unmarried.

How did it come about then that in the East clerics have been allowed to be married and to have marital relations with their wife? There are a variety of historical reasons, among them the fact that disciplinary matters were often resolved at a local level, and also that the unifying role of the Popes in the West was not felt as strongly in the East.

One of the most important reasons is the canons of the Second Council of Trullo, held in Constantinople in 691-692. The council was convoked by Emperor Justinian II and was attended only by bishops of the East, who showed disdain for the Church in the West. Misquoting one of the norms of the Council of Carthage (390) which required complete continence of all clerics, the Council of Trullo in its Canon 13 prohibited marital relations only at the time of direct service at the altar, which at that time was only once a week.

Even though the Popes never recognised the decrees of this council, the East regarded it as an Ecumenical Council and so the Orthodox Churches to this day have allowed clerics to be married and to have marital relations with their wives. Clerics of the Eastern Catholic rites have been allowed to follow the same practice.

378 Admission to the seminary of men with same-sex attraction

Can a person with same-sex attraction be admitted to a seminary to train for the priesthood? What should be done if someone already in the seminary manifests to his superiors this attraction?

This is an issue that has troubled the Church for some time, especially in the last decades when there emerged allegations of sexual abuse of boys by clergy who clearly had a certain same-sex attraction. We should always bear in mind that the percentage of priests accused was very small, only some five percent in the United States, as I explained in an earlier column. Also, the problem is not limited to the Catholic Church, with clergy of many denominations being accused. And it is not limited to the clergy, since teachers, scout leaders, sports coaches and many others have also been accused.

Responding to concerns about this matter, in 2005 the Congregation for Catholic Education, which oversees seminary formation, issued an

Instruction "Concerning the criteria for the discernment of vocations with regard to persons with homosexual tendencies in view of their admission to the seminary and to Holy Orders." On 31 August of that year Pope Benedict XVI approved the Instruction and ordered its publication. It was dated 4 November 2005.

The Instruction mentions that the question of whether to admit to the seminary and to the priesthood candidates who have deep-seated homosexual tendencies was "made more urgent by the current situation." It goes on to say that the candidate to the ordained ministry, since he is configured to Christ through the sacrament, "must reach affective maturity. Such maturity will allow him to relate correctly to both men and women, developing in him a true sense of spiritual fatherhood towards the Church community that will be entrusted to him" (n. 1).

Also, given that not only homosexual acts but also deep-seated homosexual tendencies are objectively disordered, the Instruction states that three types of men cannot be admitted to the seminary or to Holy Orders: "those who practise homosexuality, present deep-seated homosexual tendencies or support the so-called 'gay culture.' Such persons, in fact, find themselves in a situation that gravely hinders them from relating correctly to men and women. One must in no way overlook the negative consequences that can derive from the ordination of persons with deep-seated homosexual tendencies" (n. 2).

As regards men whose homosexual tendencies were "only the expression of a transitory problem – for example, that of an adolescence not yet superseded" – the Instruction says that "such tendencies must be clearly overcome at least three years before ordination to the diaconate" (n. 2). Given that in most seminaries one is not ordained a deacon until the fifth or sixth year, this allows for a man with a certain, although not deep-seated, homosexual tendency to be admitted to the seminary. But even this tendency must be overcome at least three years prior to ordination as a deacon.

As for a seminarian who still experiences homosexual tendencies in the later years of formation, the Instruction mentions the responsibility of the spiritual director to help him discern his unsuitability for the priesthood: "If a candidate practises homosexuality or presents deep-seated homosexual tendencies, his spiritual director, as well as his confessor, have the duty to dissuade him in conscience from proceeding toward ordination" (n. 3). Moreover, "It would be gravely dishonest for a candidate to hide his own homosexuality in order to proceed, despite everything, toward ordination. Such a deceitful attitude does not correspond to the spirit of truth, loyalty and openness that must characterise the personality of him who believes he is called to serve Christ and his Church in the ministerial priesthood" (*ibid.*).

Because in the following years there were numerous requests for clarification of the applicability of the Instruction, in May 2008 Cardinal Tarcisio Bertone, the Secretary of State, wrote a brief letter to the world's bishops with the specific approval of Pope Benedict. It stated that the norms of the 2005 Instruction are valid "for all houses of formation for the priesthood, including those under the Dicasteries for Eastern Churches, for the Evangelisation of Peoples, and for the Institutes of Consecrated Life and Societies of Apostolic Life." That is, the norms apply to all seminaries and houses of formation in the world. We should pray that the norms will be faithfully observed as it will be an important step towards reducing the incidence of clerical sexual abuse.

379 Wedding matters

I am confused about what is allowed and not allowed in weddings. A friend of mine asked the priest to use a certain reading, but the priest refused because he said it was not in the Bible. And she was not allowed to use a particular love song that she liked.

There are a number of issues that arise in connection with weddings that raise concern, both on the part of the couple and on the part of the celebrant. I will deal with four of the more common ones.

The first one refers to the readings. There is a general principle that in all liturgical celebrations – for example, the Mass, the celebration of the sacraments such as marriage, funerals, etc. – only readings from sacred Scripture are allowed. In his Apostolic Exhortation *Verbum Domini* (2010) Pope Benedict confirmed that in the liturgy "the readings drawn from sacred Scripture may never be replaced by other texts, however significant the latter may be from a spiritual or pastoral standpoint: No text of spirituality or literature can equal the value and riches contained in sacred Scripture, which is the word of God. This is an ancient rule of the Church which is to be maintained" (n. 69).

This is a matter of common sense. God himself speaks to us through his scriptures and the Church wants us to hear what he has to say. Weddings, like all liturgical ceremonies, are privileged opportunities to listen to the Word of God. Therefore, all non-scriptural readings are forbidden during the ceremony itself. If the couple have some favourite reading from some other source that they would like to use, there is nothing wrong with including it at the back of the wedding booklet, or reading it at the reception.

The second issue is the choice of hymns. While there is usually no official list of hymns that are allowed or forbidden, in general hymns used in liturgical ceremonies should have some religious or spiritual content so that they are appropriate for use in a church ceremony. For this reason popular love songs are usually inappropriate. Many parishes have a director of music who can help the couple choose appropriate hymns which they like.

Apart from hymns, there are a number of instrumental works that, while not strictly sacred, have a certain spiritual quality and are thus appropriate for weddings. Among them are Wagner's "Bridal March", Mendelssohn's "Wedding March", Pachelbel's "Canon in D", Bach's "Air" from Suite 3, etc.

A third issue is the formula for the exchange of consent. Some couples may have heard a particular formula in a wedding they attended, or they may have composed one themselves. Even though the formula may seem appropriate in itself, the exchange of consent is the essential act by which the couple give themselves to each other in marriage and it is very important that they use only a formula approved by the Church. The very validity of the marriage may be at stake. There are two formulas in the "Rite of Marriage" and the couple are free to choose whichever of them they prefer.

A fourth issue is the place for signing the register and the other official papers towards the end of the ceremony. While in some weddings the papers may have been signed on the altar, this is expressly forbidden by the Church. The reason is that the altar is not just a table. It represents Christ himself, it has been dedicated to God by a bishop, and hence only those objects used in the liturgy may be placed on it. Since the signing of the papers is not an official part of the liturgy of marriage, another table should be used for this purpose. It should be noted that while people consecrating themselves to God in a liturgical ceremony sign their vows or rule of life on the altar, this is because they are making their consecration to God himself, who is represented by the altar. In a wedding, the couple are committing themselves to each other, not to God.

All in all, the couple have a wide variety of texts and music from which to choose and they should respect the norms of the Church and the wishes of the celebrant in making these choices.

III. MORAL LIFE IN CHRIST

General Moral Issues

380 The natural law

I am studying law and, although we haven't studied the natural law, I have always believed in it. Recently in discussing it with some friends, one of them said the idea of the natural law was an invention of medieval Catholic theologians. Is this true?

It is most certainly not true. The concept of the natural law predates Christianity by many centuries.

For the benefit of those unfamiliar with the natural law it will be helpful if I first explain briefly what it is. In simple terms, the natural law is the series of rights and duties, or rights and wrongs, based on human nature. That is, merely by considering human nature we can deduce that certain acts are in keeping with that nature and contribute to human flourishing and are therefore morally correct, while other acts are contrary to that nature and are morally wrong. Among the latter are killing the innocent, stealing and lying. These are wrong not because the Bible says so, but because they are contrary to human nature. Or, if you like, the Bible says they are wrong because they are wrong in themselves.

If we ask what human nature is, it is simply what makes a particular being to be human rather than something else like a tree or a dog. In short, it is what all human beings have in common. We all have human nature, just as dogs have dog nature and tables have table nature.

Based on human nature are not only moral precepts about right and wrong but also human rights. For the very fact of being human a person has such basic rights as the right to life, to liberty, to follow their conscience in matters of religion, to marry and form a family, etc. Many of these human rights are listed in the United Nations Universal

Declaration of Human Rights in 1948. To believe in human rights is therefore to believe in the natural law.

Another concept based on the natural law is crimes against humanity. Even though leaders of some nations authorised practices like genocide, use of chemical weapons against their own people, or lethal experiments on the handicapped, prisoners and the insane, they were still accused of crimes against humanity, because human rights take precedence over manmade laws and decisions. The Nuremburg trials after World War II judged matters such as these and found the perpetrators guilty. The fact that the accused had acted according to the laws of their country was not a legitimate defence. The higher natural law and the human rights based on it take precedence.

Getting back to your question, belief in a law based on human nature goes back long before Christ, let alone before medieval theologians. There is evidence of belief in a universal law binding on all human beings in Oriental literature, especially in China, many centuries before Christ. But a more developed concept of the natural law is found in the ancient Greeks, in writers like Sophocles (ca. 497-406 BC), whose play *Antigone* features a clear understanding of a natural law which is higher than the law of the king. The play was first performed in 441 BC. Other ancient Greeks that presented a concept of a natural law that is universal and known to all were Thucydides (ca. 460-400 BC) and Xenophon (ca. 427-355 BC).

In the fourth century BC a great exponent of the natural law was the Greek philosopher Aristotle (384-322 BC). In his *Nicomachean Ethics* he distinguished clearly between what is just by nature and what is just by human law (Book V). And in his work *On Rhetoric* he wrote that "there is in nature a common principle of the just and unjust that all people in some way divine, even if they have no association or commerce with each other" (Book I, Ch. 13).

One of the greatest exponents of the natural law in ancient times was the Roman jurist and philosopher Cicero (106-43 BC). In his work

Laws he wrote: "What is right and true is also eternal, and does not begin or end with written statutes... From this point of view it can be readily understood that those who formulated wicked and unjust statutes for nations, thereby breaking their promises and agreements, put into effect anything but 'laws'. It may thus be clear that in the very definition of the term 'law' there inheres the idea and principle of choosing what is just and true... Therefore Law is the distinction between things just and unjust, made in agreement with that primal and most ancient of all things, nature; and in conformity to nature's standard are framed those human laws which inflict punishment upon the wicked but defend and protect the good."

Later Christian theologians like St Augustine and St Thomas Aquinas based their teaching on the natural law on these ancient writers. So the concept of the natural law is ancient indeed.

381 Workers of the eleventh hour

A few weeks ago the Sunday Gospel was about the workers called to the vineyard at different hours, all of whom received the same reward. If someone has lived all his life trying to do the right things, why should he get the same reward as one who began to do the right things only at the very end of his life? This seems unfair.

There are different interpretations of this parable. Some see it as referring to different stages of mankind, with the Jews called at the beginning to form God's people and the Gentiles called only at the end to his new people, the Church. In this sense there would be nothing unfair, since any individual who responded to the call would receive the same reward of belonging to the people of God. A more likely interpretation, however, is the one you suggest in your question. Here the hours of the day would correspond to the different stages in the life of an individual. Some are called to the Church from childhood and serve God faithfully throughout their life whereas others are called only at the end of their life. Yet all receive the same reward, eternal life with God in heaven.

Is this unfair? If we begin with the workers of the first hour, those born into Catholic families and baptised as infants, they cannot be unhappy with God when they finish their life in his grace and are taken to heaven. They expected to go to heaven, and now they receive the reward for which they laboured and longed. God is certainly not being unfair with them.

But why should people who come into the Church late in life receive the same reward as those who have been faithful all their lives? Isn't this unfair to those who have "borne the burden of the day and the scorching heat"? (*Mt* 20:12). No it isn't. As we have seen, these Catholics of the first hour were treated fairly, for they received the reward for which they longed. It is rather a manifestation of the great mercy of God, who chooses to give to the last labourers the same reward as to those who came earlier. In the parable the householder explains his action: "I choose to give to this last as I give to you. Am I not allowed to do what I choose with what belongs to me? Or do you begrudge my generosity?" (*Mt* 20:14-15).

If we are truly generous and we desire passionately that all be saved, we will never feel unhappy when we see someone come into the Church, or back to the Church, late in life. Rather, we will be delighted that God has found them and invited them into his household, his kingdom. This is especially the case when the person is a member of our own family or a close friend and we have prayed a long time for their conversion. When they enter the Church we are overjoyed. We give thanks to God and praise him for his kindness and mercy.

We should never forget either that in a real sense those of us who entered the Church as children are the ones to be envied. We have been able to live our whole lives in the light of faith, knowing that there is a God who loves us, who is always with us, and who will one day reward us with eternal life. This is a great grace. Those who come to the Church late in life have lived most of their lives without this light, this knowledge and love of God, this certainty of eternal life. They are the ones to be pitied.

Then too, we have been able to receive the grace of God in the sacraments throughout our whole life, from Baptism as infants, to Confirmation, the Eucharist and Penance, with all the benefits and graces these sacraments give. Through them we will have stored up an enormous treasure in heaven by the end of our life. I recall hearing years ago of a man who had come into the Church late in life, and when he was dying his children asked him if he had any regrets. He answered yes: that he hadn't entered the Church much earlier.

And we shouldn't forget that those who come into the Church late in life may have to spend a longer time in Purgatory atoning for their sins. We "cradle" Catholics have known from childhood that we must make up for our sins, and we have gone through many Lents and lived many acts of penance, plus we have received many indulgences, so that, God willing, we may have a short Purgatory or perhaps none at all.

All in all, God is not unfair. He is exceptionally kind and merciful to all.

382 What is grace?

Now that we are celebrating a "Year of Grace" in Australia, can you remind me what grace is?

There are two main types of grace – sanctifying grace and actual grace – and in order to do justice to your question, I will speak here of the first type and leave the second for next week.

The word grace in general refers to something freely given, to a gift. For example, we use the expression "by the grace of God", meaning by the gift that God gives us. Or we refer to an *ex gratia* payment, meaning a payment that was not due in justice, but is freely given. The Latin word *gratia* has also come to mean thanksgiving for God's gift. In this sense we say "Grace" before and after meals, meaning we thank God and ask him to bless us and the gift of the food. Likewise, the Spanish word for "thank you" is *gracias* and the Italian *grazie*. The Latin word for thanksgiving is *gratiarum actio*, literally action of graces. So the two meanings of gift and thanksgiving for the gift, which are closely related, are expressed by the same word.

The *Catechism of the Catholic Church* sums up the meaning of grace in general: "Grace is *favour,* the *free and undeserved help* that God gives us to respond to his call to become children of God, adoptive sons, partakers of the divine nature and of eternal life" (*CCC* 1996). As I mentioned above, there are two main types of grace: sanctifying grace, which remains in the soul and makes it pleasing to God, and actual grace, which is a passing help from God.

What exactly is sanctifying grace? The Catechism sums it up succinctly: "Grace is a *participation in the life of God*" (*CCC* 1997). That is, in addition to the natural life we receive from our parents, we have supernatural life, a sharing in God's own life, the life of the Blessed Trinity, in our soul. This is an awesome gift, completely undeserved. It gives us an extraordinary dignity. The Catechism describes it like this: "It introduces us into the intimacy of Trinitarian life: by Baptism the Christian participates in the grace of Christ, the Head of his Body" (*CCC* 1997).

This life of God in the soul has a number of aspects. Through it, the three divine persons come to dwell in the soul in what we call the indwelling of the Blessed Trinity. Jesus himself announces this in the Last Supper (cf. *Jn* 14:17, 23). Also, we become not mere creatures but the very children of God: "As an 'adopted son' he can henceforth call God 'Father,' in union with the only Son" (*CCC* 1997). And in what can only be termed a great mystery, we become in some way divinised or deified, "partakers of the divine nature" (*2 Pet* 1:4). That is, through grace we share in the very nature of God.

All this is truly the beginning of holiness. As the Catechism says, "The grace of Christ is the gratuitous gift that God makes to us of his own life, infused by the Holy Spirit into our soul to heal it of sin and to sanctify it. It is the *sanctifying* or *deifying grace* received in Baptism. It is in us the source of the work of sanctification" (*CCC* 1999). We receive sanctifying grace for the first time in Baptism and it remains in the soul as an "habitual grace", a stable quality, as long as we do not lose it through mortal sin. It has been called the *inchoatio vitae aeternae*, the beginning of eternal life, which is destined to reach its fulfilment in the eternal life of heaven.

What practical consequences do we derive from considering this momentous gift? First, since this grace is truly sanctifying, we do well always to strive to grow in holiness, in sanctity. What does this mean in real terms? Essentially, it means to grow in love for God: through regular times of prayer which are real encounters with God, times of loving conversation with him. Also, it means making an effort to receive the sacraments of Penance and the Eucharist more regularly, since they increase the life of grace in us and help us to grow in the love of God. And always, it means striving to do the will of God in all things since, as Jesus says, "If a man loves me, he will keep my word" (*Jn* 14:23). What is more, through our good works, we receive more grace.

Naturally, it means making a great effort not to commit sin, especially mortal sin, since sin offends the God who loves us so much. And when the soul is "dead" through mortal sin, we cannot gain merit for our good actions. So if we commit mortal sin, we should return to God as soon as possible with true contrition through the gateway to grace of the sacrament of Penance.

In this way the "Year of Grace" can be also a "Year of Holiness".

383 What is actual grace?

Now that we are celebrating a "Year of Grace" in Australia, can you remind me what actual grace is?

As I mentioned in my last answer, there are two main types of grace – sanctifying grace and actual grace. The *Catechism of the Catholic Church* says that sanctifying grace "is distinguished from *actual graces* which refer to God's interventions, whether at the beginning of conversion or in the course of the work of sanctification" (*CCC* 2000). Whereas sanctifying grace remains in the soul in a stable way, actual graces are passing helps that God gives us to draw us closer to him. Or, whereas sanctifying grace by itself makes us holy, actual grace leads us to God so that we may receive sanctifying grace and become holy.

Through actual graces God helps us understand truths that will lead us to him and to act in accordance with those truths. Thus grace acts in both the intellect and the will. St Augustine says that actual grace brings it about "not only that we discover what ought to be done, but also that we do what we have discovered; not only that we believe what ought to be loved, but also that we love what we have believed" (*De gratia Christi*, ch. 12).

To whom does God give actual grace? To everyone, absolutely everyone. Even to atheists and sinners who live far from God? Yes, to everyone. This is his goodness and mercy. As St Paul writes, God "desires all men to be saved and to come to the knowledge of the truth" (*1 Tim* 2:4). To help them, he grants everyone sufficient grace to be saved. "My grace is sufficient for you" (*2 Cor* 12:9), God answers St Paul, and we can take this as applying to everyone. Pope Alexander VIII in 1609 condemned the proposition of the Jansenists that Christ died only for the faithful and that pagans, Jews and heretics do not receive grace from him (cf. *DS* 1294 ff). More recently, the Second Vatican Council said of the salvation of those who do not know

God: "Nor shall divine providence deny the assistance necessary for salvation to those who, without any fault of theirs, have not yet arrived at an explicit knowledge of God, and who, not without grace, strive to lead a good life" (*LG* 16).

Actual grace can bring about big changes in people's lives if they respond to that grace. St Paul, for example, was changed from an ardent persecutor of the Church into the great Apostle of the Gentiles, and St Augustine was led from a life of sin to be baptised and become a priest, bishop and Doctor of the Church. In more recent times Bernard Nathanson was led from agnostic Jew and abortionist to staunch defender of life at all stages and finally to the Catholic Church. For this reason, we should never despair of the salvation of those who are living far from God or who even claim not to believe in God. Rather, we should pray for them, asking God to give them the grace necessary for their conversion and for them to correspond to that grace. We can have absolute trust in God's mercy and power. After all, the angel said to Mary after telling her that her ageing relative Elizabeth was now in her sixth month, "For with God nothing will be impossible" (*Lk* 1:37).

God's grace reaches everyone, but we are still free to correspond to it or not. It is like the rain that falls on the earth and can give life to all, but we remain free to shelter ourselves from it and not receive its benefit. It is the mysterious interplay between grace and human freedom. Coming closer to home, we are all receiving actual graces throughout the day: to get out of bed on time, to say our morning prayers, to smile at others and treat them well, to start our work, to flee from temptations to sin, to ring a friend and ask them how they are...

When we respond to these graces and do the will of God we grow in holiness and store up for ourselves treasures in heaven. When we turn a deaf ear we miss out on the opportunity and may even offend God by sin. It is up to us. God doesn't force us to do his will. He stands at the door and knocks but he doesn't enter unless we open the door to him: "If any one hears my voice and opens the door, I will come in to him and eat with him, and he with me" (*Rev* 3:20).

Let us pray that we will always be very sensitive to the promptings of God's grace in our soul, and so do his will and grow in holiness.

384 Other types of grace

Earlier you mentioned that sanctifying grace and actual grace are the two principal types of grace. I thought they were the only two. What other ones are there?

The *Catechism of the Catholic Church* mentions three more types of grace: sacramental grace, graces of state and charisms.

As regards the first, we know that all the sacraments confer sanctifying grace, which is a sharing in the very life of God, but they also confer a special grace proper to each sacrament. The Catechism describes sacramental grace as "gifts proper to the different sacraments" (*CCC* 2003). St Thomas Aquinas, in the *Summa Theologiae*, says that the sacraments confer, in addition to sanctifying grace, "a certain divine assistance in obtaining the end of the sacrament" (*STh* III, q. 62, a. 2), which he calls sacramental grace.

Sacramental grace is thus a specific grace proper to each sacrament which helps the person obtain the purpose of that sacrament. It might be considered an orientation of the person's supernatural life toward the purpose of the sacrament. Sacramental grace also involves the assurance of obtaining all the actual graces, the passing helps of God, that the person will need to fulfil the rights and duties relating to the sacrament.

Looking at the seven sacraments in particular, the sacramental grace of Baptism confers the help to live as an adopted child of God, as a brother or sister of Christ, and as a member of the Church. It helps the person to seek the holiness demanded by Baptism and to fulfil faithfully the will of God in all things.

Confirmation confers the sacramental grace which strengthens the person in professing, defending and spreading the Faith without regard to the obstacles this may entail.

The sacramental grace of the Eucharist strengthens the recipient in love for God and union with Christ, who now lives in the person and the person in him (cf. *Jn* 6:56).

The sacrament of Penance confers sacramental grace which helps the penitent to make up for their sins and to struggle to avoid falling into the same sins again.

The Anointing of the Sick strengthens the recipient to trust in the divine mercy, to be united with the Passion of Christ and to resist the temptations of the devil, which can sometimes be strong in times of sickness and impending death.

The sacramental grace of Holy Orders strengthens the bishop, priest or deacon in carrying out the duties of their order and ensures them of all the actual graces they will need for the worthy exercise of their ministry.

Finally, Matrimony strengthens the spouses in love for each other within the nuptial covenant of Christ with his Church, and ensures them of divine assistance to be faithful to the commitments of marriage throughout their lives.

In addition to sacramental grace, the Church often speaks of "graces of state". By this is meant the special grace God grants to people in certain states of life to assist them in fulfilling the duties of their state. The *Catechism of the Catholic Church* says that these graces "accompany the exercise of the responsibilities of the Christian life and of the ministries within the Church" (*CCC* 2004).

The Catechism quotes St Paul who writes: "Having gifts that differ according to the grace given to us, let us use them: if prophecy, in proportion to our faith; if service, in our serving; he who teaches, in his teaching; he who exhorts, in his exhortation; he who contributes, in liberality; he who gives aid, with zeal; he who does acts of mercy, with cheerfulness" (*Rom* 12:6-8). Thus people like teachers, principals of schools, those dedicated to helping the poor, superiors of religious communities, spiritual directors, parents, etc., can count on special graces to help them in carrying out the duties of their state in life.

Finally, the Catechism mentions "*special graces*, also called *charisms* after the Greek term used by St Paul and meaning 'favour,' 'gratuitous gift,' 'benefit'" (cf. *LG* 12). The Catechism mentions such extraordinary charisms as the gift of miracles or of tongues, and says that all charisms are "oriented toward sanctifying grace and are intended for the common good of the Church" (*CCC* 2003). Other charisms are more ordinary: the gift of teaching, generosity with the poor, etc.

385 Occasions of sin

One passage in Scripture that I have always found disturbing is Jesus' words about plucking out our eye or cutting off our hand if it should cause us to sin. How are we meant to understand this?

I think everyone finds this passage disturbing. It comes in the Sermon on the Mount: "If your right eye causes you to sin, pluck it out and throw it away; it is better that you lose one of your members than that your whole body be thrown into hell. And if your right hand causes you to sin, cut it off and throw it away; it is better that you lose one of your members than that your whole body go into hell" (*Mt* 5:29-30).

In the parallel passage in Mark, Jesus makes special reference to heaven and he adds that we should also be prepared to sacrifice a foot: "And if your hand causes you to sin, cut it off; it is better for you to enter life maimed than with two hands to go to hell, to the unquenchable fire. And if your foot causes you to sin, cut it off; it is better for you to enter life lame than with two feet to be thrown into hell. And if your eye causes you to sin, pluck it out; it is better for you to enter the kingdom of God with one eye than with two eyes to be thrown into hell, where their worm does not die, and the fire is not quenched" (*Mk* 9:43-48).

How are we meant to understand this? The first point that Jesus is emphasising is the reality of hell. As he does on so many other occasions, he is reminding his listeners, and all of us down the ages, that hell exists. To stress the horror of hell he speaks of the "unquenchable fire," "where their worm does not die, and the fire is not quenched". Because hell is such a terrifying reality and it is forever, Jesus wants us to do everything possible to avoid going there, sacrificing whatever can take us away from eternal life.

The first thing we should be prepared to sacrifice is not our limbs or our eyes but whatever can constitute an occasion of sin for us. In the passage as given in St Matthew's Gospel Jesus refers immediately beforehand to a man looking lustfully at a woman and committing adultery with her in his heart. So important is this message that he goes on to say that we should be prepared to sacrifice even our eye rather than use it to commit sin.

What sorts of occasions should we be prepared to sacrifice in order to avoid committing sins that could send us to hell? Any and all such occasions, unless they are truly necessary. For example, someone may be involved in a business where dishonesty is practised habitually, or where people are expected to lie as a matter of routine. Clearly, one cannot work in such a business. Or a married person may be working in a place where someone of the opposite sex is falling in love with them, and they too are becoming attracted to that person. Rather than end up breaking up the marriage and risking their eternal salvation, it is preferable to give up the job, no matter how much money they are earning or how promising their career prospects.

Or a person's work may involve such long hours that they don't have time to attend Mass on Sundays or even to pray, they scarcely have time for their spouse and children, and they are so stressed that they are habitually angry. This situation too could jeopardise their eternal salvation and they should be prepared to give it up. Or someone may find that their internet access leads them habitually to look at pornography and to commit sins of impurity. They should be prepared to give up the internet access.

Or someone may be reading books or articles that are gradually undermining their faith. They should be prepared to give up such readings. Or a young person may be going out with someone who leads them into sins against chastity. If they cannot avoid committing the sins, they should stop seeing that person.

It is impossible to imagine a situation where in order to avoid committing serious sin a person would have to cut off a limb or pluck out an eye. But even considering that extreme hypothetical case, as Jesus says, it would be better to go to heaven with one eye, or one hand or one foot, than to go to hell with two. The message is very clear: we should give up whatever jeopardises our eternal salvation.

386 Diminished guilt for sins

When I consider all the mortal sins people I know are committing, I wonder how they are ever going to go to heaven. How should I approach this matter?

The first thing to remember is that it is not committing a mortal sin that sends someone to hell, but rather dying without repenting of the sin. As the *Catechism of the Catholic Church* expresses it, "To die in mortal sin without repenting and accepting God's merciful love means remaining separated from him for ever by our own free choice" (*CCC* 1033).

We should always bear in mind God's merciful love, which can move the hardened sinner to repent even on their deathbed. If someone commits numerous mortal sins throughout their life and repents at the last moment, they will be saved. But of course we should pray and do all we can to help such people repent sooner, so that they can experience God's love as soon as possible and not continue to suffer the harm that every sin causes them and others.

And also we should remember that there are many factors that reduce the culpability, the subjective guilt, of the person, to a point where although they are committing an act which is objectively a mortal sin, they may not be held responsible for a mortal sin by God. As I explained earlier, one such factor is ignorance of the fact that what they are doing is a mortal sin. Unfortunately, there are many people in this state today, due to a lack of clear and systematic education in the faith. If they are ignorant of the seriousness of their sin, even though they know that what they are doing is wrong, God will not hold them accountable for a mortal sin.

Moralists distinguish between culpable ignorance and inculpable ignorance. If the person is unaware of the immorality of their acts through no fault of their own, as is often the case today, God will not hold them responsible for a mortal sin. If, however, they have doubts about their actions and they have deliberately not sought to inform themselves for fear of finding out that what they are doing is gravely sinful, their ignorance is culpable and it does not reduce the seriousness of their sin. In general people are presumed to be aware of the seriousness of sins against the basic precepts of the natural law, such as blasphemy, perjury, murder and adultery (cf. *CCC* 1756).

Another factor that can reduce the culpability of sins is habit. Thus, for example, a person trying to overcome an entrenched habit of blaspheming, drinking alcohol to excess, gambling, taking illicit drugs, committing sins against chastity with oneself or others, etc., may not be guilty of a mortal sin (cf. *CCC* 2352). Often these habits can engender a sort of sickness, an addiction, and God will judge the person more mercifully, as should their friends and relatives. In many cases, what they need is the help of doctors, psychologists or therapists, in addition to the spiritual help of priests and the support of those around them.

In addition to inculpable ignorance and entrenched habits, mental disorders can of course diminish the culpability of sins. A person suffering from depression, anxiety, schizophrenia, obsessive-compulsive disorder and other similar conditions will not be held as guilty before God as persons of sound mind (cf. *CCC* 1860).

Then there are the passions, such as anger, fear, sadness and hatred. Passions are defined as "emotions or movements of the sensitive appetite that incline us to act or not to act in regard to something felt or imagined to be good or evil" (*CCC* 1763). A strong, sudden burst of anger can make a person lose control altogether and do things they would never do in a calm state. Likewise, the fear of death or of serious harm can make a person react in a similar way. Passions, as long as they are not deliberately fostered, can thus diminish greatly the culpability of sins and sometimes take away the culpability altogether.

In short, we must be very careful in making judgments about the sinfulness of others and leave the judgment to God. But we should pray insistently that these persons may come to understand their situation and take whatever remedies they need to change their life.

387 Mortal sins

Some of my friends seem to think that the only mortal sins are murder and adultery, and since they haven't committed these they are in the state of grace and can always receive Communion. Can you give me some examples of other mortal sins?

I fear there are many people with the lack of understanding of mortal sin you mention. In fact there are quite a few mortal sins that are reasonably common and it is important to be aware of them. By mortal sin we mean a serious violation of the law of God such that the person offends God grievously and loses the state of grace. If they were to die in that state without repenting they would go to hell. In the words of the *Catechism of the Catholic Church*, "Mortal sin destroys charity in the heart of man by a grave violation of God's law; it turns man away from God, who is his ultimate end and his beatitude, by preferring an inferior good to him" (*CCC* 1855).

For someone actually to be guilty of a mortal sin, they must fulfil three conditions. First, they must violate God's law in a serious matter. For example, stealing two thousand dollars is a mortal sin, whereas stealing twenty dollars is not. Second, they must be aware that what they are doing or have done is not only wrong, but is seriously wrong so as to constitute a mortal sin. Many people today have not been properly instructed in morality and are completely unaware of the seriousness of their actions. Consequently God would not hold them responsible for a mortal sin. Third, they must consent to what they are doing, with "a consent sufficiently deliberate to be a personal choice" (*CCC* 1859). Such circumstances as a serious mental illness or a fit of rage could diminish the consent to a point where the sin would not be mortal.

Returning to your question, we can see examples of mortal sins by going through the Ten Commandments.

Against the first three commandments, which relate to God, are such mortal sins as wilfully denying a truth to be believed by all Catholics (heresy), wilful hatred of God, deliberate violation of the name of God (blasphemy), lying under oath (perjury), involvement in a satanic cult, desecration of the Eucharist through irreverent treatment of a consecrated host, the reception of Communion in the state of mortal sin, missing Mass through one's own fault without a sufficient reason, etc.

Against the fourth commandment would be, for example, a serious failure to care for one's children or parents.

The fifth commandment presents numerous possibilities of mortal sins. Among them are murder, abortion, destruction of human embryos, causing grievous bodily harm, leading another into a serious sin (scandal), euthanasia, sterilisation performed for contraceptive reasons, reckless behaviour endangering human life, complete drunkenness, habitual use of illicit drugs, etc.

All sins of action against the sixth commandment, which relates to chastity, are in themselves serious matter and hence are mortal sins: masturbation, sex outside of marriage, adultery, rape, prostitution, homosexual acts, viewing of pornography, etc. Even lustful thoughts or sexual fantasies can be mortal sins if they are deliberately consented to and prolonged in order to derive pleasure. And of course the use of contraception is a serious matter.

As regards the seventh commandment, which forbids stealing and damaging the property of others, the gravity of the sin will depend on the amount of the theft and the harm done to the other. A good rule of thumb is that the taking of the equivalent of a day's wages from someone is a mortal sin. Included in this area are fraud, the failure to honour contracts, tax evasion, corruption, etc.

The same criterion applies to lying and harming the good name of another, which are forbidden by the eighth commandment. If the harm is great, the sin is mortal.

The ninth and tenth commandments forbid internal sins against the sixth and seventh commandments and, as we have seen, these can sometimes be mortal too.

As is clear, there are many possible mortal sins, but God is merciful and he is always ready to forgive us when we come before him with contrition in the sacrament of reconciliation.

388 Does God punish us for our sins?

I have an uncle who left his wife and is now living with another woman. Everything seems to be going wrong for him. He thinks God is punishing him for his sins. Does God do this?

This is a question many people have asked, and there can be no certain answer for an individual case. Nonetheless, we do find in the Scriptures some indications which point towards an answer in general terms. In the book of Leviticus, for example, God tells the people that he will reward them if they obey his law, but he will also punish them if they disobey it (cf. *Deut* 26:1-45). We see, especially in the Old Testament, how God at times does punish his people for their waywardness.

He does it especially with the people as a whole. As one example among many, when the Israelites are in the desert after being led out of Egypt, Moses sends some men to explore the Promised Land of Canaan to see if they will be able to enter it. On their return Joshua and Caleb say they will be able to take the land, but their companions say they will not because of the size and power of its inhabitants, and the people wail all night. God then tells Moses and Aaron that as punishment the people will remain in the desert for forty years and all those over the age of twenty who murmured against him will die there: "I the Lord, have spoken; surely this will I do to all this wicked congregation that are gathered together against me: in this wilderness they shall come to a full end, and there they shall die" (*Num* 14:26-35).

At the same time God punishes two individuals, namely Moses and his brother Aaron, for their lack of faith. When the Israelites complain about the lack of water at Meribah, Moses and Aaron plead with God, who directs Moses to strike the rock to make water flow from it. He strikes the rock twice and immediately water gushes forth. But God tells Moses and Aaron: "Because you did not believe in me, to sanctify me in the eyes of the sons of Israel, therefore you shall not bring this assembly into the land which I have given them" (*Num* 20:12). Aaron dies a short time later and Moses too dies before the Israelites cross into the Promised Land under Joshua (cf. *Num* 20:28; *Deut* 34:1-6). Among the many other figures of the Old Testament who suffered for their sins is Jacob, who deceived his father Isaac by pretending to be his brother Esau and, as a result, had to endure for many years the loss of his son Joseph, who was sold into slavery by his brothers (cf. *Gen* 27:1-40; 37:12-36).

Another great punishment of the whole people comes at the time of the prophet Jeremiah, when God destroys the land and sends the inhabitants of Judah and Jerusalem into captivity in Babylon for seventy years because of their idolatry (cf. *Jer* 25:11). But while there are numerous instances of God punishing his people and some individuals for their sins, Jesus himself tells us that suffering is not necessarily a consequence of particular sins. When his disciples ask him who sinned that a man should have been born blind, he says: "It was not that this man sinned, or his parents, but that the works of God might be made manifest in him" (*Jn* 9:3).

Therefore, we should never say that a given misfortune is a consequence of particular sins that an individual may have committed. God does not always work that way. Nor should we conclude of course that just because we do not suffer misfortunes God is pleased with our life. He does not always punish us or reward us immediately for our deeds, good or evil.

At the same time, we know that we have to undergo temporal punishment for all our sins, whether venial or mortal. If we do not do it sufficiently on earth, we will complete it in Purgatory. In this light we can understand that God, moved by his mercy and love, sometimes allows us to suffer illnesses and other misfortunes in this life so that we do not have to suffer the worse pains of Purgatory. And we can always see suffering as a manifestation of God's love, who allows us to share in his Son's cross. The letter to the Hebrews says: "For the Lord disciplines him whom he loves, and chastises every son whom he receives" (*Heb* 12:6).

389 Cooperation in sin

I work as a cleaner and the firm I work for has just won a contract to look after several abortion clinics. If I am required to do so, could I work in those clinics? I am totally opposed to abortion but I don't want to lose my job.

Many people find themselves in situations like yours where they may be asked to do something which they oppose on moral grounds. This happens not only in the workplace, but also in other areas of life, so it is important to know the principles that help us resolve these moral dilemmas. Your situation is what is called in moral theology *cooperation in sin*, where a person is asked or proposes to do something in itself moral but which in some way cooperates in the sinful behaviour of another. The question then arises as to whether he or she can cooperate in this way.

A number of distinctions need to be made which help resolve the matter. First there is the question of whether the person agrees with the sinful behaviour of the other and is quite happy to cooperate in it, or is opposed to it. If the person agrees with the sinful behaviour we speak of *formal cooperation* and, as can be expected, this is always wrong. For example, a person who has no objection to abortion might take a job as a receptionist or accountant in an abortion clinic, thereby cooperating in some way in the abortions. If, however, the person is opposed to the sinful behaviour but feels compelled in some way to cooperate in it we speak of *material cooperation*. There are some circumstances in which material cooperation is permissible.

To determine this we must first ask whether the proposed cooperation is closely united to the sinful act, or is only remotely connected to it. In the first case we speak of *proximate cooperation* and in the second of *remote cooperation*. Naturally in real life there can be a whole series of degrees of proximity or remoteness. But the moral principle that applies is that the more proximate the proposed act is to the sinful act, the stronger the reason one needs to engage in the cooperation. And the more remote the cooperation, the easier it will be to justify it.

For example, staying in the case of abortion, a nurse or other clinical assistant in the abortion itself is cooperating very proximately, the receptionist or secretary more remotely, and the contract cleaner or gardener still more remotely. A good Christian should never take a job as a permanent employee in an abortion clinic since they would be cooperating on a daily basis, even though remotely, in the killing of innocent human beings. But there may be circumstances in which one could work occasionally as a cleaner or gardener.

This will depend on a further distinction. The question is asked whether if the person does not cooperate the sinful act will still go ahead or if it will not go ahead. For example, if a particular person refuses to clean the abortion clinic it is virtually certain that there will be many others who will do the cleaning and so the abortions will still go on. In this case a lesser reason is needed to justify taking the job. Or, to use another example, if the friend of a girl who is booked in for an abortion and who lives in the country refuses to drive the girl into the city for the abortion, it is quite likely that she will not be able to have the abortion. Therefore the girl who is asked to drive should refuse to do so since she can stop the abortion on that particular day and perhaps talk her friend out of the abortion altogether.

The final consideration in cooperation is the strength of the reason why one is considering cooperating. If it is a matter of losing one's job and it would be difficult to obtain another one, that can justify cooperating remotely in the case you propose. But if it were merely a matter of earning more money, that would not justify cooperating in something as evil as abortion. In general, one should try to avoid cooperating in sin altogether but, as we have seen, there can be circumstances which can justify at least remote material cooperation.

Life presents many different situations in which one can be faced with the decision of whether to cooperate in another's sin. As examples, the *Catechism of the Catholic Church* says that we have a responsibility for the sins committed by others when we cooperate in them: "by participating directly and voluntarily in them; by ordering, advising, praising, or approving them; by not disclosing or not hindering them when we have an obligation to do so; by protecting evil-doers" (*CCC* 1868). This gives much food for thought. For the case of whether one can attend a garden wedding of a Catholic see my book *Question Time 2*, q. 248.

390 What is scandal?

I have been confused for quite some time as to exactly what scandal is and whether it is a sin. For example, we say that a person was scandalised, or that someone's behaviour was scandalous, or that someone gave scandal. Is there sin in any of this?

As you say, we use the word scandal in many ways. The word, by the way, comes from the Greek word *skandalon*, meaning a stumbling block or trap. When we say that someone was scandalised, we usually mean they were shocked, or horrified, by the immoral behaviour of someone. But while shocked they were not inclined to imitate that behaviour. Quite the contrary. Similarly, when we say that someone's behaviour was scandalous, we are normally indicating our strong disapproval of what they did. Again, we are not inclined to imitate their conduct.

But when we say that someone gave scandal, we are saying that they acted in a way that was likely to lead others into sin. This is the proper sense of the term in moral theology. The *Catechism of the Catholic Church* says: "Scandal is an attitude or behaviour which leads another to do evil. The person who gives scandal becomes his neighbour's tempter. He damages virtue and integrity; he may even draw his brother into spiritual death. Scandal is a grave offence if by deed or omission another is deliberately led into a grave offence" (*CCC* 2284).

One of the worst things we can do to others is lead them into sin. If we hit them, insult them or gossip about them we do not harm them in their relationship with God, which is their most priceless possession. But if we lead them into sin we harm this relationship and can even jeopardise their eternal salvation. As the Catechism says, we become their tempter, much as Satan does, and we can draw them into spiritual death, or mortal sin. Indeed, as the Catechism says, if our behaviour leads someone else to commit a grave offence, or mortal sin, we have committed a mortal sin ourselves.

Especially serious is scandal caused by persons with authority over those led into sin. This includes parents, teachers, priests, and in general any adult with an underage person. Our Lord was particularly strong in condemning it: "Whoever causes one of these little ones who believe in me to sin, it would be better for him to have a great millstone fastened round his neck and to be drowned in the depth of the sea" (*Mt* 18:6). The Catechism teaches: "Scandal is grave when given by those who by nature or office are obliged to teach and educate others. Jesus reproaches the scribes and Pharisees on this account: he likens them to wolves in sheep's clothing" (*CCC* 2285; cf. *Lk* 17:1).

There are many ways in which one can commit scandal. The most obvious is by leading another person directly into sin. A young man who engages in sexual activity with a girl, a married man who entices a woman to commit adultery with him, a person who invites someone to attend an inappropriate film or show, someone who encourages another to commit a crime with him, a business manager who tells his staff to lie to a customer, etc., all commit scandal and are responsible not only for their own sin but also for that of the other.

Another obvious way of committing scandal is by giving bad example, without necessarily intending to lead others into sin. This can include using bad language, dressing immodestly, praising a film that contains inappropriate material, drinking alcohol to excess, etc. This is what we mean by scandalous behaviour. A girl, or a boy for that matter, who dresses or behaves immodestly can be guilty of the sins of all those who look at them with lust or have impure thoughts or desires as a result. Parents have a special responsibility to take care that their children dress and act appropriately.

Parliamentarians who vote for legislation that permits immorality in such forms as abortion, pornography or embryonic stem cell research are guilty of scandal and are responsible for all the sins committed as a result. Similarly those who make immoral films, write or publish immoral books, make or sell immodest clothing, run brothels, etc., are guilty of scandal on a grand scale.

Scandal can also be committed simply by encouraging, advising or teaching someone to do wrong, and even by not discouraging them if they tell us they are thinking of doing it.

In summary, as the Catechism explains, "Anyone who uses the power at his disposal in such a way that it leads others to do wrong becomes guilty of scandal and responsible for the evil that he has directly or indirectly encouraged. 'Temptations to sin are sure to come; but woe to him by whom they come!'" (*Lk* 17:1; *CCC* 2287).

391 New deadly sins

I understand that some years ago the Vatican issued a list of seven new "deadly sins". Do you know where I can get a copy of them as well as details about them?

The first thing I should say is that yes, someone in the Vatican did give a list of new sins, but this was not an official declaration of the Vatican. The list came from Bishop Gianfranco Girotti, Regent of the Apostolic Penitentiary, in an interview with the Vatican's official newspaper *L'Osservatore Romano* on 9 March 2008. The Apostolic Penitentiary is the tribunal responsible for such matters as indulgences and the forgiveness of sins reserved to the Holy See. The Regent is the second highest official in the tribunal. Bishop Girotti was interviewed by the Vatican's newspaper at the close of a course for confessors conducted by the Penitentiary. His statement came in answer to one of many questions put to him by the newspaper and thus carries no official status. It was given "off the cuff", not as a prepared statement.

The world's media, however, picked up on the statement and made it appear to be an official declaration of the Vatican. Some journalists even ventured to call this a new list of seven "deadly sins", following the list of seven "deadly sins" drawn up in 590 AD by Pope Gregory the Great. The traditional "deadly" or "capital" sins are pride, avarice, envy, wrath, lust, gluttony, and sloth or acedia (cf. *Catechism of the Catholic Church*, 1866).

So exactly what did Bishop Girotti say? I take the text of the interview from the English translation offered by the Istituto Acton in Rome. In answer to a previous question about why people today do not understand the Church's teaching and practice of indulgences, the bishop said: "Repentance, therefore, today takes on a (special) social dimension, due to the fact that relationships have grown weaker and more complicated because of globalisation." He was emphasising by this the social dimension of sin, and this led to the next question: "In your opinion, what are the 'new sins?'"

The bishop answered: "There are various areas today in which we adopt sinful behaviour, as with individual and social rights. This is especially so in the field of bioethics where we cannot deny the existence of violations of fundamental rights of human nature – this occurs by way of experiments and genetics modifications, whose results we cannot easily predict or control.

"Another area, which indeed pertains to the social spectrum, is that of drug use, which weakens our minds and reduces our intelligence. As a result, many young people are left out of Church circles. Here's another one: social and economic inequality, in the sense that the rich always seem to get richer, and the poor, poorer. This [phenomenon] feeds off an unsustainable form of social injustice and is related to environmental issues – which currently have much relevant interest."

This is the full text of Bishop Girotti's answer to the question. If one asks how many sins he identified, the answer could be varied. He certainly spoke of experiments and genetic modifications in the area of bioethics, drug abuse, social and economic inequality and possibly sins in the area of the environment. That is a total of five at most.

Nonetheless the media, even Catholic media, sought to find seven sins, presumably to match the traditional seven deadly sins. The new sins given by various media organisations, including CNA and Bloomberg, were bioethical violations such as birth control, "morally dubious'" experiments such as stem cell research, drug abuse, polluting the environment, contributing to the widening divide between rich and poor, excessive wealth, and creating poverty.

As is obvious, this is quite a gratuitous elaboration on what the bishop said. What are we to make of all this? Most importantly, there is no new official list of deadly sins. Certainly, we should be aware that the sins mentioned are important and we should do everything possible to avoid committing them. But they are not new in the sense that this is not the first time the Church has spoken about them. So all in all, in spite of the media hype, in the words of William Shakespeare it is a question of "much ado about nothing".

392 The seven deadly sins

Recently you wrote about the supposed "new" seven deadly sins and you mentioned the traditional ones in passing. Can you write a little more about the traditional ones and tell me where they come from and why they are important?

The phrase "seven deadly sins" is well known and has found its way into secular culture, with films, a television series and books making use of the title, as well as numerous paintings in the Middle Ages depicting them. While the name seven "deadly sins" is perhaps the best known, the sins are also known as "capital sins", from the Latin word *caput*, or head. They are called this because they are the principal ones from which others follow, or to which others are related. They are also known as "capital vices", which is perhaps a more appropriate term. Vices are bad habits which lead to sins. Likewise, they are sometimes called "cardinal sins", from the Latin word *cardo*, meaning hinge. The other sins hinge on these seven.

The list of deadly sins seems to have its origin in the eight "evil spirits", or thoughts, listed by the fourth-century monk Evagrius Ponticus. He gave them names in Greek, with the closest translation being gluttony, lust, avarice, pride, sadness, wrath, boasting or vainglory, and acedia or sloth. St John Cassian (360-435), who spent a few years in a monastic community near Bethlehem before going to southern France to found the Abbey of St Victor, brought the list of eight evil spirits to the West and translated them into Latin.

Finally, Pope St Gregory the Great in 590 gave the list that we know today as the seven deadly sins (*Moralia in Job,* 31, 45). Instead of sadness he listed envy, which is usually defined as sadness at another's success, and he included boasting or vainglory in pride. The order of his list, which was also used by Dante Alighieri in *The Divine Comedy,* is lust, gluttony, avarice, sloth, wrath, envy and pride.

The *Catechism of the Catholic Church* lists them in a different order: "pride, avarice, envy, wrath, lust, gluttony, and sloth or acedia" (*CCC* 1866). It says of them: "Vices can be classified according to the virtues they oppose, or also be linked to the *capital sins* which Christian experience has distinguished, following St John Cassian and St Gregory the Great. They are called 'capital' because they engender other sins, other vices" (*CCC* 1866).

Two things should be said about these vices or sins. First, even though they are known as deadly or capital sins, not all the sins of these seven vices are mortal sins. Some of them are mortal, like fornication and adultery resulting from lust, and stealing a large amount of money as a sin of greed. But many sins, like eating a little too much (gluttony), a degree of laziness (sloth) and envy of another's talents need not be mortal. Second, the fact of having these vices or inclinations is not itself sinful. In some way they are a disorder in our nature resulting from original sin, and as such they are not sinful. It is the acts that these vices engender that are sinful.

Looking at the sins one by one, pride may be defined as an exaggerated consideration of one's own worth. It is perhaps the most deadly sin of all since it makes the person rely on his own power rather than on God: "The beginning of man's pride is to depart from the Lord" (*Sir* 10:12).

Avarice, or greed, is the disordered love of material things, and we know the havoc this sin has brought about. Envy, or jealousy, is sadness over another's good and it often leads to hatred for that person and to the desire to obtain the good by immoral means.

Wrath, or anger, is the disordered desire to seek revenge when we have been wronged. It too can lead to great harm in human relationships. Lust, the disordered desire for sexual pleasure, again leads to serious harm, both to oneself and to others. Gluttony, the disordered desire for food and drink, shows a lack of moderation in these earthly goods. And finally, sloth, or laziness, leads to a failure to fulfill our duties, sometimes with serious consequences.

It is good to be aware of these vices or sins so that we can strive to avoid them and to grow in such virtues as humility, detachment, kindness, meekness, chastity, temperance and industriousness.

393 The value of temptations

Pardon me for my ignorance and perhaps lack of reverence, but why does God tempt us, or at least allow us to be tempted to sin? Is this a good God who allows us to be tempted?

This is a commonly asked question. Let us begin by looking at the etymology of the word temptation. It comes from the Latin word *temptatio*, which means simply a test, or a trial. We customarily use the word to refer to a situation in which we are inclined to commit a sin. As tests, temptations in themselves are not sinful. It is only when we give in to them with our will that they become sinful.

And it is not God who tempts us, in the sense of putting us in a situation in which we are strongly inclined to offend him. He is too good a Father for that. St James writes: "Let no one say when he is tempted, 'I am tempted by God'; for God cannot be tempted with evil and he himself tempts no one; but each person is tempted when he is lured and enticed by his own desire" (*Jas* 1:13-14). While God does not tempt us to sin, he does allow us to be tempted. Why would he do this? Because temptations, as tests, show us the strength of our virtue and love for God and they can be great sources of merit and sanctity.

Let us not forget that Jesus himself underwent temptations in the desert before beginning his public life (cf. *Mt* 4:1-11). After forty days of prayer and fasting, he was tempted by the devil in three different ways, but each time Jesus quoted a passage from the Old Testament and rejected the temptation. In so doing, he proved his love for the Father and gave us example so that we too would be strong in resisting temptation. The *Letter to the Hebrews* says: "For we have not a high priest who is unable to sympathise with our weaknesses, but one who in every respect has been tempted as we are, yet without sinning. Let us then with confidence draw near to the throne of grace, that we may receive mercy and find grace to help in time of need" (*Heb* 4:15-16).

We know that God always gives us sufficient grace to overcome temptations. St Paul writes: "God is faithful, and he will not let you be tempted beyond your strength, but with the temptation will also provide the way of escape, that you may be able to endure it" (*1 Cor* 10:13). Perhaps St Paul was thinking of his own experience when, tempted by a "thorn" in the flesh, he begged God three times to be freed from it. He heard the consoling words, "My grace is sufficient for you, for my power is made perfect in weakness" (*2 Cor* 12:9). In every temptation, we can be assured that God will give us sufficient grace to overcome it.

Moreover, temptations can be very beneficial in the spiritual life. St Catherine of Siena records the following words from God as to why he allows us to be tempted: "The devil, dearest daughter, is the instrument of my justice to torment the souls who have miserably offended me. And I have set him in this life to tempt and molest my creatures, not for my creatures to be conquered, but that they may conquer, proving their virtue, and receive from me the glory of victory" (*Dialogue*, 2.27). Indeed, God does not want us to be conquered, to fall into sin, but rather to conquer, to prove our virtue and receive from him the glory of victory, the crown of heaven.

St Augustine too writes: "Our pilgrim life here on earth cannot be without temptation for it is through temptation that we make progress and it is only by being tempted that we come to know ourselves. We cannot win our crown unless we overcome, and we cannot overcome unless we enter the contest and there is no contest unless we have an enemy and the temptations he brings" (*Discourses on the Psalms,* Ps 60, 2-3).

So temptations are opportunities to show God how much we love him by struggling to overcome them. We should not look for temptations, but if they come we have a great opportunity to grow in sanctity. If we pray hard when tempted – "And lead us not into temptation" (*Mt* 6:13) – and strengthen our will by penance, as Jesus did by his prayer and fasting in the desert, we will be able to win out and grow in holiness through the very temptations. Temptations are sources of sin – but they can also be sources of sanctity.

394 The influence of habits on morality

I know a man who has been an alcoholic for many years and even though he tries to give it up, occasionally he falls back into drinking. He is sincerely sorry and wonders whether he will ever get over it. How does God look on someone like that?

Your question involves an important aspect of moral life: the influence of habits on the morality of our actions. It is important to deal with it since there are many people battling to overcome entrenched habits and they may find what I have to say helpful.

We know that we form habits easily by repeating acts of any sort. For example, in driving a car, learning a language, playing a musical instrument or engaging in some sport, the more often we do it the better we get at it. We form habits that facilitate actions. Similarly in the moral sphere, we form habits by repeating acts of any type.

If our acts are morally disordered, like drinking alcohol to excess, indulging in impurity, using bad language, telling lies or gossiping, the more we do these things the more we develop a habit of doing them. This bad habit, which facilitates immoral acts, is called a vice.

On the other hand, when our actions are directed to our true last end and hence are morally good, like praying, being kind and generous or fulfilling our duties, again the more we do them the easier they become. We form good habits, called virtues, which facilitate good acts. How do virtues and vices influence the morality of our acts?

Let us begin with virtues. Obviously, the more virtues we have and the stronger they are, the easier it is to do good acts, acts which help us live a life that is pleasing to God and grow in holiness. So we should do all the good acts we can, since they will form virtues and make successive good acts that much easier. These acts are pleasing to God and they store up treasure in heaven. They speed up our journey to eternal life and they give us joy here on earth.

Turning to bad habits or vices, the more vices we have the easier it is to commit sin and the harder it is to do the will of God. But there is another aspect to bad habits that is very important. Let us consider two stages. In the first, the person willingly carries out the sins and does little or nothing to avoid them. He or she is fully responsible for those actions and for the vices they gradually form. Consider, for example, a person who habitually uses bad language or who engages in sexual activity outside of marriage and makes no effort to avoid it. Those actions and the bad habits they form are fully voluntary. Because the person is committing the sins deliberately, they have a greater malice and can be punished more severely by God. As the *Catechism of the Catholic Church* teaches, "Sin committed through malice, by deliberate choice of evil, is the gravest" (*CCC* 1860).

If, at a later stage, that person comes to realise how bad those actions are and sincerely repents of them and strives to overcome the habit, inevitably he or she will still fall into some of the bad actions, because of the entrenched habit. But those sins will have less culpability, less guilt before God, precisely because of the habit. Rather than being sins of malice, they will be more what are called "sins of weakness", sins committed with a will that desires to please God but is weakened by some factor like an entrenched habit. The culpability or guilt before God of sins of weakness is less than in sins of malice.

The *Catechism of the Catholic Church* gives as an example the sin of masturbation: "To form an equitable judgment about the subjects' moral responsibility and to guide pastoral action, one must take into account the affective immaturity, force of acquired habit, conditions of anxiety, or other psychological or social factors that can lessen, if not even reduce to a minimum, moral culpability" (*CCC* 2352). The same can be said of any bad habit. As long as we are sorry for our bad actions and are sincerely struggling to overcome the habit, there is a reduced culpability for those actions. We may have to struggle all our life to overcome the habit, but as long as we are struggling the sins have less culpability.

395 Pride – habit and acts

I have always had a problem understanding pride. They say we are all proud, and I certainly am myself, and pride is one of the seven deadly sins. How can we be humble when we are always proud, and how can we go to heaven when we are proud?

This is a very important question, and it is relevant not only to pride but to all vices, or habits of sin. But first, what is pride? It may be defined loosely as exaggerated self esteem, or an exaggerated consideration of one's own excellence. When we use the word "exaggerated" we are implying that there is a just consideration of one's excellence, and indeed there is. St Teresa of Avila says that humility, the corresponding virtue, is "to walk in truth" (*Interior Castle,* Ch. 10).

The truth is that we all have many talents and good qualities, but these are gifts from God and we should be grateful to him for them. We cannot glory in them as if they were our own achievement. St Paul writes to the Corinthians, "What have you that you did not receive? If then you received it, why do you boast as if it were not a gift?" (*1 Cor* 4:7) It is not pride to recognise that we have many talents. It is pride when we consider these gifts as our own and boast of them.

The reason why pride is such a deadly sin is that it robs God of his glory, referring the glory to oneself. Indeed, the original sin of our first parents was a sin of pride. The serpent tempted Adam and Eve to eat of the fruit of the tree, telling them, "You will be like God, knowing good and evil" (*Gen* 3:5). But while pride is a deadly sin, not all sins of pride are mortal. It will depend on the particular thoughts or actions in each case.

Since the original sin of Adam and Eve, the vice of pride remains in all of us as a habit, as a tendency to consider ourselves too highly. They say that pride will die 24 hours after we do. And St Josemaría Escrivá used to say that the best business would be to buy people for what they are worth and sell them for what they think they are worth! If we are all proud, how can we also be humble? We begin by recognising that we all have some degree of humility, some recognition of the truth of our good qualities and deeds, and of our many shortcomings and sins. Only Satan has unalloyed pride with no trace of humility.

We can think of the relationship between pride and humility – or between any other vice and its corresponding virtue, for that matter – as a spectrum, with pure pride on one end and pure humility on the other. We are not on either end, in pure pride or pure humility, but somewhere in between. The more we struggle to grow in humility the more we reduce the level of pride and the further along on the spectrum we are. Hopefully when we die we will have succeeded in reducing pride to a minimum.

But even when pride remains, always ready to lead us into an exaggerated consideration of our self-worth, by itself it is not sinful. While bad habits, or vices, can result from repeated sins, the habits themselves are not sinful. It is the acts, the sins, to which they give rise that are sinful. Therefore, as long as we succeed in not consenting to the temptations to pride – to thoughts of vainglory, to comparisons with other people, to boasting about our accomplishments, to excusing ourselves when criticised, etc. – we are not committing sins of pride, but rather are growing in humility.

This is an important truth. It is bad acts, not bad habits, that are sinful. Similarly with good habits, or virtues, it is the good acts to which they give rise that are meritorious, not the virtues themselves. We see this in the fact that all the baptised in the state of grace have the infused virtue of charity, but not all do many acts of charity. Our Lord makes this clear in his description of the Last Judgment: "Come, O blessed of my Father, inherit the kingdom prepared for you from the foundation of the world; for I was hungry and you gave me food, I was thirsty and you gave me drink..." (*Mt* 25:34-35). Similarly, St James rebukes those who show no deeds of charity: "If a brother or sister is poorly clothed and in lack of daily food, and one of you says to them, 'Go in peace, be warmed and filled,' without giving them the things needed for the body, what does it profit?" (*Jas* 2:16)

In summary, even though we all have the habit of pride, we also have the virtue of humility in some degree. It is the acts of pride that are sinful, not the vice itself. So as long as we repent of our sins and do not reject God at the end of our life through pride, we can be saved.

396 The value of suffering

I have a friend who is now confined permanently to a wheelchair. She has very little movement and finds it difficult even to talk. She is a Catholic but finds it difficult to accept her condition. How can I help her?

One of the most difficult tasks is to help others see value in their suffering. Thank God our Catholic faith sheds considerable light on this reality, which affects all of us. After all, suffering and death are a consequence of original sin and so we all experience them in one way or another. We recall how as a result of that first sin, Adam would earn his bread by the sweat of his brow, Eve would bear children in pain and both would experience death (cf. *Gen* 3:16-19).

We distinguish two main kinds of suffering: physical and moral. Physical suffering is experienced in the body in such ways as sickness, pain, tiredness, disability, hunger, thirst, cold and heat. Moral suffering is felt rather in the mind and heart: grief over the death of a loved one, the suffering of another who is close to us, marriage break-up, financial worries, upsets to our plans, loneliness, remorse over our misdeeds, unjust treatment by others...

In some way suffering will always be a mystery we cannot fully comprehend, especially when the one suffering is a child or some other very good person. But part of the answer to the mystery is given by the most innocent person ever to have lived on earth, the one who at the same time experienced the greatest suffering: Jesus Christ. Jesus' cry from the Cross – "My God, my God, why have you forsaken me?" (*Mk* 15:34; *Ps* 22:1) – expresses the anguish and bewilderment of so many suffering people down the ages.

But through his suffering, death and resurrection Jesus redeemed mankind from original sin and restored us to friendship with God. In some way he redeemed even suffering itself, giving it a new meaning and value. Jesus went so far as to call those who suffer "blessed":"Blessed are those who mourn; they shall be comforted... Blessed are those who suffer persecution in the cause of right; the kingdom of heaven is theirs" (*Mt* 5:5, 10-12). There are various ways in which suffering can be truly a blessing.

First, it strengthens character. We all know people who have overcome great adversities in life and have gone on to achieve very much. The very suffering they endured contributed greatly to forging their character.

Second, suffering helps those who suffer to be more sympathetic towards others who are suffering. It is often only when we have been through greater suffering ourselves that we can appreciate what others are going through and show them true compassion. The word compassion, after all, means literally "to suffer with".

Third, suffering helps to make up for our sins. We have all sinned and before we can enter heaven we must make up in some way for them, either here on earth or in Purgatory. Suffering is one of the best ways to do this, provided we accept it lovingly from God. It can shorten our time in Purgatory or even eliminate it altogether so that suffering becomes our "Purgatory on earth".

Fourth, suffering unites us with Jesus Christ, who suffered for us on the cross. He invited us to do this: "If anyone would come after me, let him deny himself and take up his cross daily and follow me" (*Mt* 16:24). St Paul witnesses to his own union with Christ through suffering: "I have been crucified with Christ; it is no longer I who live, but Christ who lives in me" (*Gal* 2:20).

Fifth, suffering can be offered up for others. When we offer up our suffering for someone who has wandered away from the faith, for a sick person, for someone looking for work, we know that our prayer will always be heard because it is united with the sacrifice of our suffering. This gives suffering itself a new purpose.

Finally, suffering benefits those who look after the suffering person. The kindness, patience and generosity they show to that person are shown to Christ himself: "I was sick... and you cared for me... Believe me, when you did it to one of the least of my brethren here, you did it to me" (*Mt* 25:36, 40). By showing love for Christ through a suffering person, the carer grows in holiness and merits an eternal reward.

For all of these reasons suffering is, as Jesus said, truly a blessing. It is a treasure not to be wasted.

Relations with God

397 Faith and Church teaching

I have some friends who are practising Catholics but who say they disagree with some Church teachings, like those on hell, contraception and abortion in some circumstances. This disturbs me. How can I help them?

There are probably quite a few Catholics in the situation you describe, each one with their own personal areas of disagreement with Church teaching. They are undoubtedly good people, but they fail to understand a fundamental aspect of what it means to be a Catholic. They are sometimes called "cafeteria Catholics" because they pick and choose what they want from the full menu of Church teachings, making their own intellect the standard of what is true and to be believed.

The first thing we should remember is that the Church is not a human institution, formed over the centuries, which has come to hold certain beliefs. It is a divine institution, founded by Jesus Christ himself. And Jesus is God, the second person of the Blessed Trinity, who said of himself: "I am the way, and the truth, and the life" (*Jn* 14:6). We can be certain that whatever he teaches is true.

What is more, Jesus promised the gift of the Holy Spirit to keep the Church in the truth: "When the Spirit of truth comes, he will guide you into all the truth" (*Jn* 16:13). Earlier he had told the apostles, "But the Counsellor, the Holy Spirit ... will teach you all things, and bring to your remembrance all that I have said to you" (*Jn* 14:26). As a result, we can have the assurance that whatever the Church teaches is true and that it is important for us to believe it and live it. In other words, the "menu" was written by God himself and it is not up to us to pick and choose which items we will accept and which we will not.

What is up to us is to believe whatever the Church teaches because it comes from God. If Jesus himself taught us something directly, we would believe him. And if he teaches us something through his Church, we should believe it too. After all, when he sent the disciples out to teach, he told them, "He who hears you, hears me, and he who rejects you rejects me" (*Lk* 10:16). That is, we should have faith. What does this mean? It means to accept a truth, not because we see the reasons for it, but on the authority of the person revealing it to us.

Is this reasonable? Of course it is. Virtually everything we know, we know by faith – human faith – by having read it or having been told about it by someone we trust. Almost everything we know about history, geography, science, current affairs... we know in this way. And we believe it. This is reasonable, even though sometimes human writers can be mistaken. Historians can revise earlier versions of certain events, scientists can refine and modify their previous theories, and journalists, who get it right most of the time, often give us an amended version of events in the following days. But we still trust that what they tell us is true. How much more, then, should we trust God, who is the creator of all being and truth, and who can neither deceive nor be deceived. And how much more should we trust his Church, which teaches in his name, guided by the Holy Spirit, the "Spirit of truth".

But, we may say, some of the Church's teachings are hard to understand, like how Jesus Christ can be at the same time both God and man, or how there can be three persons in one God in the Blessed Trinity, or how a merciful God can allow the existence of hell. But so many truths in the world of nature are also difficult to understand, like why light has the properties of both particles and waves, and why there should be gravity at all. We accept these truths, even though we don't fully understand them, and we know that this is reasonable. Scientists accept them and they don't understand them either.

Likewise, some of the Church's teachings are difficult to live, like those on sexual morality, contraception, abortion, honesty, sacrifice, etc. But we know that they are true, and that when we follow them we find the human flourishing that we seek, both for us as individuals and for society.

To have faith, then, is to accept all of the Church's teachings because God has revealed them through his Church, not because we personally understand them or like them. To accept a truth because we personally understand and agree with it is not faith but reason. St Edmund Campion explains this very clearly in his letter to Bishop Richard Cheney on 1 November 1571: "Whoever refuses to believe one or other article of the faith, believes in none of them. For as soon as he knowingly oversteps the bounds of the Church, which is the pillar and ground of the truth [cf. *1 Tim* 3:15], to which Christ Jesus, the highest, first, and most pure truth, the source, light, leader, measure and pattern of the faithful, reveals all these articles – whatever else of Catholic doctrine he retains, yet if he obstinately criticises one dogma, the remainder that he holds, he holds not by orthodox faith, without which it is impossible to please God, but by his own reason, his own conviction" (Cited in Richard Simpson/Fr Peter Joseph, *Edmund Campion,* Gracewing 2010, p. 75).

To believe everything the Church teaches requires humility, because we must submit our fallible judgment to that of the infallible God and his Church. This is eminently reasonable, taking into account that we are fallible and can be mistaken, whereas God and his Church are infallible. If we find it difficult to accept some teaching, we can pray for the gift of faith, for faith is always a gift from God. And we can ask Our Lord, as the apostles did, "Increase our faith!" (*Lk* 17:5).

398 Why study the faith

My teenage niece wanted to study religious education in high school but was discouraged by her dad, who said it did not carry much weight, like science. My unbelieving brother-in-law chipped in, saying there was no point in studying something if you don't know whether that something even exists. How can I help her?

We can begin by saying that your brother-in-law is right as regards the pointlessness of studying something we don't know exists. There are not any books that I know of, or university courses for that matter, on unicorns, centaurs or mermaids. Those who don't believe in these mythical beings don't waste their time writing books about them, even to debunk their existence. But there are many books and university courses on God, because every civilisation that has ever existed has believed in some form of supreme being and has had some form of religion. Even atheists can't ignore the question and have written an abundance of books on it, both to defend their own position and to try to prove that there is no God.

As we know, there is a God. If there were not, this universe would not exist, with its marvellous complexity, harmony and beauty. And we, atheists included, could not even discuss the existence of God if we did not have a rational, spiritual intelligence that did not come from the evolution of matter, but rather from the rational, intelligent pure spirit who is the very God atheists deny. What is more, since God is the very beginning and end of the universe, the study of God and religion is the most weighty of all subjects. It is the foundation of every other subject, including science. Having studied science in university, I am not biased.

What do we gain by studying God and religion? To begin with, we gain a deep sense of the meaning and purpose of life. If we were just a castoff of evolution, our life would have no meaning. But since we were created in the image and likeness of a loving God, who calls us to eternal life with him, our life is charged with meaning.

And the more we come to know about our faith, the more firm it becomes. St Anselm gave us the well-known phrase *fides quaerens intellectum*, faith seeking understanding, which expresses the desire of anyone with faith to come to know more about it. With this study, we come to know why we believe what we believe, so that our faith rests on a firm foundation that can withstand the challenges life brings, and even the doubts others may raise. Where a person with a more simple faith will be more easily persuaded by a non-believer, a person with more understanding will be able to defend the faith against these attacks.

Also, we come to have a deeper appreciation of the faith, of its wonders and mystery. Someone with no theoretical knowledge of music will be able to enjoy the music of Mozart, but one who has studied music theory and composition will have a much deeper appreciation of it. It is the same with the faith.

This deeper appreciation leads in turn to a deeper spiritual life, to a greater love for God. It is easier to pray and give thanks to God for all his gifts, if we understand them better. Our love for the Blessed Trinity, Jesus Christ, the Eucharist, the Church, Our Lady is deepened when we know more about these truths, just as our love for a human person is deepened when we know the person better.

Finally, the more we understand our faith, the more eager and able we will be to share it with others. Pope Benedict, in calling for a Year of Faith in 2012-13, invited the Church to engage in the New Evangelisation, to explain the faith to others so as to draw them closer to God. A person who has studied the faith and loves it more is in a better position to do this. For this reason, the Pope invited the whole Church "to rediscover and study the fundamental content of the faith that receives its systematic and organic synthesis in the *Catechism of the Catholic Church*" (Apost. Lett. *Porta Fidei*, 11). The Pope summed it up: "Evidently, knowledge of the content of the faith is essential for giving one's own *assent*, that is to say for adhering fully with intellect and will to what the Church proposes. Knowledge of faith opens a door into the fullness of the saving mystery of God" (*ibid.* 10).

399 Can faith be lost?

My 27 year-old godson, who was once an altar boy and quite pious, now lives with his girlfriend, says he doesn't believe in God and has nothing to do with the Church. How can this happen and is there anything I can do to help him?

I would not be able to count the number of times people have come to me with a story like yours. It is a cause of great concern to family members, especially parents, and also to us priests and others trying to help people find God.

At the outset let me say that faith is one of our most precious gifts. For those of us who have faith, life is filled with light, with meaning. No matter what happens to us, we know that God is always there looking after us in his loving providence, and that out of what appears to be evil he will bring good. In this way, even suffering has meaning, as did Our Lord's suffering on the Cross. And we know that after this life there awaits us eternal life with God, if we live and die in his love. For those with no faith, life must be very different, very empty, especially when they encounter suffering and begin to think of what awaits them after death.

Faith is the foundation of our whole spiritual life. I often represent faith, hope and love as three blocks, with faith on the bottom and love on the top. If we lose love through any mortal sin, we still have hope that God will continue to give us his grace and that he will eventually forgive us if we repent. And we still believe in God. If we lose hope, through a serious sin of despair or presumption, we lose both hope and love but we still have faith that there is a God who loves us and will forgive us. But if we sin seriously against faith, we lose love and hope and now even faith, so that nothing remains of our supernatural life. Naturally, God can still seek us out and bring us back to him through our free cooperation, but we have just severed our last link with God. So faith is extremely important.

Faith, as I said, is a gift, a gift from God himself. It is not something we can acquire by ourselves. St Paul lists faith among the variety of gifts given by God to different people (cf. *1 Cor* 12:9). I have seen more than once how faith is truly a gift. One particularly clear example came when I was instructing in the faith a woman who was going to marry a Catholic. In the first classes she was full of objections to what I was saying. But then one day she came to the class eager to become a Catholic herself and there were no more objections. Somehow, God had given her the gift of faith between one class and the next.

Although faith is a gift, there is much we can do to dispose ourselves to receive it and to preserve it and make it grow. The first thing is to learn the truths of the faith well. In the Year of Faith of 2012-13, Pope Benedict stressed this aspect, calling on Catholics to turn again to the *Catechism of the Catholic Church*. And we should make sure that our children are learning the faith well from a young age. The more we know, the better we can live our faith. Perhaps your godson lacks this knowledge.

The second thing is to live the faith fully each day, so that this priceless gift does not wane but grows ever stronger. This includes praying, doing penance, attending Mass, receiving the sacraments and showing love for others. If we do this, our faith will grow and we will be more likely to cling to God in times of trial. Also, we should protect our faith from whatever could endanger it, avoiding certain books, lectures, television programs, and people who are immoral or disbelievers. And we should reject promptly any temptations against faith, asking Our Lord to increase our faith.

If we do this, our faith will not be the flickering flame of a candle, ready to be snuffed out by the slightest puff of wind, but rather a roaring fire that will burn even hotter, the stronger the wind blows. If we do not use these means – and perhaps your godson did not – then we can easily grow lukewarm and even cold, fall into a life of habitual sin, and eventually abandon the faith altogether, throwing away God's precious gift.

As regards what to do to help those who have lost the faith, we should let them know that we – and God – love them, that we are always there for them, that we are praying for them. We shouldn't push them to do something they are not keen to do, like attend Mass with us. Occasionally we can give them something short to read, or engage them in a brief conversation about something in our own life that may help them to see the beauty of faith. And always we should pray insistently, day after day, for their conversion, like St Monica did for Augustine. God will not fail to hear us.

400 Another kind of faith

If faith, as I was taught, is the acceptance of a truth on the authority of God revealing it, why does Christ speak of faith that can move mountains? This is not the same as accepting a truth. Is there another kind of faith?

Yes, there is. While we customarily define faith in the way you did at the beginning of your question, there is another meaning of the word, which is equally biblical, completely acceptable and indeed necessary. This second kind of faith, sometimes called fiducial faith, from the word for trust or confidence, is mentioned numerous times in the Scriptures. For example, it was his complete trust, or faith, in God that led Abraham to leave his home country and set off for an unknown land (cf. *Gen* 12:1-8; *Heb* 11:8), and that moved his wife Sarah to believe that she could bear a child when she was past the age of child bearing (cf. *Gen* 18:11-14; *Heb* 11:11).

In the New Testament, when Our Lady was told that she would conceive a son by the power of the Holy Spirit while remaining a virgin, she immediately believed and accepted: "Behold, I am the handmaid of the Lord; let it be to me according to your word" (*Lk* 1:38). Although Mary did not ask for a sign, the angel Gabriel gave her one: her elderly kinswoman Elizabeth was in her sixth month with child, "For with God nothing will be impossible" (*Lk* 1:37). This assurance from the angel is the basis for our trust that God can do the impossible.

The *Catechism of the Catholic Church* calls this unquestioning response to the word of God "the obedience of faith": "To obey (from the Latin *ob-audire*, to 'hear or listen to') in faith is to submit freely to the word that has been heard, because its truth is guaranteed by God, who is Truth itself. Abraham is the model of such obedience offered us by Sacred Scripture. The Virgin Mary is its most perfect embodiment" (*CCC* 143, 144).

St Cyril of Jerusalem, in his catechesis in the fourth century, comments: "The one word faith can have two meanings. One kind of faith concerns doctrines. It involves the soul's assent to and acceptance of some particular matter... The other kind of faith is given by Christ by means of a special grace... Now this kind of faith, given by the Spirit as a special favour, is not confined to doctrinal matters, for it produces effects beyond any human capability. If a man who has this faith says to this mountain *move from here to there, it will move.* For when anybody says this in faith, believing it will happen and having no doubt in his heart, he then receives that grace" (*Cat.* 5, *De fide et symbolo*, 10-11).

It is of this second kind of faith, fiducial faith, that Christ speaks when he says: "Have faith in God. Truly, I say to you, whoever says to this mountain, 'Be taken up and cast into the sea,' and does not doubt in his heart, but believes that what he says will come to pass, it will be done for him. Therefore I tell you, whatever you ask in prayer, believe that you receive it, and you will" (*Mk* 11:22-24).

We do well to examine ourselves on how strong our faith is. Do we really believe that if we pray with faith our son or daughter will return to the practice of the faith, a sick person will get better, a troubled marriage will stay together, someone out of work will find a job, a single person will find a suitable spouse? If we feel that our faith is weak, like the apostles we can ask our Lord: "Increase our faith!" (*Lk* 17:5).

A good way to grow in faith is to pray more often and with more confidence for difficult intentions. God doesn't always answer our prayers in the way we want, but he always hears them and he answers them in the way that is best. And often he does grant what we are asking, showing us that "with God nothing will be impossible." The many miracles approved by the Vatican for causes of beatification and canonisation are proof that God can do the humanly impossible and that there were people praying with faith for those "impossible" intentions. We should be among them. After all, Jesus assures us, "All things are possible to him who believes" (*Mk* 9:23).

So often, when we have tended to doubt God's power or his willingness to help us, we have seen our prayers answered and he has had to say to us, as to St Peter, "O you of little faith, why did you doubt?" (*Mt* 14:31).

401 What is blasphemy?

I used to think that blasphemy was using the name of God in a disrespectful way but a friend recently told me it is much broader than that. What is it exactly?

Your friend is right. We tend to think of blasphemy as being limited to using the name of God in vain, which is forbidden by the second commandment, but in reality it includes a host of offences against the holiness of God. The word blasphemy, by the way, comes from a Greek word meaning "to speak harm".

What is blasphemy exactly? The *Catechism of the Catholic Church* says: "Blasphemy ... consists in uttering against God – inwardly or outwardly – words of hatred, reproach, or defiance; in speaking ill of God; in failing in respect toward him in one's speech; in misusing God's name" (*CCC* 2148). As is clear, misusing God's name is only one form of blasphemy and it is in fact mentioned last in this point of the Catechism. Examples of misusing God's name would be saying the name of Jesus Christ in anger, or asking God, who is all mercy, to damn someone. On the other hand to say "Oh my God!" when witnessing an accident is generally not sinful but rather an expression of piety.

As the Catechism says, blasphemy is not limited to spoken words against God. It can be committed inwardly, in our willful thoughts, and outwardly in such forms as books, plays and artworks that show contempt for God.

In general, blasphemy consists in any thought, word or deed that shows disrespect or contempt for God, who is all holy, all loving, all powerful. So when the second commandment forbids taking the name of God in vain, the word "name" is meant to include the very person of God and everything related to him. Thus one would commit a sin of blasphemy by showing contempt not only for God but for Our Lady or any of the saints, the Church, the sacraments, etc.

Because blasphemy shows disrespect for God himself, our creator and our all-holy Father, in itself it is a serious sin. As the Catechism puts it, "Blasphemy is contrary to the respect due God and his holy name. It is in itself a grave sin" (*CCC* 2148). Elsewhere the Catechism says: "There are acts which, in and of themselves, independently of circumstances and intentions, are always gravely illicit by reason of their object; such as blasphemy and perjury, murder and adultery"

(*CCC* 1756). We see the gravity of blasphemy in the Old Testament in the punishment ordered for it: "He who blasphemes the name of the Lord shall be put to death" (*Lev* 24:16). Naturally, while blasphemy involves grave matter, in a given case the sin may not be mortal if the person lacks sufficient knowledge or deliberate consent.

What are some more examples of blasphemy? A first one, which we find several times in the New Testament when Jesus himself is accused of blasphemy, is pretending to take upon oneself attributes or powers that belong only to God. For example, when Jesus said, "I and the Father are one", the Jews prepared to stone him to death, saying, "We stone you for no good work but for blasphemy; because you, being a man, make yourself God" (*Jn* 10:30-33). Jesus, of course, was God and so he was not guilty of the sin. In the Old Testament the Israelites themselves were accused of blasphemy for making the golden calf and worshipping it (cf. *Neh* 9:18) and for killing the prophets (cf. *Neh* 9:26). Similarly, the Assyrians were accused of mocking and reviling God by claiming to be more powerful than God (cf. *2 Kings* 19:4, 6, 22).

Someone today would be guilty of blasphemy if they hated God, were angry with him for the way he treated them, claimed that God was powerless or uncaring because he didn't answer their prayers, accused God of being unjust in some matter, said that God would never forgive them, said that the Blessed Virgin Mary or any of the saints was not holy, etc.

In short, any manifestation of contempt for the holiness of God is blasphemy.

402 Catholics and halal meat

A friend of mine recently told me that one of Australia's largest supermarket chains produces all their meat at a halal certified site, and that Catholics cannot eat halal meat. Is this true?

Firstly we should clarify what we mean by halal meat. The word "halal" in Arabic means simply "lawful" and thus halal foods are those which are considered lawful for Muslims to eat. "Halal" is distinguished from "haraam" foods, which are forbidden. Among the latter are pork, blood, animals that have been strangled or beaten to death, alcohol, meat that has not been prepared in the proper way, etc.

For meat to be halal the animal must be killed in a particular way. It must have its throat slit, and the person killing it must face Mecca and invoke the name of Allah, or God. When an abattoir can demonstrate that it follows this procedure, it may receive a certificate from the Muslim authorities as a halal certified site. Wherever possible, Muslims eat only halal foods.

Where does this leave Catholics? Can we eat such foods? The first thing we should ask is whether Scripture has anything to say about the matter. In fact it does. In the *Acts of the Apostles* we read about the so-called Council of Jerusalem, in which the apostles and elders gathered to decide what to impose on the Gentiles who had converted to Christianity in Antioch. Among other things they told these converts that they were to "abstain from what has been sacrificed to idols and from blood and from what is strangled" (*Acts* 15:29). Jews, like Muslims, regarded blood as the very life of the animal and as such it belonged to God alone. Hence they did not eat meat that had been strangled, since it would have the blood in it.

But why did the early Christians follow these Jewish practices? It must be remembered that these were the early days of Christianity and the first generation of Christians was still alive. Most of them were converts from Judaism, and it is natural that they would have felt a strong repugnance at the thought of eating meat with the blood in it, since this was prohibited by Jewish law (cf. *Lev* 17:10ff). It is probable that for some time they also abstained from pork, which Jews did not eat.

As regards food that had been offered to idols, St Paul writes that since "an idol has no real existence" and "there is no God but one", there is nothing wrong with eating such food (*1 Cor* 8:4). Nonetheless, since some Christians may be weak in conscience and think it is sinful to eat such food, others when in their company should abstain from eating lest they cause their brothers to eat as well and go against their conscience. He writes: "Therefore, if food is a cause of my brother's falling, I will never eat meat, lest I cause my brother to fall" (cf. *1 Cor* 8:13). It is probably for this reason that the Council of Jerusalem forbade the Gentile converts to each such food. St Paul sums up: "Food will not commend us to God. We are no worse off if we do not eat, and no better off if we do" (*1 Cor* 8:8).

Two chapters later St Paul confronts today's issue of halal food more directly, based on his earlier pronouncement that such food may be eaten without any qualms of conscience. As regards whether Christians should be careful not to buy certain foods at the market he writes: "Eat whatever is sold in the meat market without raising any question on the ground of conscience" (*1 Cor* 10:25).

And with respect to what to do when invited to the home of an unbeliever, he advises: "If one of the unbelievers invites you to dinner and you are disposed to go, eat whatever is set before you without raising any question on the ground of conscience" (*1 Cor* 10:27). That would apply today to accepting an invitation to eat with a Muslim.

In summary, it is clear that there is nothing in the Scriptures against Christians eating halal meat. The question of meat "sacrificed to idols" does not apply, even though not even that would present a problem, since halal meat is offered to Allah, the one God worshipped by Muslims, Jews and Christians.

403 Catholics and Halloween

Halloween seems to be gaining popularity in this country and I have a problem with it, with the witches and goblins and the trick-or-treating. Should Catholics, or other Christians for that matter, be involved in a pagan custom like this?

I don't want to tell you whether you or your children should be involved in celebrating Halloween, but I can give you some background to shed light on the matter.

First of all, the name Halloween is Christian. It means simply hallows evening, saints evening, and it refers to the vigil of All Hallows Day, All Saints Day, celebrated on November 1. "Hallow" is an old English word for saint, or holy. We use the word in the Our Father when we say "hallowed be thy name", may your name be held holy. As I wrote in an earlier column, the feast of All Saints has been celebrated on November 1 since the pontificate of Pope Gregory III (731-741). In 732 that pope consecrated a chapel in St Peter's Basilica in Rome dedicated to all the saints, and he fixed the annual celebration for November 1. A century later Pope Gregory IV (827-844) extended the feast to the universal Church and it has been celebrated on November 1 ever since (cf J. Flader, *Question Time 2*, q. 274). The feast was so important that from the beginning it was celebrated with a vigil, or liturgical celebration on the evening before the feast. The vigil came to be known popularly as Hallowe'en, hallows evening. Even today the feast of All Saints is celebrated as a liturgical solemnity with a vigil on the evening before.

But why the witches and goblins, pumpkins lit up by a candle and trick-or-treating? For this we have to go back to the early Celts. The ancient Celtic peoples of Ireland, Scotland, Wales and Brittany celebrated on November 1 the beginning of the new year and the coming of winter. On the night before the new year they celebrated the festival of Samhain, the Lord of the Dead. They believed that the spirits of the dead, both good and evil, including ghosts, witches and goblins, wandered on earth again that night, and in order to scare away the evil spirits they would light bonfires and wear masks. Thus they were not embracing the ghosts and witches and other evil spirits but rather trying to scare them away.

As regards the custom of children going from door to door asking for lollies and other types of food, commonly known as trick-or-treating, it may have its origins in an Irish custom that goes back hundreds of years. Groups of farmers would go door-to-door collecting food and other items for a village feast and bonfire. Those who gave food were assured of prosperity and those who did not were threatened with bad luck. It seems that the Irish immigrants to the United States in the nineteenth century took this custom with them and so trick-or-treating came to be associated with Halloween. As a boy I grew up with the custom in the United States, where it was completely harmless and lots of fun for everyone. But reflecting on it later in life I have come to question the aspect of playing a trick on people who did not give treats. This could consist in rubbing their windows with a bar of soap or other equally harmless acts.

What I do not like about it is the fact that it introduces children to what in adults would be called a protection racket: threatening people with harm if they do not pay a sum of money. I do not want to give this undue importance, because children are innocent and do not understand the full implications of what they are doing, but simply to point out its possible implications. If children today do not play a trick on those who do not give them anything, so much the better. Naturally too, it would not be good for children to dress up as demons or witches or to use diabolical imagery.

And as for the pumpkins, again we go back to the Irish, who would hollow out a turnip and place a lighted candle inside to ward off evil spirits. When the Irish went to America, they found the much larger pumpkin a better solution.

So that is the background to Halloween, which has both pagan and Christian origins. If children want to live the custom, they can be told about the Christian origins of the name and the feasts of All Saints and All Souls. They might be suggested to give some of the treats they receive to their brothers and sisters, or to poor children through a charity, so that they do not see the feast as an opportunity to indulge themselves.

Relations with our neighbour

404 Love of self

God tells us to "love your neighbour as yourself", yet the Universal Prayer attributed to Pope Clement XI says "Give me, good God, love for you, hatred for myself..." It seems to be a contradiction. Can you shed some light on this?

As you say, Our Lord commands us to love our neighbour as ourselves: "You shall love the Lord your God with all your heart, and with all your soul, and with all your mind. This is the great and first commandment. And a second is like it, You shall love your neighbour as yourself" (*Mt* 22:37-40).

The command to love our neighbour as ourselves implies that we should first love ourselves. And indeed we should. Everything God made is good, including ourselves. We should love the goodness in all God's creatures, including ourselves. What is more, God loves each one of us and we are special to him. We read in the prophecy of Isaiah: "Can a woman forget her sucking child, that she should have no compassion on the son of her womb? Even these may forget, yet I will not forget you. Behold I have graven you on the palms of my hands" (*Is* 49:15-16).

Indeed, God loves us so much that he became man and died on the Cross for us. He has a place for us in heaven and he constantly showers graces upon us so that we will live in such a way as to be with him there forever. If God loves us so much, how can we not love ourselves?

As if to emphasise this, the *Catechism of the Catholic Church* teaches: "Everyone is responsible for his life before God who has given it to him. It is God who remains the sovereign Master of life. We are obliged to accept life gratefully and preserve it for his honour and the salvation of our souls. We are stewards, not owners of the life God has entrusted to us. It is not ours to dispose of" (*CCC* 2280). If we are stewards of our life, surely we should love it and look after it.

Indeed, love for oneself even takes precedence over love for our neighbour in certain circumstances. For example, we may go so far as to kill another who is attacking us if this is necessary to save our own life. The Catechism teaches: "Love toward oneself remains a fundamental principle of morality. Therefore it is legitimate to insist on respect for one's own right to life. Someone who defends his life is not guilty of murder even if he is forced to deal his aggressor a lethal blow" (*CCC* 2264). For the same reason love for oneself demands that we not end our life through suicide. As the Catechism says, suicide "is gravely contrary to the just love of self" (*CCC* 2281). So there is a justified love of self based on everything we have considered.

How then can a popular prayer written by a Pope ask for the grace to hate oneself? The word "hate" here should be understood in the same sense as Jesus used it when he said, "If anyone comes to me and does not hate his own father and mother ... he cannot be my disciple" (*Lk* 14:26). Obviously we should not hate our parents. Jesus clearly means "to love less", as in the parallel passage when Jesus says, "He who loves father or mother more than me is not worthy of me" (*Mt* 10:37).

The prayer to "hate" ourselves must be understood in light of the common tendency to love ourselves too much. As an effect of original sin we all have a certain disorder in our nature which inclines us to pride, exaggerated self-love, laziness, disordered love of pleasure, etc. For this reason the prayer asks for the grace to "hate" oneself, to avoid the excessive and exaggerated self-love which puts our own interests before those of others and even before God.

At the same time, we should bear in mind that there are some people for whom self-love is not a problem. On the contrary they tend to look down on themselves and even hate themselves, sometimes being moved to self-harm. They lack the healthy love for self we should all have. They may have been put down by others when they were growing up, even by family members, and they should strive to forgive those who have hurt them and to remember how much God loves them.

Sometimes they need to seek professional help, and those close to them should encourage them to do this. God loves every one of us and he doesn't want anyone not to love himself or herself. We were made in his image and likeness and he wants us to reflect his love and goodness in the world. In short, we are all good and we should love ourselves in a healthy, balanced way.

405 Tattoos and body piercing

In recent years I have seen more and more young people with large tattoos and ear rings on all parts of their face. Personally I find them repugnant. Are they immoral?

Tattooing is an ancient practice. The body of a man found frozen in a glacier between Italy and Austria in 1991, dating to around 3300 BC, had several tattoos on it, among them a cross and six straight lines, some fifteen centimetres long. Tattooed mummies have also been discovered in Egypt, dating to around 2000 BC. Also in ancient Egypt, captives were sometimes branded with the name of a god or of Pharaoh. Because the practice was widespread among the peoples around the Israelites and was sometimes associated with idolatry or other immoral practices, God specifically forbade certain body markings at the time of Moses, around 1200 BC: "You shall not make any cuttings in your flesh on account of the dead or tattoo any marks upon you: I am the Lord" (*Lev* 19:28).

The general moral framework within which tattoos and other body markings and piercings are to be evaluated is the fact that man is made in the image and likeness of God and he should reflect this image in all his actions. Not only the soul but also the body is a masterpiece of God, and it should be treated with great respect, reflecting the beauty God gave it. Even more, as St Paul teaches, "Do you not know that your body is a temple of the Holy Spirit within you, which you have from God? ... So glorify God in your body" (*1 Cor* 6:19).

In certain cultures, body markings such as cuts in the skin, marks on the forehead, tattoos and of course piercings for ear rings are regarded as manifestations of beauty, or they may signify something about the status of the person within society. As long as they are not dangerous to health and are not extreme, they are morally acceptable. But there can be reasons why some tattoos and body piercings are immoral, and hence each case must be evaluated on its own.

The first consideration to bear in mind is the motivation for having the tattoo or body piercing. While some people may do so moved by the desire to enhance their beauty or their standing in the community, others may do it moved by a rejection of society and what it stands for, or by self-hatred or loathing, just as they may deprive themselves of food or cut their skin, leaving scars, for this reason. This latter motivation is certainly sinful, as would be mere vanity or the immature desire to be accepted by others at almost any price.

A second consideration is what is depicted in the tattoo. Historically, and even today, some Christians may have discreet tattoos of Christian symbols including the Cross, Our Lady, etc. If the other moral criteria are fulfilled, such tattoos may be morally acceptable. However, many people choose to depict symbols of death, evil, violence or even Satan in their tattoos. Among the common objects in this regard are skulls, snakes, demons, spiders, knives, etc. These often manifest a rejection of God and his love, and are of course sinful.

In general, anything which truly enhances the beauty of the body, made in the image of God, will reflect God himself and hence be acceptable. But some body markings are in bad taste and are an attempt to destroy the beauty of God's creation, thus becoming an attack on God himself.

A third consideration is the extent of the tattooing or body piercing. While one or two discreet tattoos may be acceptable, tattoos covering a large part of the body are excessive. The body has a natural beauty that can be hidden by tattoos. Similarly, while body piercings for ear rings are common and acceptable, those for rings or studs on other parts of the face such as the eyebrows, nose, lips and tongue only detract from one's natural beauty and some are downright ugly. Moreover, many such body markings are not socially acceptable and may prevent the person from obtaining a job or position in society.

A fourth consideration is the possible danger to health. Some tattoos and many facial rings other than on the ear lobes are prone to infection and thus constitute an unnecessary danger to health. What is more, they are often permanent, or their removal can itself be a danger to health and leave permanent scars. As such they are forbidden by the fifth commandment. While the *Catechism of the Catholic Church* says nothing about tattoos or body piercings, the criteria just mentioned can be useful in evaluating their morality in individual cases.

406 The morality of cosmetic surgery

I know a few people who have had cosmetic surgery, including breast implants, and I have always wondered about the morality of this. Does the Church have a position on it?

To my knowledge, there is no Church document that deals with the matter as such, but the following considerations can help to clarify the issues.

First of all, I take cosmetic surgery, sometimes called aesthetic surgery, to mean surgery aimed merely at improving a person's appearance. Here the person's present condition does not constitute a threat to their health or life, but they are unhappy with their appearance and want to improve it. In this sense, cosmetic surgery is very different from the plastic surgery that may be necessary following trauma to restore bodily integrity or function. For example, after suffering burns a person may need skin grafts, or after an accident a severed limb may be sewn back on, the face may be reconstructed, etc. There is nothing morally objectionable with such procedures.

Among the common cosmetic procedures are breast implants, breast reduction, liposuction, nose reshaping, "tummy tucks", chin implants, face lifts, cheek implants and many more. Are these morally justified? Obviously, there are many different situations and motivations so one cannot give a blanket answer that covers all cases.

We can begin with persons born with a serious deformity that affects their quality of life and mental well-being. Often these deformities can be disturbing for others to look at, as well as being a source of distress for the persons themselves. If surgery can restore the person to a more "normal" appearance and the risks and cost of the surgery are proportionate to the benefits to be obtained, there is nothing morally objectionable. One could say the same for small irregularities such as birth marks, facial moles or other growths, as well as for liposuction to remove excess fat where exercise and diet have proven unsuccessful. This in addition improves one's health and quality of life.

Then there are irregularities of appearance that fall within the range of what is considered "normal", even though they are somewhat exceptional. For example the person may have a somewhat exceptional nose, ears, chin or breasts. While most people simply accept their condition, some may feel very self-conscious or distressed. Before proceeding to surgery, they should pray about the matter and discuss it with those close to them, including in some cases a psychologist. If they decide to go ahead and surgery offers good hope of success without disproportionate cost and risks, cosmetic surgery can be morally justified. In his three-volume work *The Way of the Lord*

Jesus, reputable moral theologian Germain Grisez argues that such procedures as reducing the size of unusually large ears or breasts is morally justified (Franciscan Press 1993, II, p. 543). As regards breast implants where the person is particularly flat-chested, it should be borne in mind that this may interfere with breast-feeding should the person later have children.

But what if the person's appearance would be considered by others as perfectly normal and they just want to look prettier or more handsome? Cosmetic surgery in this case would be hard to justify morally. We should always remember that God made us the way we are and we should not rush into rejecting the body he gave us and want to change it.

Also, we must beware of pursuing a "cult of the body", a form of "idolatry" which is very prevalent in modern society. Bodily beauty, while important, is only "skin deep". Spiritual beauty is what truly matters. Addressing himself to women, St Peter writes: "Let not yours be the outward adorning with braiding of hair, decoration of gold, and wearing of robes, but let it be the hidden person of the heart with the imperishable jewel of a gentle and quiet spirit, which in God's sight is very precious" (*1 Pet* 3:3).

There is nothing wrong, of course, with enhancing one's appearance through make-up, jewellery, stylish clothes, an appropriate hairstyle, etc. What is more important, though, is the inner beauty of soul. There are many truly "beautiful" people whose outward appearance is quite plain.

407 The morality of in-vitro fertilisation

I know several women, including Catholics, who have had children through IVF. Why is the Church opposed to this?

You are not alone in wondering why the Church is opposed to in-vitro fertilisation (IVF). I suspect there are many Catholics who are unaware of the Church's teaching on this issue, so it is good to answer your question for the benefit of others as well.

First we should explain what IVF is and how it is performed. The expression "in-vitro fertilisation" means literally fertilisation "in glass". A woman with blocked Fallopian tubes or who is infertile for some other reason goes into a clinic where several eggs are extracted from her ovaries through a needle. These are placed in a liquid medium in a glass vessel, and sperm from her husband or from some other man is then added to the dish. In due course one or more eggs will be fertilised.

If the man's sperm on its own is not able to fertilise the eggs, the sperm may be injected into the eggs by a procedure known as Intracytoplasmic sperm injection (ICSI). This is simply a variation of IVF and has the same moral considerations. When the eggs have been fertilised, one or more are inserted several days later into the woman's womb, where it is hoped they will implant and the woman will be able to give birth to a baby. Often unused embryos are frozen for future use or they are discarded. It should be remembered that once fertilisation has taken place the zygote or embryo is now a human being and must be treated with the same respect as a child or an adult.

Why is the Church against this procedure? The reasons are given in the Instruction *Donum vitae* of the Congregation for the Doctrine of the Faith, dated 22 February 1987 and signed by the Prefect, Cardinal Joseph Ratzinger, later Pope Benedict XVI. The document quotes Pope Paul VI's encyclical *Humanae Vitae* (1968), which established the important principle that the unitive and procreative meanings of the marriage act can never be separated. The unitive meaning is the physical one flesh union of the husband and the wife, who give themselves to each other in an act of mutual love, and the procreative meaning is the openness of that act to life. "By safeguarding both these essential aspects, the unitive and the procreative, the conjugal act preserves in its fullness the sense of true mutual love and its ordination toward man's exalted vocation to parenthood" (*HV* 12; *DVitae* II, 4).

If the parents resort to IVF there is no one flesh union, since the sperm and egg are brought together by scientists in a laboratory. God intended that children should come into being through an act of mutual love of the parents, not through an act of technicians in a laboratory. When fertilisation takes place in this way, the child becomes more a product of science than a human being with the dignity of a person: "The one conceived must be the fruit of his parents' love. He cannot be desired or conceived as the product of an intervention of medical or biological techniques; that would be equivalent to reducing him to an object of scientific technology. No one may subject the coming of a child into the world to conditions of technical efficiency which are to be evaluated according to standards of control and dominion" (*DVitae* II, 4).

Through IVF, fertilisation "is brought about outside the bodies of the couple through actions of third parties whose competence and technical activity determine the success of the procedure. Such fertilisation entrusts the life and identity of the embryo into the power of doctors and biologists and establishes the domination of technology over the origin and destiny of the human person. Such a relationship of domination is in itself contrary to the dignity and equality that must be common to parents and children" (*DVitae* II, 5).

While infertile couples suffer if they cannot have children, they should always remember that "a child is not something *owed* to one, but is a *gift*. The 'supreme gift of marriage' is a human person. A child may not be considered a piece of property, an idea to which an alleged 'right to a child' would lead. In this area, only the child possesses genuine rights: the right 'to be the fruit of the specific act of the conjugal love of his parents,' and 'the right to be respected as a person from the moment of his conception'" (*CCC* 2378; *DVitae* II, 8).

408 Vaccines from aborted foetuses

A friend of mine, a young mother like me, recently raised the issue of whether it is moral to have our children vaccinated against childhood illnesses when the vaccines are made from aborted foetuses. This was new to me. Does the Church teach anything on this?

Many people would be unaware, as you were, that some of these vaccines are in fact made from cell lines obtained from tissues from aborted foetuses. This naturally raises the question of whether it is moral to use such vaccines for one's children. The Church has in fact dealt with the issue, stating that it is lawful to use these vaccines under certain conditions. The ruling came in the Congregation for the Doctrine of the Faith's Instruction on Certain Bioethical Questions *Dignitas personae*, issued on 8 September 2008. The Instruction made a distinction between the use by researchers of "biological material" derived from aborted foetuses and its use by parents in the vaccination of their children.

As general criterion the Instruction insists on "the duty to avoid cooperation in evil and scandal" (n. 32). As regards cooperation in evil, in this case the grave evil of abortion, those actually involved in the abortion bring about the evil directly or cooperate immediately in it, while researchers using biological material obtained from the abortion would be cooperating more remotely. Nonetheless, even though the researchers have not been directly involved in the abortion, they should still not benefit from it through use of biological material obtained from it, since this would imply acceptance of the abortion. Indeed, the Instruction says this involves a "contradiction in the attitude of the person who says that he does not approve of the injustice perpetrated by others, but at the same time accepts for his own work the 'biological material' which the others have obtained by means of that injustice" (n. 34).

This would seem to rule out researchers using this material to make vaccines in the first place. However, Fr John Fleming, in his book *Dignitas Personae Explained* (Connor Court 2010), says that "in cases where tissue has been preserved for some time from a past abortion, it may be possible to use that material because of the remoteness of the researcher from the injustice of the abortion" (pp. 70-71). Indeed, the cell lines used for some vaccines, in particular that for German measles, come from foetuses aborted more than 40 years ago.

But what about parents using vaccines derived from this material? Obviously their cooperation in the abortion is extremely remote, and it is presumed that they are opposed to the immorality of abortion. Thus, following the general criterion for cooperation in evil, if the cooperation is remote and the person is opposed to the original evil – i.e. their cooperation is material, not formal – they may cooperate provided there is a proportionate reason to justify it.

In this case the need to vaccinate children against potentially life-threatening illnesses would justify the use of vaccines obtained from aborted foetuses if no other vaccine is available. In the words of the Instruction, "Grave reasons may be morally proportionate to justify the use of such 'biological material'. Thus, for example, danger to the health of children could permit parents to use a vaccine which was developed using cell lines of illicit origin, while keeping in mind that everyone has the duty to make known their disagreement and to ask that their healthcare system make other types of vaccines available" (n. 34). While they can make use of these vaccines, parents should tell their doctor or health insurer that they would prefer that the vaccines did not come from aborted foetuses.

And while some parents do not have their children vaccinated at all because of this moral issue or because of the danger of death due to the vaccination itself, they should be aware that the danger of death later on due to not vaccinating them is much higher, and moreover their children may later contaminate other children and adults with their illness.

409 Living together outside marriage

My cousin, in her twenties, is sharing a flat with a young man. She says they are just friends and there is nothing intimate between them. Nonetheless their living together somehow doesn't seem right to me. Is it?

The situation you describe is becoming more and more common. Forty or fifty years ago people frowned upon such a living arrangement, and few people would have adopted it, but these days it is socially quite acceptable. What are we to make of it?

There can be different reasons why people might choose to embrace that lifestyle. For example, someone may have rented a two-bedroom flat and now rents out the other room to someone of the opposite sex. Or two friends, workmates or classmates of the opposite sex decide to share a house or flat together. Or a young man and woman who are engaged to marry decide to live in the same flat in order to avoid paying rent on two flats and thus save money. Or a man and a woman are in a *de facto* relationship with no intention of marrying, at least for the time being.

The moral life of the people involved may thus range from those in the first cases, where there is no sexual intimacy, to the last case, where there clearly is. Obviously, any use of sexuality outside of marriage is gravely sinful (cf. *CCC* 2353). But is it morally acceptable to live together even when there is no sexual activity? Here there are two important considerations.

The first is the danger that, even though for the time being the man and woman have no attraction for one another and no intention of indulging in sexual activity, their very living together may give rise to the temptation to do so. Years ago I remember hearing of an elderly priest who had warned a younger priest about the danger of living in the same house with his housekeeper without proper separation of their living areas. He had given the wise advice that "propinquity is more dangerous than beauty". That is, the mere fact of living in close proximity to the housekeeper, even if she was much older than he was, was more dangerous to his chastity than being in occasional contact with someone who was very beautiful.

I recall too the response of a wise Dominican priest who was the Master of a residential college for university students where the rule was that women were not to visit the men in their bedrooms. When some innocent students asked him, "Don't you trust us?" he replied, "If I were in your situation, I wouldn't trust myself!"

Thus an unmarried man and woman sharing a flat would ordinarily be putting themselves voluntarily without good reason in what is called an "occasion of sin". They would be increasing the likelihood that one day they might give in to the temptation to sleep together. And there is no proportionate reason for them to be in that situation. Saving money is never a sufficient reason to put oneself in an occasion of committing a serious sin. If a couple who are engaged wish to save money they can each share a flat with someone of the same sex, or they might choose to live at home or in some other arrangement. What is more, living self-discipline in the area of chastity is the best preparation for the self-control needed in marriage.

The other consideration to bear in mind is scandal. That is, others knowing that a good Catholic girl is living together with a man without being married to him might be led to think that it is a perfectly acceptable arrangement and to try it themselves. They might then be led into sin, whereas the first couple might not be committing any sin. By living together they would thus be giving bad example and ultimately they would be held accountable before God for the sins committed by others who naively decided to imitate them. For these reasons, it is wrong for unmarried persons to live together, even if they do not intend to engage in sexual intimacy.

410 Adultery and divorce

In my Bible in Chapter 19 of St Matthew's Gospel it says that whoever divorces his wife, except in the case of adultery, and marries another, commits adultery. Does this mean that adultery is a ground for divorce and remarriage?

The text you cite has been a cause of confusion and misunderstanding for a long time. The phrase "except in the case of adultery" is translated differently in different versions of the Bible. For example, the Knox version reads "not for any unfaithfulness of hers", and the Revised Standard Version, Second Catholic Edition has "except for unchastity". But while the wording varies, the idea remains the same.

Before we venture into the meaning of the text, however, we should say two things. First, only Matthew includes this phrase. The parallel passages in Mark and Luke omit it and read more succinctly: "Whoever divorces his wife and marries another, commits adultery against her" (*Mk* 10:11, *Lk* 16:18). Here the meaning is very clear: there are no grounds that would allow for divorce and remarriage. Second, even though the Gospel of Matthew seems to allow for a situation in which it would be permissible to divorce and remarry, this must always be interpreted in light of the living tradition of the Church. And the tradition has been constant from the beginning: the Church has never allowed divorce and remarriage for any reason. While many Protestant denominations have used this passage to justify divorce and remarriage, the Catholic Church has always maintained the indissolubility of marriage.

Pope Pius XI affirmed it clearly in his encyclical *Casti connubii* (1930): "This is the teaching of Sacred Scripture; it is the constant and universal Tradition of the Church; it is the solemnly defined doctrine of the Council of Trent, which uses the words of Holy Scripture to proclaim and establish that the perpetual indissolubility of the marriage bond, its unity and its stability, derive from God himself." What then is the meaning of the phrase "except for unchastity"? Scott Hahn, in his *Ignatius Catholic Study Bible* that there are three possible meanings, all of which exclude divorce and remarriage.

First, several Fathers of the Church interpret this as meaning that when there has been adultery or unfaithfulness on the part of one of the spouses, the couple can separate, or "divorce", but the marriage bond remains intact and the spouses are not free to marry again. In this case the Greek word for "unchastity", *porneia*, would mean adultery, which is one of its various meanings. St Paul confirms this: "To the married I give charge, not I but the Lord, that the wife should not separate from her husband (but if she does, let her remain single or else be reconciled to her husband) – and that the husband should not divorce his wife" (*1 Cor* 7:10). Likewise, the *Code of Canon Law* mentions adultery as a grounds for separation at the same time as it earnestly recommends the other spouse to forgive the adulterous partner (cf. Can. 1152). But in no way does it authorise divorce.

The second interpretation is that "unchastity" refers to invalid unions, where the "spouses" are living together in a relationship prohibited by law, for example where they are closely related by family ties. In this case *porneia* refer to the unchaste relations of persons living together who are not validly married, and who can therefore separate and remarry validly. This view is supported by two passages in the New Testament where *porneia* to incest (cf. *Acts* 15:20, 29; *1 Cor* 5:1-2). The Old Testament background for this interpretation refers to prohibited marriages between closely related persons (cf. *Lev* 18:6-18).

The third interpretation is that "except for unchastity" means "regardless of the Old Testament grounds for divorce", of which one was unchastity on the part of the wife (cf. *Deut* 24:1). According to this interpretation Jesus is abolishing the Old Testament permission of divorce in certain circumstances and does not want even to discuss it. He is not clarifying or reaffirming Moses' permission but doing away with it altogether. By this teaching, Christ is taking marriage back to the way it was "in the beginning", before the fall of Adam and Eve, when it was a lifelong commitment and a mirror of God's faithful love for his people.

411 Impure thoughts

I have several questions regarding impure thoughts. Can they be mortal sins? How should I confess them? Do I need to go into detail?

These are very commonly asked questions, and it is good that I have the opportunity to answer them, both for you and for many others.

First of all, what do we mean by impure thoughts? We mean thoughts of actions or situations which if acted upon by the particular person would involve committing a sin against chastity. Thus the thought a young man has of going to bed with a young woman would be an impure thought, whereas the thought a married man has of going to bed with his wife would not be. But if the married man had thoughts of going to bed with some other woman they would be impure thoughts.

In the genesis of impure thoughts one can distinguish several stages, which are helpful in judging their morality. In a first stage the thoughts simply appear in the imagination without being sought. The fact that they are in the mind does not mean that the person has sinned. The thoughts at this stage are not voluntary, they have just appeared, and there can be no sin until the person consents to them. But there may have been prior sins that led to the thoughts. For example, if someone has watched an unchaste film on television the night before, or has looked at pornography on the internet, that in itself is putting oneself in an occasion of sin without good reason, and is therefore sinful. In this sense, the person is responsible in some measure for the present impure thoughts, even though the thoughts in themselves are not yet sinful.

In a second stage the person becomes aware that he or she is having thoughts which are impure. At this moment the possibility of sin enters, because the will can now reject the thoughts or consent to them. If the person consents to them and continues dwelling on them voluntarily, there is certainly sin. Will it be venial or mortal? If the person takes great pleasure in the thoughts, imagines in some detail committing an impure act, prolongs the thoughts for some time, "fantasises" in the imagination, often experiencing bodily pleasure, the sin will most likely be mortal.

Jesus alluded to this when he said, "But I say to you that every one who looks at a woman lustfully has already committed adultery with her in his heart" (*Mt* 5:28). It is not merely looking at a woman that is sinful, but the lustful thoughts in the mind, the impure desires, that constitute the sin. And it is clear from Jesus' words about committing adultery in the heart, that the sin is mortal.

If, however, on adverting to the impure thoughts the person recognises their immorality and rejects them, there will be no sin. It can be helpful in these situations to imagine Jesus suffering excruciating pain in the scourging at the pillar or on the cross, as an incentive to avoid offending him by seeking illicit pleasure. Likewise, it can be helpful to pray to Our Lady, "Mother most pure", "Mother most chaste", in order to obtain the graces necessary to reject the temptation.

And always, it is important to distract the imagination away from the impure thoughts by thinking about something that truly engages the mind and is not sinful; for example, thinking about one's work, one's recreation, one's plans for the weekend, etc. If the person struggles with determination to reject the thoughts, he or she will actually grow in sanctity and acquire great supernatural merit through the struggle. The person has been tested and found worthy, and God will reward them for their fidelity. If the person recognises that, even though they are trying to reject the thoughts, they have given in to some extent, there will be venial sin but certainly not mortal sin.

How should these thoughts be confessed? It is not good to say "I have had impure thoughts", since the thoughts in themselves are not sinful. The person should give some indication as regards the extent to which they think they have consented to the thoughts. And if the thoughts have involved particular persons in special relationships, for example impure thoughts towards a family member, towards a person dedicated to God in a vocation to celibacy, towards someone of the same sex, towards someone other than one's spouse, etc., this aggravating circumstance should be mentioned.

412 The sexual abuse scandal

In the face of the child sexual abuse scandal and now the Royal Commission into it, I have frankly sometimes felt my faith weakening, above all when talking with friends who are very critical of the Church, some of whom no longer go to Mass. How should I respond?

The following observations may be of help in facing up to this most serious problem.

First, we must acknowledge that child sexual abuse is always a great evil, but especially when carried out by a member of the clergy. It is a deplorable act with devastating consequences, especially for the victim but also for many others. Among the "victims" are some priests who have been falsely accused, or accused of very minor offences, who have been sidelined from their ministry and sometimes suffer psychological damage as well. We should have the greatest sympathy for all those involved and affected by this lamentable situation.

Second, while the media are fond of highlighting the sexual abuse carried out by priests and others in the Catholic Church, the problem is very widespread and includes clergy of other denominations, teachers, sports coaches, scout leaders and many others. There is no reason to believe that Catholics were any more involved than those in other institutions. The Royal Commission is looking into abuse in all institutions, not only in the Catholic Church. And it is not investigating child sexual abuse in families, where the immense majority of cases occur.

Third, we should remember that priests too are human and that they carry the effects of original sin as much as everyone else. While they have a commitment to live chastity, they are still subject to temptation and they sometimes fall. It is consoling in this sense to look at the twelve men chosen by Christ himself as his apostles. One of them denied Our Lord and betrayed him for thirty pieces of silver, the "Prince of the Apostles" denied three times even knowing him, and they all ran away in fear in the Garden of Gethsemane. Weakness among the ministers has been with the Church from the beginning, but the Church has continued to go forward steadily, bearing abundant fruits.

Pope Pius XII was not afraid to describe the situation in his encyclical *Mystici corporis* (1943): "And if at times there appears in the Church something that indicates the weakness of our human nature, it should not be attributed to her juridical constitution, but rather to that regrettable inclination to evil found in each individual, which its Divine Founder permits even at times in the most exalted members of his Mystical Body, for the purpose of testing the virtue of the Shepherds no less than of the flocks, and that all may increase the merit of their Christian faith. For, as we said above, Christ did not wish to exclude sinners from his Church; hence if some of her members are suffering from spiritual maladies, that is no reason why we should lessen our love for the Church, but rather a reason why we should increase our devotion to her members" (*MC* 66).

Fourth, we should never forget that it is a very small percentage of priests who have abused their ministry. The second report of the John Jay College of Criminal Justice into sexual abuse by Catholic clergy in the U.S. reported that in the period 1950-2010 there had been accusations of sexual abuse against only 5% of priests, and that less than 4% of these involved paedophilia. The report acknowledged that the rate of abuse by clergy is lower than that in comparable professions. While figures of abuse by clergy in Australia are not available, it is probable that they are similar to those in the U.S. The immense majority of priests have been faithful to their ministry.

Fifth, at the time that most of the offences occurred, many years ago, neither the Church nor people in secular society understood, as we do today, the seriousness of paedophilia as a mental condition that is not easily treated. The tendency then was to regard it as an isolated case of sexual weakness, for which the perpetrator had repented and was resolved not to commit it again, and so the priest was simply moved to a different parish where he could begin his new life of chastity in different surroundings. This was gravely mistaken but those who responded in that way were usually acting in good faith and cannot be judged by standards that have changed in the light of new findings. Obviously, when it was clear that a priest had offended multiple times drastic action should have been taken, and this did not always happen.

Sixth, once the nature of sexual abuse of minors became more clear the Church responded vigorously, setting up protocols and institutions to deal with it. The national *Towards Healing* protocols for dealing with complaints were first published in 1996 and then revised in 2010. In addition, the document *Integrity in Ministry* sets out a code of conduct for those in ministry and the National Committee for Professional Standards oversees the procedures in response to complaints.

Seventh, the Church is now far more careful in vetting candidates for the priesthood, so that it is highly unlikely that a man with a tendency to sexual abuse would be admitted to the seminary.

With all of this, we should acknowledge that there has been a serious problem and we should pray and make reparation for the great harm that has been caused. We should support our priests and show appreciation for their fidelity and generosity in serving us. We should pray very much for all priests, and we should have great faith in and love for the Church. Our Lord is still the head of his Mystical Body, the Holy Spirit is just as active as on that first Pentecost and Our Lady is very much Mother of the Church. The Church will move on from this crisis purified and renewed.

413 Keeping secrets

A girl friend recently told me something in secret and I feel that if I don't tell someone else, harm could come to her or possibly others. Can I tell someone what she told me?

I will first give the general teaching on secrets and then answer your question. By a secret we understand the knowledge of something that ought not be revealed to others. We all know many things, most of which we feel no obligation to keep hidden, but there are some things that, for various reasons, we feel we ought not reveal. These are what we call secrets. Secrets can be divided broadly into three general categories.

First there are what we can call *natural* secrets. These are things we come to know in the normal course of life but which should not be revealed to others because the knowledge of them could cause harm to someone. For example, we might see someone drunk or we might be aware that a married person is having an affair with someone at our work place.

Then there are secrets that we come to know after an explicit or tacit agreement to observe secrecy. These are sometimes called *entrusted* secrets. To this category belong *professional secrets* between professionals and their clients where confidentiality is to be observed. For example, doctors, accountants, lawyers, counsellors, psychologists and many others know that what they hear through their work is to be kept confidential. It is a matter between them and their client.

Another obvious example of an entrusted secret is the secret of the confessional. Priests are under a strict and grave obligation never to reveal to anyone the sins they hear in confession. This is a very serious matter, so much so that the punishment for violating it is automatic excommunication which can be lifted only by the Holy See (cf. *Code of Canon Law,* Can. 1388 §1). Apart from these general categories of entrusted secrets there can be individual cases in which an explicit agreement is made not to reveal what is about to be disclosed. That is, before hearing the secret the person promises not to reveal what he or she is about to hear.

The third type of secret is sometimes called the *promised* secret. Here one promises to keep the secret after hearing it.

In principle there is an obligation to keep all secrets. The *Catechism of the Catholic Church* teaches: "*Professional secrets* – for example, those of political office holders, soldiers, physicians, and lawyers – or confidential information given under the seal of secrecy must be kept, save in exceptional cases where keeping the secret is bound to cause very grave harm to the one who confided it, to the one who received it or to a third party, and where the very grave harm can be avoided only by divulging the truth" (*CCC* 2491).

While in your question you have not given any details of what your friend told you in secret, it is easy to imagine cases in which you could reveal to others what you have heard. For example, if your friend said she was using drugs, you would try to dissuade her, but if you saw you were not succeeding you could tell her parents or some other person close to her so that they could help her. Likewise, if she said she was feeling depressed and suicidal you would be right in telling someone close to her. Or if she said she was planning to hurt someone in a serious way, you could inform that person.

There are situations too in which even the law requires people to disclose what they have heard in secret. In many places, for example, if a person comes to know that someone has committed a crime, the person is obliged to report it to the police or they will be guilty themselves of the offence of not reporting a crime. Naturally, the seal of confession takes precedence over all other norms, so that the priest can never divulge for any reason what he has heard in confession.

As regards the natural secret, this too must be kept unless there is a grave reason to make it known. So if one became aware that someone was having an affair, it would be reasonable to inform that person's spouse so they could take measures to save their marriage.

We should remember too that when others tell us something without asking us to keep it secret, it is often understood by the very nature of the information that it is to be kept confidential. In summary, we should be careful to keep confidential information confidential and only reveal it when there is a serious reason to do so.

IV. CHRISTIAN PRAYER

Prayer and Devotions

414 The Sign of the Cross

I recently attended a Catholic seminar in which, although prayers were said at the beginning, the Sign of the Cross was not made. I find it disturbing that this centuries-old tradition is being pushed aside. Should I be concerned or am I just old fashioned?

I wrote a column on the history and meaning of the Sign of the Cross some years ago (cf. *Question Time 1*, q. 124), but your question affords me the opportunity to elaborate on the importance of this traditional act of piety.

The custom of making the Sign of the Cross goes back to the very first centuries of the Church. As I mentioned in that earlier column, one of the oldest written testimonies comes from Tertullian at the end of the second century: "In all our travels and movements, in coming in and going out, in putting on our shoes, at the bath, at the table, in lighting our candles, in lying down, in sitting down, whatever employment occupies us, we mark our foreheads with the sign of the cross. These practices are not commanded by a formal law of scripture, but tradition teaches them, custom confirms them, and faith observes them" (*De cor. mil.,* 3).

As Tertullian says, this was not a custom imposed by the Church but rather one which arose out of the piety of the early Christians. What moved them to adopt this custom? They obviously recognised that the cross was their distinctive sign. After all, it was through the cross that Jesus redeemed mankind, and they wanted to remind themselves constantly of this fact. For them, the cross was not a reminder of an agonising death but rather a sign of victory, of the triumph of God's love over sin, death and the devil.

The early Fathers of the Church also saw the cross as a symbol of the union Christ had brought about by his death and resurrection. In the vertical bar they saw the union between heaven and earth, and in the horizontal bar the union between Jews and Gentiles. For this reason the early Christians had crosses everywhere: in their homes, in churches, on tombstones and in the Sign of the Cross they made over themselves.

St John Chrysostom explains: "No one can be ashamed of the holy symbols of our salvation, the greatest of all goods, to which we owe our life and existence. Rather, we take the cross of Christ with us everywhere, like a crown. In fact everything is done in us through the cross. When we are reborn, the cross is there. When we feed on the mystical food, when the sacred ministers are consecrated, when any ministry is performed, the victorious symbol is always present. That explains our fervour in tracing and forming it on our houses, walls and windows, and on our forehead and over our heart. For this is the sign of our salvation, the sign of mankind's freedom, the sign of the Lord's goodness towards us" (*In Matth. hom.* 54, 4).

The cross and the Sign of the Cross are still present everywhere in the Church. On entering and leaving a church, we sign ourselves with holy water. The celebration of every sacrament begins with the Sign of the Cross. In Baptism the minister, parents and sponsors make the Sign of the Cross on the forehead of the infant being baptised, the water is poured in the form of a cross, and the two anointings are done by making a cross with the oil.

In the Mass there are numerous Signs of the Cross, from the one which begins the Mass to the final blessing, passing through the signing which all do on their forehead, lips and heart before the Gospel. All blessings involve the Sign of the Cross over the persons or objects blessed. And of course we have crucifixes everywhere: on the walls of our churches, both inside and outside, in our homes, in our pockets and handbags, on our rosary beads, along the roads in many countries...

Therefore, we should feel happy and privileged to live this custom, which has been with the Church from the beginning. We begin all our prayers with the Sign of the Cross, including the blessing of meals, we may use it on entering or leaving our homes, on beginning trips…

And let us not be afraid to manifest our faith with the Sign of the Cross when we bless our meals in restaurants and other public places. After all, we see so many sports people making the Sign of the Cross before thousands of spectators and millions more watching on television. In summary, the Sign of the Cross is our badge of identity as Christians, the symbol of Christ's triumph over sin and death. It will never be old fashioned.

415 Distractions in prayer

I find that I have many distractions in prayer and don't know what to do about it. Can you help me?

This must be one of the questions most frequently asked of priests. What this tells us is that everyone has distractions. Everyone. Distractions are part of our human nature. The imagination presents us with thoughts and images completely foreign to what we were thinking about, without our seeking them. What is more, the frequency of these distractions can increase, the more busy we become. There are many things to think about and it is only natural that they enter into our conversations with God in prayer, just as they enter our work, our leisure and even our sleep.

A first line of defence can be to discipline our imagination outside of prayer. If we allow it to run wild when we are working or resting or conversing with other people, it is only natural that we will not be able to control it in our prayer. This means that we should make a real effort to concentrate on what we are doing and ignore the distractions. If we ignore them they will go away. If, on the contrary, we allow our mind to go along with the distractions each time they appear, we will become dissipated and scatter-brained, and will lack efficacy. It is important to learn how to concentrate on what we are doing and ignore the distractions. The mental discipline we acquire in this way will help us in everything we do, including our prayer.

When we speak of distractions in prayer, we of course include all forms of prayer: meditation, the Rosary, the Mass, spiritual reading, etc. The first thing to remember is that distractions, of themselves, are not sinful. They are simply part of our human condition, the fruit of our imagination. They can plague us like flies at any time, but as long as we do not dwell on them voluntarily we are not sinning. Even when the mind is drawn away from what we were doing and dwells for a time on the distraction, this is involuntary and not sinful.

If we did let the distractions linger briefly and wilfully turn our mind to them, for example in saying the Rosary, this would normally be only an imperfection, a lack of love for God, not a sin. Therefore, there is usually no need to say in confession that we had distractions in our prayer, since these are a normal part of life. Only if we convert them into voluntary distractions by freely choosing to dwell on them for some length of time at a serious moment in our lives, such as just after receiving Communion, might they be sinful.

The best way to deal with distractions is to ignore them and concentrate more intensely on the prayers we were saying. If they persist, as they often do, Our Lord will see the effort we are making to concentrate on him and he will be very pleased. Moreover, persistent distractions can lead us to say an act of sorrow to Our Lord for the fact that our mind wandered involuntarily in prayer or in Mass, and this act of sorrow is very pleasing to him too. In this sense, distractions can be a great means of sanctification. They force us to struggle harder in our spiritual life and this added effort is very pleasing to God.

If the distraction comes in our meditation and refers to an important matter such as a difficult family relationship, it may be good to turn our prayer to that topic and ask Our Lord for lights as to how to resolve it. Alternatively, we can abandon the matter into his hands and ask him for the grace to resolve it at another time.

During other forms of prayer such as the Rosary or Mass, we shouldn't turn our mind to the distraction, or even ask ourselves why we have so many distractions or complain about them. As the *Catechism of the Catholic Church* puts it, "To set about hunting down distractions would be to fall into their trap, when all that is necessary is to turn back to our heart: for a distraction reveals to us what we are attached to, and this humble awareness before the Lord should awaken our preferential love for him and lead us resolutely to offer him our heart to be purified. Therein lies the battle, the choice of which master to serve" (*CCC* 2729).

416 Spiritual dryness

I don't know what is happening at the moment but I just don't seem to be able to pray as I did before. I have no fervour and I feel as if God is very far from me. Sometimes I wonder whether it is worthwhile praying at all in this state. What is going on?

You are the second person who has asked me this in the last month and I am sure there are many others who share your experience. Hence this answer. What you are going through is a fairly common experience known as spiritual dryness, or aridity. In this state the person experiences little or no fervour, may have many distractions and somehow does not feel close to God. They look back to other times when it was very easy to pray and they felt close to God. Now, on the contrary, they wonder whether it is worthwhile praying at all because they feel their prayer is not pleasing to God.

This is a state that we can all go through at times and that God allows even the saints to suffer. It is well known that for the last fifty years of her life Mother Teresa of Calcutta experienced a sort of "dark night of the soul" in which she felt God very distant from her. Similarly, St Teresa of Avila describes a long period during which she suffered dryness in her prayer: "It would have been impossible, I think, for me to persevere during the eighteen years for which I had to bear this trial and these great aridities due to my being unable to meditate. During all these years, except after receiving Communion, I never dared to begin to pray without a book. My soul was as much afraid to engage in prayer without one as if it were having to go and fight a host of enemies... For it was not usual for me to suffer from aridity: this only came when I had no book, whereupon my soul would at once become disturbed and my thoughts begin to wander. As soon as I started to read they began to collect themselves and the book acted like a bait to my soul" (*Life*, 4).

Spiritual dryness can last for a short time – days, weeks or months – or it may last for many years. What should we do if we go through it? The first thing is to keep up our prayer life, no matter how we feel about it. The devil wants us to think that if we do not feel close to God our prayer is not worthwhile. We cannot play into his hands and give up. Then too we should realise that our prayer can be even more pleasing to God when we pray while spiritually dry. When God grants us fervour and we feel close to him it is as if he is carrying us along and it is easy to pray. Anyone will pray in those circumstances.

But when we are dry and do not feel close to God, we have to make a greater effort to pray and this sacrifice has great merit before God. Then we are praying not to please ourselves but to please him. We can be sure that he values this prayer very much. If we are inclined to say that we don't pray because we are dry and we do not get anything out of it, God can answer: "I don't value your prayer by what you get out of it, but by what you put into it".

Indeed, the *Catechism of the Catholic Church* tells us that prayer always involves a struggle: "Prayer is both a gift of grace and a determined response on our part. It always presupposes effort. The great figures of prayer of the Old Covenant before Christ, as well as the Mother of God, the saints, and he himself, all teach us this: prayer is a battle. Against whom? Against ourselves and against the wiles of the tempter who does all he can to turn man away from prayer, away from union with God" (*CCC* 2725).

Finally, when we are spiritually dry we have a great opportunity to exercise faith. The Catechism says: "Dryness belongs to contemplative prayer when the heart is separated from God, with no taste for thoughts, memories, and feelings, even spiritual ones. This is the moment of sheer faith clinging faithfully to Jesus in his agony and in his tomb... If dryness if due to the lack of roots, because the word has fallen on rocky soil, the battle requires conversion" (*CCC* 2731).

In short, spiritual dryness can be a very beneficial and meritorious state, from which great spiritual profit can be derived. What is important is not to stop praying.

417 Praying in tongues

I was recently invited to a charismatic prayer meeting and, among other things, saw people praying in tongues. I found it very strange and was wondering what to make of it. Does the Church approve of this?

First, let us look at what the Scriptures have to say. Jesus himself prophesied that those who believed in him would be able to speak in tongues: "And these signs will accompany those who believe: in my name they will cast out demons; they will speak in new tongues..." (*Mk* 16:17).

The most well known manifestation of this gift took place on Pentecost, when the Holy Spirit came down on the apostles: "And they were all filled with the Holy Spirit and began to speak in other tongues, as the Spirit gave them utterance. Now there were dwelling in Jerusalem

Jews, devout men from every nation under heaven. And at this sound the multitude came together, and they were bewildered, because each one heard them speaking in his own language" (*Acts* 2:4-6).

Later, when St Peter went to the house of the Roman centurion Cornelius in Caesarea and many were converted, this gift of the Holy Spirit was poured out even on converts from the Gentiles. "For they heard them speaking in tongues and extolling God" (*Acts* 10:45-46). Something similar happened in Ephesus when a group of men spoke in tongues after St Paul laid his hands upon them and they received the Holy Spirit (cf. *Acts* 19:6).

St Paul himself writes at length to the Corinthians about the gift of tongues, including it among the variety of gifts given by the Spirit: "to another various kinds of tongues, to another the interpretation of tongues" (*1 Cor* 12:10). He goes on to distinguish between the gift of tongues and the gift of prophecy, each of which has a different purpose: "For one who speaks in a tongue speaks not to men but to God; for no one understands him, but he utters mysteries in the Spirit. On the other hand, he who prophesies speaks to men for their upbuilding and encouragement and consolation. He who speaks in a tongue edifies himself, but he who prophesies edifies the Church. Now I want you all to speak in tongues, but even more to prophesy. He who prophesies is greater than he who speaks in tongues, unless some one interprets, so that the Church may be edified" (*1 Cor* 14:2-5).

Paul acknowledges that he too spoke in tongues: "I thank God that I speak in tongues more than you all; nevertheless, in church I would rather speak five words with my mind, in order to instruct others, than ten thousand words in a tongue" (*1 Cor* 14:18-19). Later he summarises this relationship between tongues and prophecy: "So, my brethren, earnestly desire to prophesy, and do not forbid speaking in tongues; but all things should be done decently and in order" (*1 Cor* 14:39).

In these passages we find the answer to your question. First, there is nothing wrong with speaking in tongues, which is a gift of the Holy

Spirit. If the apostles had the gift on Pentecost and St Paul also had it, there can be nothing wrong with it. Naturally it would be very wrong for someone to pretend to be talking in tongues, moved not by the Holy Spirit but by themselves.

Second, speaking in tongues is primarily directed to God in prayer, not to those present, and it is not meant to be understood by them. Many charismatics will acknowledge that this is exactly what happens in their meetings. Someone prays in tongues and the others recognise that the Holy Spirit is truly present, moving the person to pray in that way. It fills the others with faith and gratitude for this manifestation of the Spirit.

Third, while the gift of tongues is important, much more important is the gift of prophecy, of communicating to others the word of God in order to instruct them. After all, this is what happened on Pentecost, when the apostles used the gift of tongues to enable those present to understand God's message.

Finally, in a real sense the whole Church today has the gift of tongues in that it speaks the language of every nation. A sixth century homily from an unknown African preacher expresses this truth: "Therefore if somebody should say to one of us, 'You have received the Holy Spirit, why do you not speak in tongues?' his reply should be, 'I do indeed speak in the tongues of all men, because I belong to the body of Christ, that is, the Church, and she speaks all languages" (*Sermo* 8, 1-3).

418 Is the Rosary boring?

We have recently tried to reintroduce the family Rosary but my sons, aged 11 and 13, say they find it boring. I have not been able to convince them otherwise. Can you help me?

Experience tells us that children will always say that something is boring when they don't want to do it. How many times have we heard that the Mass is boring, or the Stations of the Cross, or even visiting the grandparents or other older relatives?

There are a number of things we can say about this. First, we shouldn't look on the Rosary, or the Mass or visiting relatives, for that matter, as a form of entertainment. It was never meant to be that. If we are going somewhere to be entertained we can rightfully say that we find it boring. But if we are doing something to please someone else, or for some other noble reason it doesn't make any difference whether we find it boring. We still do it.

Thus we visit relatives whom we may find boring because we want to show them our love, and we take subjects in school that we don't find particularly interesting, because they are necessary for our overall education. And we wash the dishes after a meal and work in the garden to please our parents who have done so much for us, even though we may not particularly enjoy these activities. So too in our relationship with God we do such things as go to Mass and pray the Rosary not to please ourselves, but to show our appreciation for all God's blessings and to grow in love for him.

As regards the Rosary in particular, Our Lady herself asked us to say it. In the apparitions in Lourdes in 1858, she appeared with the Rosary beads in her hands and she recited it together with St Bernadette. At Fatima in 1917, in the first apparition on 13 May Our Lady appeared holding the beads and she asked the three children to pray the Rosary everyday. In the July apparition she again asked the children to pray the Rosary everyday for peace in the world and for the end of the war. In the final apparition, on 13 October before the great miracle of the sun, Mary identified herself as "the Lady of the Rosary" and she showed the children three tableaux, or visions, representing the joyful, sorrowful and glorious mysteries of the Rosary. If it were only to please our heavenly Mother, who loves us so much and who asked us to pray the Rosary, we should do it, no matter how boring we find it.

But the Rosary not only pleases Our Lady. We derive much benefit from it ourselves. If in saying the Rosary we meditate on the mysteries, we come to know Our Lady and Our Lord much better. After all, the mysteries of the Rosary consider the principal events in the life of Christ, from his conception in the virginal womb of Mary, through his infancy and public life to his suffering, death and Resurrection and finally his glorification, along with that of Our Lady. For this reason, the Vatican's Directory on the Pastoral Ministry of Bishops, *Ecclesiae imago,* says that the Rosary "has been ceaselessly recommended by the popes as a kind of compendium of the Gospel and therefore as a model devotional practice recommended for the Church and splendidly confirmed by the practice of the saints."

When we meditate on the mysteries we do not find the Rosary boring. Rather, we find it short as we have only some three minutes to meditate on each mystery. In order to make this meditation more practical, it can be good to focus on some particular aspect of the mystery, such as a virtue, a sacrament, a truth or a devotion suggested by it. In this regard writings like my booklet *Understanding the Rosary* can be helpful. It has a section at the end with five different themes for meditation on each mystery. Using it we see that the Rosary is not only a compendium of the Gospel but a compendium of the entire Catholic faith.

When saying the Rosary with children, it is good to let each child lead a mystery and suggest the intention for which the family will offer that mystery. When the children suggest these intentions – peace in some country, children who have lost a parent, a sick friend or relative, someone who has just died – they are more inclined to say the Rosary willingly, and they find it more meaningful.

Finally, we should remember that people in love do not tire of saying the same things over and over again: "I love you." "I love you too." They do not find it boring. Nor should we find boring our loving reflection on the life of Christ and Mary contained in the Rosary.

419 The Angelus

In my daughter's school they say the Angelus every day at noon. I was not familiar with the prayer but am very happy to know that they say it. My mother remembers saying it when the parish bells were rung at 6 pm each day. What is the origin of this prayer and the bells?

The Angelus is in fact a very traditional prayer, going back almost 800 years. For those unfamiliar with it, the name comes from its first word in Latin, *Angelus*, meaning angel. The prayer commemorates the archangel Gabriel's annunciation to Mary of her vocation to be the mother of God and her response. It consists of three verses and responses each followed by a Hail Mary, with a longer prayer at the end. The verses and responses are:

V. The angel of the Lord declared unto Mary,

R. And she conceived of the Holy Spirit.

V. Behold the handmaid of the Lord.

R. Be it done unto me according to thy Word.

V. And the Word was made flesh.

R. And dwelt amongst us.

The Angelus has its origin in the thirteenth century in the recitation of three Hail Marys by the lay faithful when the evening bell was rung in the monasteries to announce the praying of Night Prayer, or Compline. A decree of the Franciscan General Chapter in 1263 or 1269, at the time of St Bonaventure, directed preachers to encourage the faithful to say three Hail Marys at the time of the Compline bell. It was believed that it was at this hour that the angel appeared to Our Lady.

It was not long before the custom grew up of ringing a bell also in the morning and saying the same prayers. This coincided with the monks saying the office of Prime. The earliest mention of this custom seems to be in a chronicle of the city of Parma in 1318, where the town bell, not that of the monastery, was rung. The local bishop exhorted the people to say three Our Fathers and three Hail Marys for the preservation of peace, and the bell became known as the "peace bell". The custom of the morning prayers soon became popular all over Europe and England.

The midday Angelus with a ringing of the bell was the last to be introduced. It seems to have appeared first in the fourteenth century and was also known as a peace bell. King Louis XI of France commended the custom in 1475 for the cause of peace. The midday prayers were often associated with the veneration of the Passion of Christ, and so at first the bell was rung only on Fridays, although it gradually spread to the other days of the week. In some places, including England and Germany at the beginning of the sixteenth century, longer prayers commemorating the Passion were said in addition to the three Hail Marys.

The recitation of the verses and responses that we say today, although without the final prayer, seems to have begun in the sixteenth century. An Italian catechism printed in Venice in 1560 has these verses. An English manuscript of 1576 suggests that the Resurrection should be commemorated in the morning, the Passion at noon and the Incarnation in the evening.

The Angelus can be said in the morning, usually around 6 am, at noon and at 6 in the evening. It is usually said standing and some people have the custom of genuflecting or bowing at the words "And the Word became flesh." In summary, the Angelus is a beautiful prayer honouring Our Lady's response to the angel which brought about the Incarnation of Christ. The more it is said, the better.

420 The Hail, Holy Queen

Is anything known about the origin of the Hail, Holy Queen that we say at the end of the Rosary? I have always liked this prayer.

The Hail, Holy Queen, or *Salve Regina* in Latin, is traditionally said at the end of the Rosary and it is one of the four Marian hymns said after Compline in the Divine Office. It is a rich and much loved prayer and it goes back many centuries.

As with some other prayers there is an element of uncertainty about who wrote it, historical writings attributing it to at least three persons. According to the Catholic Encyclopedia, one such person is Petrus of Monsoro, Bishop of Compostella in Spain, who died about 1000. Another is Adhemar, Bishop of Podium (Puy-en-Velay) in France, who was the first to ask permission to go on the Crusades. Adhemar is said to have composed the hymn to invoke the protection of Our Lady, Queen of Heaven, before leaving for the Crusades in 1096. But the most probable writer is Blessed Hermann Contractus, or Hermann the Cripple, who died in 1054. What is clear is that the hymn dates back to at least the eleventh century.

Blessed Hermann has an interesting story. He was born in 1013 at Altshausen in Swabia, Germany, one of fifteen children of Count Wolverad II. Hermann was deformed, crippled and very small, whence the name in Latin Contractus. He could not stand or walk unaided, and he could barely sit upright in the special chair they made for him. His fingers were so twisted that it was almost impossible for him to write, and his mouth and tongue were so deformed he could hardly be understood when he spoke. Yet he gradually overcame these difficulties to a point where he was able not only to write but also to make clocks and astronomical and musical instruments, and to help the many people who sought his advice. He was extraordinarily gifted intellectually, so much so that when he was only seven his parents entrusted him to the learned Benedictine Abbot Berno on the island of Reichenau in Lake Constance, where he later took monastic vows as a Benedictine.

In spite of his handicaps Hermann excelled in such disciplines as theology, mathematics, astronomy, music, Latin, Greek and Arabic. Students flocked to him from all over, attracted not only by his learning but also by his virtue and pleasant personality. His biographer describes him as pleasant, friendly, cheerful and never complaining, always trying to cooperate.

Hermann wrote many books on a variety of subjects and is considered one of the most gifted minds of the eleventh century. He also wrote religious hymns, and to him are attributed not only the Hail, Holy Queen but also another great Marian hymn, the *Alma Redemptoris Mater*, also used in the Divine Office. At the age of forty-one he contracted pleurisy and died ten days later on 21 September 1054. He was beatified by Pope Pius IX in 1863. Hermann is a testimony to what can be achieved in spite of severe physical handicaps.

The Hail, Holy Queen quickly became popular all over Europe. St Bernard of Clairvaux, who had great love for Our Lady, did much to promote it. There is a touching story of him entering the cathedral of Speyer on Christmas Eve in 1146 while the hymn was being sung. At the words "O clement, O loving, O sweet Virgin Mary" he is said to have genuflected three times in veneration of Mary. A book on St Bernard records that brass plates were later laid in the pavement of the cathedral to mark the spot where the saint showed this devotion.

By the middle of the twelfth century the Hail, Holy Queen had been introduced in shrines and monasteries in many places, including Cluny and Citeaux. In the thirteenth century it was used after Compline in the Divine Office of the Dominicans and later the Franciscans. Pope Gregory IX (1227-1241) prescribed it for the universal Church.

The hymn is a heart-felt plea for mercy from the "poor banished children of Eve" to Mary, addressed as "Queen, Mother of Mercy, our life, our sweetness and our hope". The petition ends: "Turn then, most gracious advocate, thine eyes of mercy toward us; and after this our exile, show unto us the blessed fruit of thy womb, Jesus, O clement, O loving, O sweet Virgin Mary." Our Lady will not to fail to answer those who pray to her with such humility and faith.

421 The *Trisagium Angelicum*

A friend recently told me about a prayer called the Trisagium Angelicum which she prays in a group to which she belongs. I had never heard of it. What is it?

I think few people would be aware of this ancient prayer to the Blessed Trinity, so it is good that you ask the question. After all, we Catholics should be familiar with the many aspects of our rich cultural and spiritual heritage.

The *Trisagium Angelicum*, or Angelic Trisagion, is a prayer of devotion to the Blessed Trinity elaborated by the Order of the Blessed Trinity, better known as the Trinitarians. The *Trisagium* is their official prayer, and it has been recited by them and many others for centuries. The Trinitarians were founded in 1198 by St John de Matha and St Felix of Valois with the special mission of ransoming Christians held captive by nonbelievers as a result of the Crusades and the activities of pirates along the Mediterranean coast. They also served the people of their local communities by performing works of mercy. From the outset, a special dedication to the mystery of the Blessed Trinity was an essential element of their spirituality.

Returning to the *Trisagium*, the devotion begins with some brief opening prayers concluding with the Glory be to the Father. This is followed by the Trinitarian antiphon "Holy is God, Holy and strong, Holy Immortal One, have mercy on us" and the Our Father. The heart of the devotion is a verse and response repeated nine times: "To you,

O Blessed Trinity, be praise, and honour, and thanksgiving, for ever and ever! Holy, holy, holy Lord, God of hosts. Heaven and earth are filled with your glory," followed by the Glory be to the Father. These prayers, from the antiphon to the Glory be to the Father are said three times in honour of the three divine Persons.

The final prayers begin with another prayer to the Blessed Trinity: "God the Father unbegotten, only-begotten Son, and Holy Spirit, the Comforter: holy and undivided Trinity, with all our heart and voice we acknowledge you, we praise you, and we bless you: glory to you forever." Then another verse and response: "Let us bless the Father, and the Son with the Holy Spirit. Be praised and exalted above all things forever."

The concluding prayer is: "Almighty, ever-living God, who has permitted us your servants, in our profession of the true faith, to acknowledge the glory of the eternal Trinity, and in the power of that majesty to adore the Unity, grant that by steadfastness in this same faith, we may be ever guarded against all adversity: through Christ our Lord. Amen." Then all say: "Set us free, save us, vivify us, O Blessed Trinity!"

Why is this devotion called the Angelic *Trisagion*? The Greek word *trisagion* means "thrice holy." It refers especially to the threefold "Holy, holy, holy Lord, God of hosts" at the heart of the devotion. These words come from the prophet Isaiah, who saw a vision of the Lord sitting on a throne with the seraphim calling out: "Holy, holy, holy is the Lord of hosts; the whole earth is full of his glory" (*Is* 6:3). The same words come in the book of Revelation, where the four living creatures never cease to sing "Holy, holy, holy" to the Lord God almighty (cf. *Rev* 4:8). The liturgy of the Church takes up this praise of God in every Mass in the Sanctus, or Holy, holy, holy.

But why is it called the *Angelic* Trisagion, when there is no express mention of angels in any of the prayers? The answer undoubtedly comes in the fact that it is the angels, the seraphim, who cry out "Holy, holy, holy" in the prophecy of Isaiah, an image of their praise of God in heaven.

The praise of Christ, "Holy is God, Holy and strong, Holy Immortal One" is found in the Eastern liturgies, both Orthodox and Catholic, before the reading of the New Testament and in the Divine Office. It is also used in the liturgy of the Latin rite on Good Friday in the reproaches that may be recited during the adoration of the Cross.

So the *Trisagium* has a long history, going back to the Old Testament, and it expresses exalted praise of the Blessed Trinity. It can be found in many prayer books and even on apps for mobile phones. It is a beautiful devotion to use in families, parishes and other groups before the feast of the Blessed Trinity.

422 The *Akathistos* hymn

The Catechism of the Catholic Church *speaks of the* Akathistos *in connection with devotion to Our Lady. I had never heard of it. Can you tell me what it is?*

The Catechism mentions this prayer in Part Four, "Christian prayer", in Article Two on "The Way of Prayer". After commenting on the words of the Hail Mary the Catechism goes on to say: "Medieval piety in the West developed the prayer of the Rosary as a popular substitute for the Liturgy of the Hours. In the East, the litany called the *Akathistos* and the *Paraclesis* remained closer to the choral office in the Byzantine churches, while the Armenian, Coptic, and Syriac traditions preferred popular hymns and songs to the Mother of God" (*CCC* 2678).

Those of us familiar with Marian devotion in the Western tradition, with its emphasis on such devotions as the Rosary, the Angelus, the Memorare, etc., have probably never heard of the *Akathistos*. We are thus grateful to those who wrote the Catechism for including much material on the Eastern tradition, broadening our horizons and making us aware of a whole dimension of the Church of which we were quite unaware.

Returning to your question, the *Akathistos* is one of the most well known prayers or hymns to Mary in the Eastern tradition. It is chanted in Eastern Catholic and Orthodox Churches on the five Fridays of Lent, in preparation for Holy Week and the Easter services, as well as at other times. The hymn seems to have originated in the sixth century, and has been added to over the years. It is associated with a great favour attributed to Our Lady in Constantinople in the year 626. In that year, during the reign of the Emperor Heraclius, Constantinople was besieged by the Sassanid Persians and Avars, who came with a fleet of ships and over 80,000 soldiers. There were only some 12,000 soldiers to defend the city.

After several months of the siege, with the people of Constantinople becoming desperate, the Patriarch Sergius led a procession around the city carrying an icon of the Theotokos, the God-bearer Mary, praying for deliverance. According to the accounts, a great storm arose and in the huge waves most of the ships of the attackers were sunk and the enemy retreated. The people then spontaneously filled the Church of the Theotokos at Blarchernae and spent the night giving thanks to Our Lady, chanting praises including the *Akathistos* while standing. The name *Akathistos* in Greek means literally not seated. In the Eastern tradition the people always stand while reciting the prayer, as they do while listening to the Gospel.

The *Akathistos* is divided into four sections, corresponding to the themes of the Annunciation, the Nativity, Christ and finally the Theotokos herself. In Lent one part is used on each of the four first Friday evenings and the entire *Akathistos* is recited on the fifth Friday. The prayer consists of 24 stanzas, each consisting of a *Kontakion*, or prayer, followed by an *Oikos*, with responses of the people. The first word of each *Oikos* begins with a different letter of the Greek alphabet, from the first to the last.

The first *Kontakion* makes reference to Our Lady's power in defending the people: "Queen of the Heavenly Host, defender of our souls, we thy servants offer to thee songs of victory and thanksgiving, for thou, O Mother of God, hast delivered us from dangers. But as thou hast invincible power, free us from conflicts of all kinds that we may cry to thee." The people respond: "Rejoice, unwedded Bride!" This is followed by the *Oikos*, which says: "An Archangel was sent from Heaven to say to the Mother of God: Rejoice! And seeing Thee, O Lord, taking bodily form, he was amazed and with his bodiless voice he stood crying to her such things as these." The people respond with a series of chants, beginning: "Rejoice, thou through whom joy will flash forth! Rejoice, thou through whom the curse will cease! Rejoice, revival of fallen Adam!..."

Fr Vincent McNabb, who translated the hymn into English in London in 1934, wrote in his foreword that no apology was needed for introducing the *Akathistos* to the Christian West and, indeed, that the West might well be apologetic about its neglect, or ignorance of such a liturgical and literary masterpiece.

423 What is a litany?

A convert friend of mine recently asked me what a litany was and where they came from. How do I answer him?

As with so many questions I answer in this column, this one has led to the discovery of unsuspected riches in the treasure house that is the Catholic Church. But then again, when the Church has two thousand years of history and spans the entire globe, it is only natural that there should be a multitude of traditions of which many people are unaware.

For those unfamiliar with the name, a litany in general is a series of statements or prayers with some element of repetition. The word comes from the Greek word *litaneia*, meaning prayer or supplication. In the strict sense, it is a series of short petitions or exhortations said by one person or a group of persons, answered by a short response such as "Pray for us", "Deliver us, Lord" or "Lord, have mercy", said by the rest of the people.

Litanies have their origin in the Old Testament. For example, Psalm 136 is written in the form of a litany, with each phrase ending with "for his mercy endures for ever." Similarly, the prayer of the three young men in the fiery furnace is a litany, with each act of praise followed by "sing praise to him and highly exalt him for ever" (*Dan* 3:35 ff).

Litanies found their way into the liturgy in the East, around the fourth century in Antioch. From there they passed to Constantinople and the rest of the East and then to Rome and the West. They are an important feature of Eastern liturgy. The Divine Liturgies of St Basil, St John Chrysostom and St James have numerous litanies, as do other liturgical rites and the Divine Office.

Among the popular early litanies in the East were those in honour of Our Lady. They include the *Epitaphian Threnos* recalling Mary's suffering on Good Friday, associated with Symeon Metaphrastes; the dogmatic Canon of John Monachos Zonaras in honour of the *Panhagia Theotokos*; the "Canon to the Mother of God in time of imminent war", probably by John Mauropous; and the "Canon to the Theotokos" by Euthymos Monachos Synkellos, referring to the confession of a sinner.

Another early Marian prayer interspersed with litanies was the *Akathistos*.

In the West the word litany was very early associated with processions, often with prayers begging God for such causes as delivery from a plague, from war, etc. Thus in Rome there was a series of processions of the Pope, priests and people to a different station church each day for the celebration of Mass, especially in Lent. The *Litania Maior*, or Major Litany, was a procession with prayers for a successful harvest held in Rome each year on the feast of St Mark, 25 April.

The *Litania Minor*, or Minor Litany, was introduced in 477 by St Mamertus, Bishop of Vienne, before the feast of the Ascension of Our Lord into heaven, on account of the earthquakes and other afflictions at that time. These litanies were associated with what came to be called Rogation Days, or Ember Days (cf. J. Flader, *Question Time 2*, q. 277).

An example of a litany in the modern Mass is the "Lord, have mercy" in the penitential rite, with its repetition of "Lord, have mercy, Christ, have mercy". It was introduced into the Mass in the fifth century by Pope Gelasius I (492-496) and originally consisted of a three-fold recitation of each petition, in honour of the Blessed Trinity. The original language was Greek – *Kyrie eleison, Christe eleison, Kyrie eleison* – as it is in the Latin Mass today, pointing to its Eastern origins. Another litany is the Prayer of the Faithful, with its repeated "Lord, hear our prayer".

The more well-known litanies, properly so-called, are of relatively recent origin. The Litany of Loreto, which is said after the Rosary, was approved in 1587, and the Litany of the Saints, used in ordination ceremonies, was also in use at that time. Other officially approved litanies are those of the Holy Name of Jesus (approved in 1886), the Sacred Heart of Jesus (1899), St Joseph (1909) and the Precious Blood (1960).

The Divine Praises recited in Benediction with the Blessed Sacrament are another example of a prayer in the form of a litany, with its repetition of the word Blessed: "Blessed be God, Blessed be his Holy Name... So, as you can see, litanies have a long and rich history.

424 The Litany of Loreto

I like very much the litany to Our Lady that is often said after the Rosary but I am intrigued by where the Church got it. Who wrote it and for how long have we had it?

The litany you describe is known as the Litany of Loreto, because it was used at the shrine of Loreto in Italy at least since the year 1531. It was officially approved in 1587 by Pope Sixtus V. But its origin goes back to long before then. Some writers trace it back to the transporting of the Holy House from the Holy Land to Loreto in 1294, while others suggest an origin as far back as Pope St Gregory the Great at the end of the sixth century or Pope Sergius I (687).

The earliest known printed copy is that of Dillingen in Germany, dating from 1558. It bears the title "Order of the Litany of Our Lady as said every Saturday at Loreto" and it is the same text we have today with a few slight variations. It contains the invocation "Help of Christians", which does not appear in some other early copies of the litany. The Litany of Loreto clearly owes its inspiration to earlier litanies of Our Lady.

For example, there is a Marian litany in a twelfth-century codex in the Mainz Library in Germany with the title "Litany of Our Lady, Mother of God, the Virgin Mary: a truly good prayer, to be recited daily in any tribulation." The Mainz litany begins, as does the Litany of Loreto, with "Lord, have mercy" followed by invocations of the Blessed Trinity such as "God, the Father of heaven, who chose Mary ever Virgin, have mercy on us." It also contains, like the Litany of Loreto, prayers to Our Lady in her relationship with the patriarchs, prophets, apostles, martyrs, confessors and virgins, and has such invocations as "refuge of sinners" and "health of the sick". The litany concludes with a prayer to the Lamb of God, who takes away the sins of the world, like the Litany of Loreto.

Another early litany of Our Lady, dating from the late thirteenth or early fourteenth century, appears in a codex in the Library of St Mark in Venice. It has seventy-five invocations, all beginning with "Holy Mary", many of which are also in the Litany of Loreto with some variations. Among them are "Mother inviolate", "Queen of Heaven", "Mistress of the Angels", "Star of Heaven", "Gate of Paradise", "Mother of true Counsel", "Unfailing Rose" and "Immaculate Virgin." It too speaks of Mary in her relation with the patriarchs, prophets, apostles and martyrs.

While numerous other Marian litanies prior to that of Loreto are known, special mention should be made of one found in a manuscript of prayers, copied in 1524 by Fra Giovanni da Falerona. It has fifty-seven praises of Mary, many from earlier litanies and others new. The first ones address Mary as "Mother", then come some expressing her love for mankind, then the titles given to her in the Creeds, then those beginning with the title "Queen", which are identical to those in the Litany of Loreto. Two new titles are introduced as in the Litany of Loreto: "Cause of our joy" and "Spiritual vessel". Thus the Litany of Loreto is clearly based on these earlier litanies going back at least four hundred years.

While the Litany of Loreto is well known, it is perhaps useful to remind ourselves of its structure and content. It begins with "Lord, have mercy", "Christ, have mercy", and then asks the three divine Persons and the Blessed Trinity to have mercy on us. These prayers are followed by three invocations highlighting Mary's holiness, twelve addressing her as Mother, six addressing her as Virgin, thirteen calling her by various symbolic titles taken mostly from the Old Testament, four extolling her as our advocate in works of mercy, and finally thirteen invoking her as Queen. These are followed by three petitions to the Lamb of God.

Over the years new titles of Our Lady have been added by the Popes: "Queen of the most Holy Rosary" in 1675, "Queen conceived without original sin" in 1883, "Mother of good counsel" in 1903, "Queen of peace" in 1917, "Queen assumed into heaven" in 1950, "Mother of the Church" by Pope John Paul II in 1980 and "Queen of the family" by the same Pope in 1995. While we can't say who wrote this litany or its predecessors, it expresses deep Marian piety and filial trust in the Mother of God. It is good to say it after the Rosary whenever possible.

425 The Litany of the Saints

I have attended various functions in which the Litany of the Saints was used, but each time with different saints. Is there a standard form of this litany, and what is its origin?

Like the Litany of Loreto, the Litany of the Saints has been in use for a long time. In fact it goes back to the early Church. It is one of the oldest prayers in continuous use, with different versions of it dating from the third century in the East. There is historical evidence of litanies invoking the saints at the time of St Gregory the Wonderworker, who died around the year 270, and St Basil, who died in 379.

In the West, the saints were invoked in the litany used in the procession of St Mamertus, Bishop of Vienne, in 477, beseeching God for help at a time of earthquakes and other calamities. Through a decree of the Council of Orleans in 511 the devotion then spread to the rest of France. At the end of the sixth century, a litany of the saints was used in the *Litania Septiformis* of Pope Gregory the Great, a procession through Rome in 590 following the flood and pestilence that swept the city. By that time, the Litany of the Saints had substantially the form it has today.

It is understandable that when the faithful wanted to obtain special favours from God, they would call upon the saints in heaven to intercede for them, naming them one by one. This early prayer to the saints is thus part of the Tradition of the Church. It shows the lack of substance in the Protestant objection to this custom, based largely on scriptural passages including St Paul's statement that there is only one mediator between God and man, Jesus Christ, himself a man (cf. *1 Tim* 2:5).

As with other litanies, it is not known exactly when or by whom the Litany of the Saints was composed. But the order in which the Apostles are named, corresponding to that of the Roman Canon of the Mass, is proof of its antiquity. The Roman Canon can be traced back to the fourth century, and it was given its present form during the pontificate of Pope Gregory the Great.

At the present time, the Litany of the Saints is prescribed on various occasions, among them the ordination of deacons, priests and bishops, and in the Easter Vigil prior to Baptism. A very abbreviated form is used in the Rite of Baptism of children.

The original official version of the Litany is very long and much more involved than the versions used in most ceremonies today. It begins with "Lord, have mercy; Christ, have mercy; Lord, have mercy" and then calls upon Christ twice to hear us, and then on the Father, Son and Holy Spirit and finally the Blessed Trinity to have mercy on us. Then, following the traditional "hierarchy" of the saints in heaven, it calls upon the Blessed Virgin Mary under various titles to pray for us. This is followed by the invocation of the three Archangels and then all the angels.

The first saints to be invoked are St Joseph, St John the Baptist and all the patriarchs and prophets. They are followed by St Peter, St Paul, and then all the other Apostles and Evangelists, one by one. Next come the martyrs of the early Church, then Fathers, Doctors and Bishops of the early centuries. These are followed by other early saints including St Anthony, St Benedict, St Bernard, St Dominic and St Francis, the latest saints being from the thirteenth century. Then come holy women saints, starting with St Mary Magdalene and early martyrs.

After the invocation of the saints comes a long series of petitions to be delivered from various forms of evil, then petitions that God will grant a series of blessings, and finally petitions to the Lamb of God to have mercy on us and Christ to hear us. The Litany concludes with a long prayer, or series of prayers, begging God for mercy and favours.

The Litany of the Saints, as recited in various ceremonies today, is much shorter and may have petitions specific to the occasion. Also, newer saints and blesseds may be added, including those most recently canonised, according to the wishes of those organising the ceremony. This is why the list of saints can be so varied. In summary, the Litany of the Saints is a beautiful expression of faith in the powerful intercession of the saints for all our needs, and it takes us back to the early centuries of the Church.

Seasons and Feast Days

426 The Advent wreath

In recent years I have seen more and more Advent wreaths, both in homes and in churches. Is this just a nice decoration like a wreath on a door, or does it have some spiritual meaning?

For those who may not know, an Advent wreath is a ring of greenery, preferably from an evergreen tree, with four candles. Usually three of the candles are purple and one rose. One of the purple candles is lit on the first Sunday of Advent, this one plus another one on the second Sunday, these two plus the rose one on the third Sunday, and all four on the fourth Sunday.

The wreath may have its origin in pre-Christian times when people in northern Europe used wreaths with lit candles in the dark, cold months of winter as a sign of life and of hope in the coming warmth and light of spring. Advent wreaths have been used by Christians since at least the Middle Ages. By the end of the sixteenth century both Catholics and Lutherans in northern Europe had formal practices associated with them.

The wreath is rich with symbolism. For example, the evergreen boughs can be seen as a symbol of everlasting life. The fir tree, such as the pine or spruce, is green even in the winter and can therefore be a symbol of the everlasting life that Christ brought to the world. This is seen in the popular German Christmas carol "O Tannenbaum" ("O Christmas Tree"), which speaks of the truth, or faithfulness, of the tree's needles, which are green not only in the summer but also in the winter. Another verse speaks of the "clothes" or needles of the tree teaching us of hope and steadfastness, and providing comfort and strength at any time. This can aptly refer to the long years of hopeful waiting for the Messiah, who brings us comfort and strength.

The fact that the wreath is round and unending also speaks of everlasting life, or eternity, brought by Christ. The four candles represent the four Sundays of Advent. The length of Advent can vary, depending on which day of the week Christmas falls, but it always begins on a Sunday and comprises the four Sundays before Christmas plus whatever number of days remain until Christmas.

As regards their colour, in the Catholic tradition the vestments worn by the priest in Mass during Advent are purple, except for the third Sunday, when they may be rose, or pink. For this reason the candles have the same colours, and the rose candle is lit on the third Sunday. The colour purple, which is also used in Lent, symbolises the prayer, penance and good works carried out in preparation for the coming of Christ. Rose is a joyful colour and is used on the third Sunday of Advent, also called "Gaudete" (Rejoice) Sunday. The Entrance Antiphon for this Sunday begins with the word "Rejoice", taken from St Paul's letter to the Philippians: "Rejoice in the Lord always; again I say, rejoice" (*Phil* 4:4). We rejoice on this Sunday because we are now beginning the second half of Advent and we are drawing closer to Christmas.

The light given off by the candles symbolises the light brought by Christ, who is "the light of the world" (*Jn* 8:12). As the candles are progressively lit on the four Sundays, this light increases, symbolising Christ drawing ever nearer.

The Church recognises the Advent wreath officially in its *Book of Blessings,* which contains a blessing for the wreath, to be carried out on the first Sunday of Advent. One of the blessings provided asks that the light of the candles may reflect the splendour of Christ, and another asks that the wreath and its light may be a sign of Christ's promise to bring us salvation.

And the Vatican's *Directory on Popular Piety and the Liturgy* says that the wreath, with the progressive lighting of its four candles, "is a recollection of the various stages of salvation history prior to Christ's coming and a symbol of the prophetic light gradually illuminating the long night prior to the rising of the Sun of Justice" (cf. *Mal* 4:2; *Lk* 1:78); n. 98).

All in all, the Advent wreath is a beautiful custom and it is much to be encouraged. It focuses our attention on the very heart of the season, on the coming of Christ who brings light and everlasting life, and thus helps us avoid becoming distracted by the more material aspects of the preparation for Christmas.

427 Why is Christmas so important?

Recently my five year-old son asked me why Christmas is so important and while I think I gave him some good answers I suspect there may be more. How would you answer him?

Actually, the *Catechism of the Catholic Church* answers your son's question under the heading "Why did the Word become flesh?" It is a somewhat more sophisticated way of putting it but in the end it is the same question. Christmas is important because it celebrates the birth into the world of the Word of God, the second person of the Blessed Trinity, and his birth brought many blessings. Many centuries ago St Anselm (1033-1109) wrote a whole treatise on the question entitled *Cur Deus Homo? – Why the God man?*, so it is a question that has been thought about down the ages.

Before we look at the answers the Catechism gives we should remind ourselves that the child Jesus lying in the manger is not just one more child – he is God the Word who has become man. As Pope Benedict XVI says in his Apostolic Exhortation *Verbum Domini,* "'The Lord made his word short, he abbreviated it' (*Is* 10:23; *Rom* 9:28) ... The Son himself is the Word, the *Logos*: the eternal word became small – small enough to fit into a manger... Now the word is not simply audible; not only does it have a *voice,* now the word has a *face,* one which we can see: that of Jesus of Nazareth" (n. 12).

Returning to your son's question about why Jesus' birth is so important, we find the first and most important answer in the Creed we say in Mass on Sundays: "For us men and for our salvation he came down from heaven, and by the Holy Spirit was incarnate of the Virgin Mary, and became man." That is, Jesus came to us in that first Christmas for our salvation – to redeem us from original sin and from our personal sins. In the words of the Catechism, "The Word became flesh for us *in order to save us by reconciling us with God,* who 'loved us and sent his Son to be the expiation for our sins': 'the Father has sent his Son as the Saviour of the world,' and 'he was revealed to take away sins'" (*1 Jn* 4:10, 4:14, 3:5; *CCC* 457).

The second reason for the Word becoming flesh is "so that we might know God's love" (*CCC* 458). We know that God loves us but it is especially in his becoming man and living among us that we see the love of God made visible. St John writes: "In this the love of God was made manifest among us, that God sent his only Son into the world, so that we might live through him" (*1 Jn* 4:9). And Our Lord said to Nicodemus, "For God so loved the world that he gave his only Son, that whoever believes in him should not perish but have eternal life" (*Jn* 3:16). Truly Christmas is a great manifestation of God's love for mankind. The infant lying in the manger is God in the flesh, God who so loved us that he became man and dwelt amongst us in order to redeem us by his death on the cross. And by coming into the world as a new-born infant he is easy to love in return. Christmas is a good time to grow in love for Jesus.

The third reason for the Word becoming flesh is "to be our model of holiness" (*CCC* 459). We are all called to holiness, to be saints in our own state in life, but how do we achieve this? What is the model we are to imitate? The model is Jesus Christ himself, "perfect God and perfect man", as we say in the Athanasian Creed. Just as many people have a hero that they try to imitate, studying their way of being and mannerisms in order to imitate them and be more like their hero, so our hero is Jesus Christ. We make the effort to get to know him better by reading the Scriptures and other books about him, so that we can become more like him, more Christ-like. He is the model of holiness. He himself said, "Learn from me" (*Mt* 11:29), and "I am the way, and the truth, and the life" (*Jn* 14:6).

The fourth reason why the Word became flesh was "to make us 'partakers of the divine nature'" (*2 Pet* 1:4; *CCC* 460). That is, by assuming our human nature, and making us members of his Mystical Body through Baptism, Jesus allows us to share in the divine nature. Many Fathers of the Church express this truth, each one in slightly different words. For example, St Athanasius says: "For the Son of God became man so that we might become God" (*De inc.* 54, 3; *CCC* 460).

As we see in these four reasons, Christmas is very important. It is truly a feast to be celebrated for the many lessons it teaches us and the benefits it brings.

428 Nativity scenes

My daughter came home from school recently saying that it was St Francis of Assisi who had first built a nativity scene. Is this true? Also, is it appropriate to put the child Jesus in the crib before Christmas?

Yes, St Francis was responsible for the first nativity scene, in Greccio, Italy, in the year 1223. The mind of St Francis was to portray the birth of Christ so that the scene would enter through the senses.

Thomas of Celano, in the first book of his biography of St Francis, describes the events. About two weeks before Christmas St Francis called his good friend Giovanni Vellita, a local land owner, and said to him: "If you want us to celebrate the present feast of our Lord at Greccio, go with haste and diligently prepare what I tell you. For I wish to do something that will recall to memory the little Child who was born in Bethlehem and set before our bodily eyes in some way the inconveniences of his infant needs, how he lay in a manager, how, with an ox and an ass standing by, he lay upon the hay where he had been placed."

Giovanni prepared everything as the saint had requested, with live animals and humans, except for the child Jesus, made out of wood. The biography relates how many people from the surrounding area came to the nativity scene on Christmas Eve carrying candles and torches which lit up the night. An ox and an ass were led in, and a figure of the child Jesus lay on the hay. Finally St Francis himself arrived, dressed in his robes of a deacon. He saw the scene and was overjoyed. "The saint of God stood before the manger, uttering sighs, overcome with love, and filled with a wonderful happiness." Mass was then celebrated over the manger and St Francis sang the Gospel and preached "charming words concerning the nativity of the poor king and the little town of Bethlehem."

Scenes like this soon became popular throughout Christendom. Within a hundred years every church in Italy was expected to have a nativity scene at Christmas, with statues eventually replacing live participants. The scenes were often very elaborate, with richly robed figures placed in intricate landscape settings.

Nativity scenes then spread from churches into homes, where they are still very popular. In an Angelus message in Advent 2005 Pope Benedict XVI spoke of their value: "To set up the crib at home can be a simple but effective way of presenting the faith and transmitting it to one's children. The manger helps us to contemplate the mystery of God's love who revealed himself in the poverty and simplicity of the Bethlehem cave."

He spoke of St Francis' living nativity scene, which made him "the initiator of a long popular tradition which still keeps its value for evangelization today. The crib can help us, in fact, to understand the secret of the true Christmas, because it speaks of humility and the merciful goodness of Christ, who 'though he was rich, yet for your sake he became poor' (2 *Cor* 8:9). His poverty enriches those who embrace it and Christmas brings joy and peace to those who, as the shepherds, accept in Bethlehem the words of the angel: 'And this will be a sign for you: you will find an infant wrapped in swaddling clothes and lying in a manger'" (*Lk* 2:12).

On Gaudete Sunday, 14 December 2008, Pope Benedict commented, "Standing before the crèche, we will be able to taste Christian joy, contemplating in the new-born Jesus the face of God who out of love made himself close to us".

As regards when to place the Christ child in the manger, this is up to each parish and family. There is no official norm. Many prefer to wait until Christmas Eve, praying "Come, Lord Jesus" (*Rev* 22:20) or some other prayer when they see that the child is not there. Others place the child when they set up the crib. Some also live the custom of having the figures of the wise men gradually approach the stable so as to arrive on the feast of Epiphany. One beautiful custom is for children to place a piece of hay or straw in the manger every time they do a good deed during Advent, so that at Christmas the baby Jesus will have a soft bed on which to lie.

The Vatican's *Directory on Popular Piety and the Liturgy* says of nativity scenes: "Their preparation, in which children play a significant role, is an occasion for the members of the family to come into contact with the mystery of Christmas, as they gather for a moment of prayer or to read the biblical accounts of the Lord's birth" (n. 104).

429 The feast of St Stephen

I have always been intrigued by the fact that on the day after Christmas, December 26, the Church celebrates the feast of St Stephen, martyr. There must be some reason for this, and friends have asked me about it, but I am at a loss. Can you help me?

First, a few words about St Stephen. He was a Jew of Greek background – his name in Greek means "crown" – who was probably born somewhere outside Palestine in a place where Greek was spoken, and who later went to Jerusalem.

The *Acts of the Apostles* tell how the Jews of Hellenist, or Greek, background, felt that their widows were being neglected in the distribution of alms, moving the Apostles to have seven men selected by the disciples to dedicate themselves to looking after the poor. The first one mentioned is Stephen, who is described as "a man full of faith and of the Holy Spirit" (*Acts* 6:5).

The *Acts* go on to describe how St Stephen became the first Christian martyr. When certain Jews accused Stephen of blasphemy against Moses and God, he was brought before the council of the Jews. There he explained in a long discourse how Jesus was the promised Messiah, but the Jews had killed him as they had killed the prophets in earlier times (cf. *Acts* 6:11-7:53). Enraged, they took Stephen outside the city and stoned him to death, laying down their garments at the feet of Saul, who would later become St Paul (cf. *Acts* 7:58-60).

Returning to your question, why does the Church celebrate the martyrdom of St Stephen on the very day after the celebration of the birth of Christ? In the absence of an authoritative statement from the Church, one can only speculate.

To begin with, the celebration of the feast on this day is very ancient. The second reading in the Office of Readings of the breviary for the feast is from St Fulgentius of Ruspe, who died around the year 532. In a sermon on the feast, St Fulgentius relates Christmas and the feast of St Stephen: "Yesterday we celebrated the birth in time of our eternal king; today we celebrate the triumphant death of a soldier. Yesterday our king put on the robe of flesh, and coming out of the court of the virgin's womb, deigned to visit the earth. Today a soldier leaves the earthly tabernacle of his body, and goes up in triumph to heaven...

The love then that brought Christ down from heaven to earth, lifted Stephen from earth to heaven."

Another possible explanation for the date goes back to the ancient custom of distributing food and other gifts to the poor on the day after Christmas. Since one of the roles of deacons, like St Stephen, was precisely to distribute alms to the poor, his feast may have been assigned to this date for that reason. In any case, the popular Christmas carol "Good King Wenceslaus", written around 1850, makes mention of the Bohemian king, who ruled in the early tenth century, going out in the snow to give alms to a poor man on the feast of St Stephen: "Good King Wenceslaus looked out on the feast of Stephen, when the snow lay round about, deep and crisp and even. Brightly shone the moon that night, though the frost was cruel, when a poor man came in sight, gathering winter fuel."

St Wenceslaus called his servant to go out with him to take food and drink to the poor man: "Bring me food and bring me wine, bring me pine logs hither. You and I will see him dine, when we bear them thither." The carol uses the melody of a much earlier thirteenth century song about Spring, *Tempus adest floridum*. It had some verses, written in the ninth century, referring to martyrs and was sung on the feast of St Stephen and other martyrs: "Joy that martyrs won their crown, opened heaven's bright portal, when they laid the mortal down, for the life immortal."

St Stephen's day is commonly known as "Boxing Day" in the United Kingdom and other Commonwealth countries. The name may refer to the practice of the wealthy "boxing up" food and other gifts for their servants and the poor on the day after Christmas. Also, it was on that day that the alms box in English churches was opened and the contents distributed to the poor.

In any case we do well to heed the last verse of "Good King Wenceslaus: "Therefore, Christian men, be sure, wealth or rank possessing, you who now will bless the poor shall yourselves find blessing."

430 The feast of the Holy Innocents

I have always been intrigued by King Herod ordering the killing of all boys under the age of two after the birth of Christ. What made him fearful about the birth of Our Lord, why would he order the killing of all those under two and why do we celebrate this massacre?

The events to which you refer are related in the Gospel of St Matthew: "Now when Jesus was born in Bethlehem of Judea in the days of Herod the king, behold, Wise Men from the East came to Jerusalem, saying, 'Where is he who has been born king of the Jews? For we have seen his star in the East, and have come to worship him.' When Herod the king heard this, he was troubled, and all Jerusalem with him..." (*Mt* 2:1-3). Herod then asked the leaders of the Jews where the Christ was to be born and, following the teaching of the prophet Micah (cf. *Mic* 5:2), they told him in Bethlehem, so he sent the Wise Men off to that city, telling them to come back to tell him where they had found the child. Sometime later, when the Wise Men did not return, Herod "was in a furious rage, and he sent and killed all the male children in Bethlehem and in all that region who were two years old or under, according to the time which he had ascertained from the Wise Men" (*Mt* 2:16).

What made Herod so fearful? This was Herod the Great, the first of four Herods who appear in the New Testament. He was born in 73 BC, the son of non-Jewish parents, and died in 4 BC. He had curried the favour of Octavian, who later became the emperor Augustus Caesar, and it was through him that the Roman Senate appointed Herod King of Judea, a position he held for 37 years. He practised the Jewish faith but was not considered Jewish by the Pharisees.

Herod had a persecution complex and saw rivals to his throne everywhere. He was notorious for his cruelty and killed over half of his ten wives, some of his children and various high ranking people. These facts come largely from Flavius Josephus, a Jewish historian who wrote at the end of the first century, and they confirm what is related in the Gospels. This makes it understandable that Herod would regard the "King of the Jews", as the Wise Men reported to him, a threat to his rule, even though this new King was just an infant.

Why did he have all the boys under two years of age put to death? As St Matthew records, he did it "according to the time which he had ascertained from the Wise Men" (*Mt* 2:16). One can surmise that the Wise Men told Herod they had first seen the star over a year before they arrived in Jerusalem, and that Herod would have waited some months for the Wise Men to return to him before he ordered the massacre. Just to be sure, he probably added some months to his calculations and so the period came to two years.

Why do we celebrate this tragic event in the liturgy? The answer is that the Church regards these infants as the first martyrs to give their lives for Christ. Their death is considered a Baptism of blood, which brought their justification and salvation. St Thomas Aquinas comments: "How can it be said that they died for Christ, since they could not use their freedom? ... God would not have allowed that massacre if it had not been of benefit to those children. St Augustine says that to doubt that the massacre was of benefit to those children is the same as doubting that Baptism is of use to children. For the Holy Innocents suffered as martyrs and confessed Christ *non loquendo sed moriendo*, not by speaking but by dying" (*Comm. on St Matt.*, 2,16).

The feast of the Holy Innocents has been celebrated in the West since at least the fifth century, where it appears in the Leonine Sacramentary around 485. It is celebrated on December 28, in the octave of Christmas, as is the feast of St Stephen, who also gave his life for Christ. Today the feast is often associated with the important work of protecting human life from the moment of conception.

431 Epiphany and the magi

My daughter and son attended World Youth Day 2005 in Cologne and came back saying they had visited the tomb of the three wise men in the Cathedral there. Frankly, this sounded far-fetched. What do we know about the three kings, or magi, that came to adore Our Lord?

These men are known commonly by three quite different names: magi, wise men, and kings. What do we know about them? First of all, that they existed and that they did go from the East to adore the Christ child. St Matthew records the event: "Now when Jesus was born in Bethlehem of Judea in the days of Herod the king, behold, Wise Men from the East came to Jerusalem, saying, 'Where is he who has been born king of the Jews? For we have seen his star in the East, and have come to worship him'" (*Mt* 2:1-2). These men were obviously not of the Jewish people and yet they were mysteriously moved to travel from a distant land somewhere in the East to worship the newly born king of the Jews.

The Greek version of St Matthew's Gospel calls them *magoi*, which we usually render in English as magi, or wise men. The word is sometimes used in the Bible to refer to magicians (cf. *Acts* 8:9; 13:6, 8), but it more likely refers to a caste of priests among the ancient people known as the Medes. They were credited with having profound religious knowledge, including astrology, whence the name "wise men".

It seems that after some magi attached to the court proved to be expert in the interpretation of dreams, Darius the Great established them over the state religion of Persia. Thus the magi became the supreme priestly caste of the Persian empire but they also enjoyed secular powers. We see this in the prophet Jeremiah's account of the fall of Jerusalem to Nebuchadnezzar, king of Babylon. Jeremiah calls Nergal-sharezer, one of the "princes" who served the king, the "Rabmag", or chief of the magi (cf. *Jer* 39:3, 13). This was a predominantly civil or military role.

Later, when the Jews were taken to Babylon, King Nebuchadnezzar made the prophet Daniel the Rab-mag, or "chief of the magi" (cf. *Dan* 5:11; 4:9). Even though their power ebbed and flowed in the following centuries, at the time of Christ there was a magi priesthood in Media, Persia, Assyria, and Babylon. So it is likely that the magi who came to worship Christ were from one of these nations.

Although the magi are sometimes referred to as the three kings, there is no historical evidence that they were kings. None of the Fathers of the Church calls them kings, although Tertullian does refer to them in Latin as *fere reges*, which translates as "almost kings" (cf *Adv. Marcion*, III, 13). The fact that the Mass for the feast of Epiphany uses Psalm 72:10, which says, "May the kings of Tarshish and of the isles render him tribute, may the kings of Sheba and Seba bring gifts!", does not mean that the Church is calling the wise men kings. The psalm, which is clearly messianic, simply expresses very appropriately what the magi were doing.

How many magi went to worship Our Lord? St Matthew does not give us the number but it has become traditional in the West to say there were three, undoubtedly based on the three gifts of gold, frankincense and myrrh. In the East, tradition favours twelve.

Neither does St Matthew give us their names. Nonetheless, in the West from the seventh century on they have been commonly called Gaspar, Melchior and Balthasar.

There is a tradition that after their return home the magi were baptised by St Thomas and did much to spread the faith, dying as martyrs. The Martyrology, or list of the saints, includes their names in the month of January: St Gaspar on January 1, St Melchior on January 6 and St Balthasar on January 11. The cathedral of Cologne contains what are claimed to be the remains of the magi. According to the tradition the remains were discovered in Persia, brought to Constantinople by St Helena, taken to Milan in the fifth century and finally laid to rest in Cologne in 1163.

432 The spirit of Easter

I always look forward to Easter after the long season of Lent, but fear I do not appreciate the season in all its fullness as I do in Lent. What should I be thinking or doing at this time?

This is a good question, which reveals a desire to live your spiritual life attuned to the spirit of the Church. I think many of us have a real and practical sense of how to live Lent but then we fail to appreciate the richness of the season of Easter.

The Easter season, by the way, extends from Easter Sunday through to Pentecost Sunday, a total of seven full weeks. During this time we say the Regina Caeli instead of the Angelus at noon or at other times of the day (cf. J. Flader, *Question Time 1,* q. 130). So here we have a very practical way to live the Easter season, rejoicing with the Blessed Virgin over the resurrection of her divine Son.

Another practical reminder of Easter is the frequent use of "Alleluia" in the liturgy. As I explained in an earlier column (cf. *Question Time 2,* q. 268), the word in Hebrew means "Praise the Lord" and it is used frequently during the Easter season to praise and thank God for redeeming us through the death and resurrection of Christ. St Augustine comments: "So now, my brethren, I urge you to praise God: this is what we all say to one another when we say Alleluia. 'Praise the Lord,' you say to the one you are addressing, and he says the same to you; and by urging one another in this way, people do what they are urging the other to do. Praise God with the whole of yourselves; it is not only your tongue and your voice that should praise him, but your conscience, your life, your deeds" (*On Psalm 148,* 1-2).

Another beautiful way to live Easter is the Eastern custom of greeting another person with the words, "Christ is risen", to which the other answers, "He is risen indeed" or "Truly, he is risen". The more common greeting in the West is of course simply "Happy Easter".

St Augustine explains that the Easter season looks forward to the joy of eternal life in heaven: "We celebrate two seasons, one before Easter and one after. The season before Easter signifies the tribulation in which we now live; the present season after Easter signifies the happiness which will be ours hereafter. What we celebrate before Easter, we already experience; what we celebrate after Easter signifies that we do not yet possess what we celebrate. And so we keep the season before Easter in fasting and prayer; but in the present season we relax our fast and devote ourselves to praise. This is the meaning of the Alleluia which we sing" (*On Ps 148,* 1-2).

Following St Augustine's suggestion, we do well during this time to raise our hearts and minds often from the earthly joy of the resurrection to the eternal happiness that awaits us in heaven. St Paul invites us to do this: "If then you have been raised with Christ, seek the things that are above, where Christ is seated at the right hand of God. Set your minds on things that are above, not on things that are on earth. For you have died, and your life is hidden with Christ in God. When Christ who is our life appears, then you also will appear with him in glory" (*Col* 3:1-4).

Apart from joy, another great theme of the Easter season is hope, typified by the experience of the two disciples of Emmaus. Like the apostles and holy women, they were devastated when the one they had hoped would redeem Israel died on the cross. Their whole life revolved around following Jesus and now he was dead. As a result, they left Jerusalem, full of sadness. On the way, "Jesus himself drew near and went with them. But their eyes were kept from recognising him" (*Lk* 24:15-16). A short time later they recognise him in the breaking of the bread and, overjoyed, return immediately to Jerusalem where Jesus appears to all the apostles, to their overwhelming joy. We should never lose hope in the midst of our difficulties. Sadness can turn into joy. God is with us.

Pope Francis comments in his homily on Easter Sunday, 2013: "Are we often weary, disheartened and sad? Do we feel weighed down by our sins? Do we think that we won't be able to cope? Let us not close our hearts, let us not lose confidence, let us never give up: there are no situations which God cannot change, there is no sin which he cannot forgive if only we open ourselves to him."

Let us live always, not only at Easter, in the hope and joy of knowing that God is with us, that he can turn sadness into joy, that Christ has risen and he awaits us in heaven.

433 The date of Easter

Why is it that the date for the Catholic celebration of Easter and that of the Orthodox are different and is anything being done to celebrate on the same day?

There is a very interesting history to your question. In the early Church in some places, especially the Roman province of Asia, the date of Easter was determined in conjunction with the Jewish feast of Passover, which was celebrated on the fourteenth day of the lunar month of Nisan, the day of the full moon. Easter was celebrated on that day so that it could fall on any day of the week. In other places, especially Rome and Alexandria, Easter was always celebrated on the Sunday following the Jewish Passover.

In the second century several synods were held to resolve the matter and, according to the early historian Eusebius, they all ruled in favour of celebrating Easter on a Sunday. Council of Nicaea in 325 determined, among other things, that the Church would no longer follow the Jewish calendar and that Easter was to be celebrated on a common day throughout the world. The Council did not say what that day was to be but at the time Easter was celebrated on a Sunday virtually everywhere.

In 725 AD the English monk St Bede wrote that Easter was to be celebrated on the Sunday following the full moon which falls on or after the Spring equinox. This is the formula that is now followed. The equinox is the day twice a year on which the sun passes over the equator and so there are equal periods of day and night all over the world, hence the name equinox, or equal night. While this day in the northern Spring can fall on March 19, 20 or 21, to facilitate in advance the determination of the date of Easter the Church fixed it as March 21 and so Easter was always celebrated after that.

Since different formulas were used in different places to calculate the exact date of the full moon, it took some centuries before East and West were finally able to agree on a common date for Easter. By the end of the eighth century the Christian world was united in its celebration, with Easter falling anytime between March 22 and April 25.

In 1582 that was to change. Until then the whole Roman world was following the Julian calendar, which had been introduced by the Emperor Julius Caesar in 46 BC. That calendar had a year of 365 days divided into 12 months, with an extra day added in February every four years. A year therefore had 365.25 days. The calendar did not allow for the fact that the real astronomical year is a few minutes shorter than 365.25 days, even though this had been known since the time of the Greek astronomer Hipparchus, who died around 120 BC. As a result the calendar gained about three days every four centuries compared to what was observed astronomically.

To correct this, Pope Gregory XIII in 1582 reformed the calendar, removing ten days, so that Thursday, 4 October in the Julian calendar was followed by Friday, 15 October in the new Gregorian calendar. While the West on the whole adopted the Gregorian calendar, the Orthodox Christian Churches continued after 1582 to follow the Julian calendar. As a result their dates were initially ten days later than those of the Gregorian calendar and at present they are thirteen days later.

Another important difference between the Churches is that while the Catholic Church determines the day of the full moon and of the equinox by definition, not astronomically, most of the Eastern Churches follow the astronomical full moon and equinox as they occur in Jerusalem. As a result, even though the Orthodox Easter is usually after the Western one, in some years it may coincide.

To agree on a common date, in recent years there has been dialogue between the Catholic Church, the Coptic Orthodox Pope, the Ecumenical Patriarch of Constantinople and the Archbishop of Canterbury. They have expressed the hope that a common date can be agreed upon relatively soon. We can pray for this to come about, as a gesture of good will and as a step towards eventual reunion of at least some of these Churches with Rome.

434 The Jewish feast of Pentecost

I have always been intrigued by the fact that the Holy Spirit came down on the apostles on the Jewish feast of Pentecost. What exactly was this feast and is there any connection between it and our celebration of the coming of the Holy Spirit?

This is indeed an intriguing question and I am happy to answer it. It is good for all Catholics to know the history and customs of the Jewish people, since they are our ancestors in the faith. After all, Jesus, Mary and Joseph formed part of the Jewish people. The Old Testament prepares for the New and contains numerous prophecies of Christ. We recall how Jesus, "beginning with Moses and all the prophets" explained to the two disciples of Emmaus "in all the Scriptures the things concerning himself" (*Lk* 24:27). It is in the Old Testament that we find the answer to your question.

As you say, the day on which the Holy Spirit came down on the apostles was the Jewish feast of Pentecost, which had brought to Jerusalem "Jews, devout men from every nation under heaven" (*Acts* 2:5). What were the Jews celebrating on that day and why was it called Pentecost? The name Pentecost is Greek, meaning fiftieth, and it was the name given to the Jewish feast by the Greek-speaking Jews. On that day the Jews were celebrating two different events.

The first and original feast celebrated the end of the harvest (cf. *Ex* 23:16) and so it was called *Hag ha-Bikkurim* (the Festival of the First Fruits). It was also known as *Shavu'ot*, the Festival of Weeks (cf. *Ex* 34:22; *Deut* 16:10). For that feast, as for the Passover and for another harvest feast at the end of the year, all males were to present themselves before the Lord (cf. *Ex* 23:17; 34:23). This explains why so many people from all over that part of the world were in Jerusalem.

But why was the harvest feast also called Pentecost, and what does it have to do with the number fifty? The answer is found in the book of Leviticus. There God tells the Israelites that once they entered the promised land they were to bring a sheaf of the first fruits of their harvest to the priest and wave it before God on the day after the Sabbath, that is on Sunday. He goes on: "And you shall count from the day after the Sabbath, from the day that you brought the sheaf of the wave offering; seven full weeks shall they be, counting fifty days to the day after the seventh Sabbath; then you shall present a cereal offering of new grain to the Lord" (*Lev* 23:10-15). Because it was celebrated fifty days after the wave offering it was called Pentecost, and because it was seven weeks afterward it was also called the Festival of Weeks.

The feast was celebrated on a Sunday, the day on which we celebrate it today. And it was to be celebrated for all time: "And you shall make proclamation on the same day; you shall hold a holy convocation; you shall do no laborious work; it is a statute for ever in all your dwellings throughout your generations" (*Lev* 23:21). In fact the Jews continue to celebrate *Shavu'ot* to this day.

Although the text from Leviticus does not say so expressly, the Sabbath of the wave offering was the first one after the celebration of Passover, so that the fiftieth day closed both the harvest season and the Passover season. This is significant for us today as our feast of Pentecost closes the Paschal, or Easter, season, just as it did for the Jews.

The second event celebrated in the Jewish Pentecost feast was the giving of the Torah, or the Law, to Moses on Mount Sinai. For this reason it was called *Hag Matan Torateinu* (the Festival of the Giving of our Torah). According to the book of Exodus (cf. *Ex* 19:1), God gave Moses the Law on Mount Sinai fifty days after the first Passover, when the Israelites left Egypt. The Jews see a close connection between the Passover and the giving of the Law. Just as in the Passover they were freed from over 400 years of slavery in Egypt, so the Torah freed them spiritually from their slavery to idolatry and immorality. On the night before the feast it is customary for the Jews to stay up the entire night studying the Torah and then to pray as early as possible in the morning.

Why did the Holy Spirit come down on the apostles precisely on this feast? Without presuming to know the mind of God, we can see some reasons. Just as the giving of the Torah made the Israelites the people of God with a new religion, so the coming of the Holy Spirit gave "birth" to the Church of the new people of God. And just as the Jewish Pentecost closes the Passover season, so the coming of the Holy Spirit closes our Paschal or Easter season. Finally, the offering of the first fruits of the harvest to God by the Jews is replaced by the offering of the first fruits of the spiritual harvest on Pentecost, when some three thousand were converted that very day (cf. *Acts* 2:41).

435 The Octave of Prayer for Christian Unity

In my parish we have special prayers before Pentecost for the Octave of Christian Unity. I have never fully understood what this is about. Is it something new?

The Octave of Prayer for Christian Unity is a week of prayer for the union of all Christian denominations in the one Church of Jesus Christ. An octave, in this sense, is a period of eight days, beginning on a particular day of the week and ending on the same day the following week. The Octave of Prayer for Christian Unity is a response to Our Lord's prayer to the Father in the Last Supper "that they may be one, even as we are one" (*Jn* 17:11, 22). Christ founded only one Church and he wanted all his followers to be united, even as he was united with the Father (cf. *Jn* 17:21).

At the beginning the Church was truly united under the apostles, but then over the centuries different groups separated so that today there are literally thousands of communities calling themselves Christian. The largest communities to separate were several Orthodox Churches in the fifth century, many more in the eleventh to thirteenth centuries and then the Anglican and many Protestant communities in the sixteenth century.

The effort to bring about reunion is known as the ecumenical movement and it has been going on ever since the first rupture of communion. Over the centuries it has borne numerous fruits, especially in the return to union with the Catholic Church of large groups of faithful from the Orthodox Churches to form many of the Eastern Catholic Churches (cf. J. Flader, *Question Time 2*, q. 180). More recently, many Anglicans have been admitted to union with the Church through the Anglican Ordinariates established following Pope Benedict's Apostolic Constitution *Anglicanorum coetibus* in 2009.

The Second Vatican Council (1962-65) gave great impetus to the ecumenical movement, especially through the Decree *Unitatis redintegratio*, and then in 1995 Pope John Paul II encouraged the promotion of Christian unity yet again in the encyclical *Ut unum sint.*

The Octave of Prayer for Christian Unity, however, has its origin a long time before the Second Vatican Council. It began in 1908 as the Octave of Christian Unity at the suggestion of Fr Paul Wattson, cofounder of the Graymoor Franciscan Friars and a convert from Anglicanism. The octave was to begin on January 18 and end on the feast of the conversion of St Paul, January 25. In 1909 Pope Pius X officially blessed the initiative, and Pope Benedict XV, who succeeded him, encouraged its observance throughout the entire Church.

In 1926 the Faith and Order movement of Protestants also embraced an annual octave of prayer for unity among Christians in the week leading up to Pentecost Sunday. In 1941 the Faith and Order Conference, a Protestant group, accepted the Catholic dates for the week so that it would be held in January. With the founding of the World Council of Churches in 1948, the Week of Prayer for Christian Unity became increasingly recognised by non-Catholic communities throughout the world.

In 1958 the French Catholic group Unité Chrétienne and the Faith and Order Commission of the World Council of Churches worked together to prepare materials to be used jointly for the week. In 1968 the cooperation went to a higher level when the Faith and Order Commission and the Vatican's Pontifical Council for Promoting Christian Unity prepared materials together. Since then, these two bodies have collaborated more and more in promoting prayer for Christian unity.

In Australia, as in many other countries in the Southern Hemisphere, where January is a time of summer holidays, the octave is celebrated in the week before the feast of Pentecost. This is an appropriate time, since Pentecost is often regarded as the birth of the Church, when the Holy Spirit came down on the apostles to breathe life into it.

We should always bear in mind that the restoration of Christian unity is not so much a human work as a divine one. Pope Benedict XVI, in his homily on the feast of the conversion of St Paul, 25 January 2008, in the Basilica of St Paul Outside the Walls in Rome said: "At the end of the Week of Prayer for Christian Unity, we are even more conscious that the task of restoring unity, which demands all our energy and efforts, is infinitely above our own possibilities. Unity with God and our brothers and sisters is a gift that comes from on high, which flows from the communion of love between Father, Son and Holy Spirit in which it is increased and perfected. It is not in our power to decide when or how this unity will be fully achieved. Only God can do it!"

436 The Presentation of Mary in the Temple

What exactly does the Church celebrate in the feast of the Presentation of Mary on November 21? And why does the Church celebrate a feast which seems to have no basis in Scripture?

I have to say I have always wondered about the origins of this feast myself. As you say there is no basis in Scripture for the presentation of Our Lady in the temple.

The tradition for the feast seems to stem rather from apocryphal writings of the first centuries, principally the so-called *Protoevangelium of James,* sometime in the second century. In the seventh chapter of that document we read how Mary's father, Joachim, tells his wife Anne that he would like to take Mary to the temple in Jerusalem to live there and be trained in virtue. Anne replies that they should wait until Mary is three years old, lest she long too much for her parents. By the way, it is only from the apocryphal literature that we have the names of Mary's parents, whose feast we celebrate on July 26.

When the day arrived, other girls were invited to accompany Mary with burning lamps to the temple. There the priest received her, blessed her and kissed her, saying: "The Lord has magnified your name in all generations. In you the Lord will manifest his redemption to the sons of Israel." As planned, Mary stayed behind and her parents returned to Nazareth glorifying God.

Significantly, the basic facts of Mary's presentation in the temple from the apocryphal literature agree with those supposedly revealed by Our Lady herself to the Venerable Mary of Agreda (1602-1665), a Spanish nun and mystic. In her *Mystical City of God*, the Venerable Mary writes that Joachim and Anne took Mary up to Jerusalem when she was three years of age, to entrust her into the care of the priests, to be brought up in piety and virtue along with other girls who were the first-born daughters of the tribes of Judah and Levi. The girls lived in special quarters alongside the temple until they were ready to marry.

Upon arriving at the temple, Joachim and Anne offered Mary to God and Mary likewise offered herself to the service of God. According to Mary of Agreda's account, St Simeon, who later appears when Mary and Joseph present Jesus in the temple (cf. *Lk* 2:25-35), received Mary and entrusted her into the care of her teachers, one of whom was the elderly prophetess Anne, who also appears at Jesus' presentation, and who is described there as spending her days in the temple (cf. *Lk* 2:36-38). It was in the temple of Jerusalem, according to Mary of Agreda, that Our Lady took a vow of chastity (cf. *The Mystical City of God*, Two, Chapters 1-2). While we have no historical proof other than the documents mentioned for these events, they make clear that even in childhood Mary was completely given over to God.

In any case, in the sixth century the Emperor Justinian I built a church dedicated to Mary in the temple area of Jerusalem. It was dedicated on 21 November, 543, giving rise to the feast of the Presentation of Mary on that day each year. The church was destroyed by the Persians in 614.

Some eighth century Fathers of the Church, among them St Germanus, Patriarch of Constantinople, and his contemporary St John Damascene, preached beautiful homilies on this feast. They referred to Mary as a special plant planted in the House of God, nourished by the Holy Spirit, and keeping her body and soul spotless to receive God in her womb. They said that he who is all-holy rests among the holy.

In the Byzantine Church this feast is regarded as one of the twelve great feasts of the liturgical year. It celebrates the same values as the Immaculate Conception of Mary does in the Western Church. In the West the feast came to be celebrated in the ninth century in the monasteries of southern Italy, which had been influenced by the Byzantine tradition. By the fourteenth century it had spread to England and France. In 1472 Pope Sixtus IV extended the celebration to the universal Church. Although it was not included in the calendar of Pope Pius V in 1568, it was reintroduced by Pope Sixtus V in 1585.

The feast was retained in the revised calendar of 1969 after the Second Vatican Council. The description of the feast in the *Liturgy of the Hours* reads: "We celebrate that dedication of herself which Mary made to God from her very childhood under the inspiration of the Holy Spirit who filled her with grace at her Immaculate Conception."

Devotion to the Saints

437 St Michael the Archangel

St Michael the Archangel is often depicted with a spear or a sword and overcoming the devil. Why is this?

Along with St Gabriel and St Raphael, St Michael is one of the three archangels whose feast we celebrate each year on September 29. The name Michael in Hebrew means "Who is like God", alluding to his special place among the angels and his power over Satan.

St Michael appears four times in the Bible, two of them in the book of Daniel. In the first, Daniel has a vision of a powerful man or angel who tells him, "The prince of the kingdom of Persia withstood me twenty-one days; but Michael, one of the chief princes, came to help me, so I left him there with the prince of the kingdom of Persia and came to make you understand what is to befall your people in the latter days... There is none who contends by my side against these except Michael, your prince" (*Dan* 10:13, 21). The second is more succinct: "At that time shall arise Michael, the great prince who has charge of your people" (*Dan* 12:1). In these texts we see St Michael as a prince, the prince of the heavenly host, a powerful warrior doing battle against the enemy.

In the New Testament letter of St Jude we again find St Michael, now called an archangel, battling against the devil: "But when the archangel Michael, contending with the devil, disputed about the body of Moses, he did not presume to pronounce a reviling judgment upon him, but said, 'the Lord rebuke you'" (*Jude* 9). St Jude alludes here to an ancient Jewish tradition of a dispute between St Michael and Satan over the body of Moses, mentioned in an apocryphal book on the assumption of Moses (cf. Origen, *De Principiis* III.2.2). According to the tradition, St Michael concealed the tomb of Moses but Satan revealed its location in an effort to entice the Jewish people to worship Moses as a hero.

The most well known biblical reference to St Michael is in the book of Revelation: "Now war arose in heaven, Michael and his angels fighting against the dragon; and the dragon and his angels fought, but they were defeated and there was no longer any place for them in heaven. And the great dragon was thrown down, that ancient serpent, who is called the Devil and Satan, the deceiver of the whole world – he was thrown down to the earth, and his angels were thrown down with him" (*Rev* 12:7-9). It is especially on account of this text that St Michael is often depicted as a warrior, with a helmet and shield, standing over the dragon and striking him with a lance.

Christian tradition has attributed to St Michael such roles as fighting against Satan, rescuing souls from the enemy especially at the hour of death and defending them in the judgment, and being the patron of the Church and of the orders of knights in the Middle Ages. To protect the Church against Satan Pope Leo XIII in 1886 ordered the prayer to St Michael to be said after every Low Mass (cf. J. Flader, *Question Time 1,* q. 137).

The veneration of St Michael goes back to the early centuries of the Church. In Phrygia, in modern-day Turkey, where he was first venerated, St Michael was regarded more as a healer of the sick than as a warrior against Satan. According to one tradition, St Michael caused a medicinal spring to spout near Colossae so that all the sick who bathed there and invoked the Blessed Trinity and St Michael were cured. At Constantinople too St Michael was regarded as the heavenly physician. A shrine dedicated to him, the Michaelion, was located at Sosthenion, some eighty kilometres south of Constantinople, where St Michael is said to have appeared to the emperor Constantine. Another famous church dedicated to St Michael in Constantinople was at the thermal baths of the emperor Arcadius. The feast of the archangel was celebrated there on November 8 and this feast soon spread throughout the East.

In Rome the feast of St Michael has been celebrated since at least the fifth century. In that century the Leonine Sacramentary has a feast of the Basilica of the Angel on the Via Salaria celebrated on September 30. Of the five Masses for the feast, three mention St Michael. The Gelasian Sacramentary of the seventh century has a feast of St Michael the Archangel on September 29, and the eighth century Gregorian Sacramentary has a feast on the same day, commemorating the Dedication of the Basilica of St Michael the Angel.

So devotion to St Michael is very ancient and we do well to pray to him for protection against the snares of the devil, both for ourselves and for the Church.

438 Mary, Star of the sea

I am interested to know the history behind the title of Our Lady "Star of the sea" and especially the hymn "Ave Maris Stella". Would you happen to know who composed the hymn, when and under what circumstances, or any other information?

The title "Star of the sea" as applied to Our Lady is very ancient. It seems that it appeared first in St Jerome's work *Liber de nominibus hebraicis*, or Book of Hebrew Names, written probably around 390 AD to explain the etymology of Hebrew names. In that work St Jerome rejects the name *smyrna maris,* bitterness of the sea, which is related to Our Lady's Hebrew name Miriam, which can mean bitterness. Jerome rather proposes the title *Stella Maris,* "Star of the sea", for Mary. In support he quotes a certain Syrus, probably his contemporary St Ephraem Syrus, who had insisted on Mary's status as *domina,* or lady.

The Latin hymn *Ave Maris Stella* is also very ancient. While its authorship is uncertain, it dates back to at least the ninth century since the text of the hymn is preserved in the so-called *Codex Sangallensis*, a ninth-century manuscript kept in the Monastery of St Gallen in Switzerland. Over the years the hymn has been attributed to different people. Among those suggested but clearly to be rejected are St Bernard of Clairvaux (1090-1153) and Hermanus Contractus, of the eleventh century.

In the ninth century Paschasius Radbertus wrote of Mary, Star of the sea, as a guide to be followed on the way to Christ "lest we capsize amid the storm-tossed waves of the sea." He may be the author of the hymn. Also suggested as possible are Venantius Fortunatus, who died in 609, and Paul the Deacon, who died in 787.

The hymn is found in ancient manuscripts of the Divine Office for Vespers on feasts of Our Lady. Today it is still used in the Divine Office and in the Little Office of the Blessed Virgin. The hymn is set out in stanzas of four verses, which have a rhyming pattern in the original Latin.

Some of the stanzas are particularly beautiful. For example, the first two say: "Hail, Star of the sea! Blessed Mother of God, yet ever a virgin! O happy gate of heaven! Thou that didst receive the Ave from Gabriel's lips, confirm us in peace, and so let Eva be changed into an Ave of blessing for us." Two later stanzas say: "Show thyself a mother, and offer our prayers to him, who would be born of thee, when born for us. O incomparable Virgin, and meekest of the meek, obtain for us the forgiveness of our sins, and make us meek and chaste."

The next verse points to the meaning of the title "Star of the sea": "Obtain for us purity of life, and a safe pilgrimage; that we may be united with thee in the blissful vision of Jesus." As "Star of the sea", Mary is the heavenly light that guides us on our pilgrimage, our journey through the storms and swells of life to the safe harbour of heaven.

The popular Marian hymn "Hail, Queen of heaven" is based loosely on *Ave, Maris Stella* and echoes this theme: "Hail, Queen of heaven, the ocean star, guide of the wanderer here below; thrown on life's surge, we claim thy care, save us from peril and from woe. Mother of Christ, star of the sea, pray for the wanderer, pray for me."

St Bernard too takes up the theme and offers the comforting advice: "You, whoever you are, who find yourself in the rushing torrent of this world ... do not take your eyes off the brightness of this star if you do not want to be overwhelmed by the squalls. If the winds of temptation rise, if you are in the midst of the reefs and shoals of tribulation, fix your gaze on the star, call upon Mary. If you are tossed by the waves of pride, of detraction, of ambition or envy, look at the star, call upon Mary...

"If you follow her, you will not go astray; if you call upon her, you will not despair; if you think of her, you will not be lost. If she takes you by the hand, you will not fall; if she protects you, you will have nothing to fear; if she guides you, you will not give up; if she shelters you, you will reach safe harbour. Then you will experience in your own life the truth of those words: 'and the name of the virgin was Mary'" (*Lk* 1:27; *Homiliae super "missus est"* 2, 17).

439 The sorrows and joys of St Joseph

I have often heard people speak of the seven sorrows and joys of St Joseph, but I don't know anything about them. Can you tell me something about this devotion?

The devotion of the seven sorrows and joys of St Joseph is traditional in the Church. It may have its origin in the following story, which is often recounted in relating the history of the devotion. It seems that two Franciscan fathers were once aboard a ship sailing along the coast of Flanders when a great storm arose, sinking the ship with its three hundred passengers. The two Franciscans seized hold of a plank and clung to it for three days, tossed on the waves and fearing for their lives. All this time they begged St Joseph to save them. A young man of good appearance then appeared to them and encouraged them to trust in him, as he led them safely into a harbour. When they asked his name, he told them he was St Joseph, and he advised them to recite the Our Father and Hail Mary seven times each day, in memory of his seven sorrows and seven joys. Then he disappeared.

Whether or not the story is authentic, the devotion of the seven sorrows and joys has deep roots. It consists in reciting seven prayers, each referring to one of the sorrows and joys, followed by an Our Father, Hail Mary and Glory be to the Father. The wording of these prayers varies from one version to another, but they all mention the same sorrows and joys.

The first is St Joseph's immense sorrow on discovering that Our Lady is carrying a child which he knows is not his, and his decision to separate from her whom he loves so much (cf. *Mt* 1:18-19). The corresponding joy comes when an angel appears to him in a dream and tells him, "Joseph, son of David, do not fear to take Mary your wife, for that which is conceived in her is of the Holy Spirit" (*Mt* 1:20). Overjoyed, St Joseph takes Mary as his wife.

The second sorrow comes when St Joseph considers that Jesus is to be born in the poverty of a stable and laid in a manger, a feeding trough for animals (cf. *Lk* 2:7). His sorrow turns to joy when he sees the Son of God born in the flesh and the magi come to worship him, offering him gifts of gold, frankincense and myrrh (cf. *Mt* 2:11).

St Joseph's third sorrow comes eight days after Jesus' birth when he sees the blood flowing during the circumcision. This is followed by his great joy when the child is given the name Jesus, "the name given by the angel before he was conceived in the womb" (cf. *Lk* 2:21).

The fourth sorrow and joy come during the presentation of Jesus in the temple, forty days after his birth. The sorrow is the prophecy of Simeon that a sword would pierce Mary's heart, and the joy is Simeon's saying that the child would bring about the rising of many in Israel (cf. *Lk* 2:35).

The fifth sorrow, a great one indeed, is the message to Joseph from an angel in a dream to take Our Lady and Jesus and flee into Egypt because Herod wants to kill the child (cf. *Mt* 2:13). Joseph responds to this message by rising while it is still night and beginning immediately the journey into Egypt. The joy comes with the arrival of the Son of God in Egypt, signifying the superseding or overthrowing of the idols which had been worshipped there.

The sixth sorrow again responds to a message from an angel in a dream. After some time in Egypt, an angel appeared to Joseph and told him that those who sought Jesus' life are dead and that he can return to Israel. "But when he heard that Archelaus reigned over Judea in place of his father Herod, he was afraid to go there, and being warned in a dream he withdrew to the district of Galilee" (*Mt* 12:22). This fear is the sixth sorrow and the corresponding joy is the arrival of the Holy Family safely in Nazareth, fulfilling the prophecy that "He shall be called a Nazarene" (*Is* 11:1; *Mt* 2:23).

The seventh sorrow is the loss of Jesus in the temple in Jerusalem at the age of twelve, and the joy is finding him again after three days (cf. *Lk* 2:41-51).

It is interesting to note that Pope Pius VII, who was Pope from 1800 to 1823, granted indulgences for living the devotion of the seven sorrows and joys. The indulgence was greater if the devotion was lived on Wednesdays or in a novena preceding the great feasts of St Joseph. And it was a plenary indulgence on those feasts or when the devotion was lived daily for a month. We see from these indulgences how the Church has blessed the devotion and how it is of longstanding tradition.

440 The Sabbatine privilege

My daughter was recently enrolled in the scapular at her school but the priest didn't say anything about the Sabbatine privilege, that anyone who dies wearing the scapular will be taken to heaven on the first Saturday after their death. Does the Church teach this?

First, we should remind ourselves that the devotion of the scapular was revealed to St Simon Stock, Prior General of the Carmelites, on 16 July 1251. I wrote about it in an earlier column (cf. J. Flader, *Question Time 1,* q. 136) but I didn't include the Sabbatine privilege because of the uncertainty surrounding it. The word Sabbatine, by the way, comes from the word for Saturday. So what do we know about the Sabbatine privilege?

The idea of the privilege stems from a supposed Bull of Pope John XXII entitled *Sacratissimo uti culmine* and dated 3 March 1322. In this Bull the Pope purportedly declares that Our Lady appeared to him and said, among other things, that she would free from Purgatory on the first Saturday after their death all those enrolled in the scapular and therefore members of the Confraternity of Our Lady of Mount Carmel. According to the *Catholic Encyclopedia*, the first information on the Bull is in a work of the French Carmelite Baudouin de Leers, who died in 1483. The authenticity of the Bull was strongly contested, especially in the seventeenth century, and today it is universally regarded as not authentic. It does not appear in the register of the works of Pope John XXII.

While some provisions of the Bull were ratified by Popes in the sixteenth century, neither the Bull itself nor its general contents were thereby declared authentic. In particular, the ratification by Pope Gregory XIII on 18 September 1577 must be interpreted in light of a decree of the Holy Office in 1613. That decree expresses no opinion about the authenticity of the Bull and confines itself to declaring what the Carmelites may preach about its contents. Importantly, it forbids the painting of pictures representing Our Lady descending into Purgatory to free souls detained there.

The decree allows the Carmelite fathers to preach that the Christian people "may piously believe in the help which the souls of brothers and members, who have departed this life in charity, have worn in life the scapular, have ever observed chastity, have recited the Little Hours [of the Blessed Virgin Mary], or, if they cannot read, have observed the fast days of the Church, and have abstained from flesh meat on Wednesdays and Saturdays (except when Christmas falls on such days), may derive after death – especially on Saturdays, the day consecrated by the Church to the Blessed Virgin – through the unceasing intercession of Mary, her pious petitions, her merits, and her special protection."

This text was reproduced in a summary of indulgences and privileges of the Confraternity of the Scapular of Mount Carmel approved by the Congregation of Indulgences on 4 July 1908. No mention was made there of the Bull of Pope John XXII nor, as is clear, of Our Lady taking someone to heaven on the first Saturday after their death. But there is mention of Our Lady helping those souls after death especially on Saturdays, which are traditionally dedicated to her, through her petitions, merits and special protection. One would always expect Our Lady to intercede for the faithful departed who have had devotion to her in life, and so this privilege is unexceptional.

As regards the conditions to benefit from Our Lady's help – observing chastity, reciting the Little Office of Our Lady or observing the fast days and abstaining from meat on Wednesdays and Saturdays – we could say that the more closely someone fulfils them, the more they can count on the help of Our Lady. But Our Lady will always intercede for anyone who has devotion to her, especially when they are enrolled in the scapular. In any case Pope Leo XIII, by a decree of the Congregation of Indulgences in June 1901, granted all confessors the faculty to commute for a good reason the obligation to recite the Little Office and to abstain from meat. A typical alternative might be to say the Rosary everyday and anyone is free to undertake this on their own.

In any case those enrolled in the scapular can say with special confidence, "Holy Mary, Mother of God, pray for us sinners now and at the hour of our death", with the assurance that Our Lady will hear and answer them, both at the hour of death and afterwards if needed.

441 The history of canonisations

Recently I was speaking with a friend about six early saints from the same family when my friend said that it was much easier for someone to be declared a saint in those days. It raised the question of how saints were actually canonised in the early centuries. What is the answer?

It is a very good question and, as usual, a little research reveals a fascinating answer. By the way, for the benefit of readers, the six saints were all brothers and sisters, the most famous of them Basil the Great and Gregory of Nyssa. And their grandmother Macrina the Greater, with whom they spent much time on their holidays, is also a saint. All of them lived in the fourth century.

As your friend says, the process of "canonisation", such as it was, was very different from the process today (cf. J. Flader *Question Time 2,* q. 279). The word "canonisation", by the way, comes from the word "canon", meaning list, so that canonisation is the inclusion of the person in the list of recognised saints.

A saint is someone who died in the grace of God and is now in heaven and can be held up to the faithful as an example of Christian virtue. The recognition as a saint involved demonstrating that the person had a reputation for holiness and that their holiness was confirmed by convincing arguments. This does not mean that the person always lived a saintly life. St Augustine, for example, lived with a woman and had a son by her before his conversion to Christianity. St John Vianney, the Curé of Ars, sums it up: "The saints did not all begin well, but they all ended well" (*Catechesis on Salvation*, Ch 1).

Going back to the early Church, the first persons to be included in the canon of saints were the martyrs. When it was clear that someone had been put to death for holding firmly to their faith, they were honoured as martyrs, or "witnesses" to the faith, their remains were collected and safeguarded, and their anniversary of death was celebrated. In order for there to be public veneration of a martyr, the intervention of the bishop was required. The Church did not grant permission for liturgical veneration to everyone, not even to all the martyrs. For this reason the bishop would conduct an investigation into the circumstances of the life and death of the person, and only when he was satisfied that there was fame of sanctity and that the person had indeed died for the faith did he grant this permission.

It was customary for the bishop to send an account of the martyrdom to other neighbouring churches, so that, if their bishops approved, they too might honour the martyr in the liturgy. In effect this was equivalent to today's beatification, since it granted veneration of the saint only within a limited area. In exceptional cases, like those of St Lawrence, St Cyprian and Pope St Sixtus of Rome, the veneration quickly spread to the whole Church.

The Roman Canon, or first Eucharistic Prayer, which dates back to Pope Gregory the Great at the end of the sixth century, includes numerous saints who by their inclusion were regarded as worthy of public veneration. Apart from the Apostles, they are Linus, Cletus, Clement, Sixtus, Cornelius, Cyprian, Lawrence, Chrysogonus, John and Paul, Cosmas and Damian, John the Baptist, Stephen, Matthias, Barnabas, Ignatius, Alexander, Marcellinus, Peter, Felicity, Perpetua, Agatha, Lucy, Agnes, Cecilia and Anastasia.

Later on, confessors too came to be regarded as saints (cf. J. Flader,

Question Time 2. q. 282). Initially the name confessor was given to those who had suffered for the faith but had not died for it, but later it came to be applied to all saints who were not martyrs, as at present. As early as the fourth century, liturgical veneration was granted to such confessors as St Anthony, St Ephrem and St Martin of Tours. Again, this required episcopal approval and it was restricted to the local area.

Toward the end of the eleventh century, Popes including Urban II, Calixtus II and Eugenius III decreed that the sanctity of anyone to be honoured publicly should be declared not just by the local bishop but by regional councils of bishops. Only with the consent of the Pope could the person be venerated in the universal Church, as in today's canonisation.

Finally, in 1170, Pope Alexander III decreed that no one could be declared a saint without the permission of the Roman Pontiff. This was formally incorporated into Church law by Pope Gregory IX in 1234. Since then only the Pope can declare someone a Blessed or Saint. So yes, it was somewhat easier for a person to be declared a saint in the early Church. But that person still needed to be of exceptional holiness and with fame of sanctity.

442 Saints in the Roman Canon

I don't mean to be disrespectful but why does the first Eucharistic Prayer have the names of so many saints I, and presumably many others, have never heard of? Why are they mentioned and who were they?

At the outset we should remember that the first Eucharistic Prayer, otherwise known as the Roman Canon, is very ancient, having been in existence in substantially its present form since the pontificate of Pope Gregory the Great (590-604). The saints mentioned, therefore, were all from the centuries before that time and understandably many of them may be little known today.

The reason for invoking the saints is simple. The Mass is celebrated in communion with the whole Church: the Church militant on earth, the Church suffering in Purgatory and the Church triumphant in heaven. It is thus united with the eternal liturgy offered by the angels and saints in heaven, who sing "Holy, holy, holy" (*Is* 6:3). It is therefore only natural to mention by name some of those saints, who intercede for us here on earth and present our prayers to the Blessed Trinity.

The first Preface of Saints explains this reasoning in a prayer addressed to the Father: "For you are praised in the company of your Saints and, in crowning their merits, you crown your own gifts. By their way of life you offer us an example, by communion with them you give us companionship, by their intercession, sure support, so that, encouraged by so great a cloud of witnesses, we may run as victors in the race before us and win with them the imperishable crown of glory, through Christ our Lord. And so, with the Angels and Archangels, and with the great multitude of the Saints, we sing the hymn of your praise, as without end we acclaim: Holy, Holy, Holy..."

Since it is impossible to mention all this great multitude by name, the Roman Canon mentions only a few. It has two lists, one before the Consecration and one after it. Here I will comment only on the first list and will leave the others for the following answer.

The list begins with Our Lady and St Joseph, whose name was added to the Roman Canon by Pope John XXIII in 1962. They are followed by Saints Peter and Paul and the other ten apostles. Then come another twelve names. The first three are considered to be the first three successors of St Peter as head of the Church. Linus, from Tuscany, reigned from around 67 to 76 AD and St Irenaeus suggests he was consecrated a bishop by St Paul. Cletus, or Anacletus (76-88), was a Roman. And Clement I (88-97), who Tertullian says was ordained by St Peter, was a martyr and the author of the well-known letter to the Corinthians.

The next two, Sixtus and Cornelius, were also Popes. There were two Popes who took the name Sixtus in the early Church: Sixtus I (115-125) and Sixtus II (257-258). It is generally held that the one mentioned in the Canon is Sixtus II, who was martyred under the Emperor Valerian on 6 August 258, a few days before his deacon Lawrence. His feast is celebrated on August 7. St Cornelius, Pope from 251 to 253 and very close to St Cyprian, was banished by the Emperor Gallus and is considered a martyr. His feast is celebrated along with that of St Cyprian on September 16.

After these five Popes come another seven saints, all of whom were martyrs. St Cyprian, one of the great Fathers of the Church and a bishop in North Africa, was martyred in Carthage in 258.

St Lawrence (cf. J. Flader, *Question Time 2,* q. 287) was one of the seven deacons of the Church in Rome and was martyred under the Emperor Valerian in 258, a few days after Pope Sixtus II, whom he served. His feast is celebrated on August 10.

St Chrysogonus was martyred at Aquileia under Diocletian, who was Emperor from 284 to 305. It would seem that more is known of his death than of his life.

Next come Saints John and Paul, who suffered martyrdom at the time of the Emperor Julian the Apostate (361-363), the half brother of the Emperor Constantine. This was well after Constantine's Edict of Milan in 313 that gave Christianity legal status in the Roman Empire. In spite of the Edict, there were still persecutions from time to time.

The last two saints are Cosmas and Damian, twin brothers and physicians, who were martyred in Cyrus, Syria, around 287 during the persecution of Diocletian. Their three brothers Anthimus, Leontius and Euprepius were put to death with them. Their feast is observed on September 27.

443 More saints in the Roman Canon

Following your column on some of the saints in the Roman Canon, who are the saints mentioned after the Consecration?

After the Consecration in the Roman Canon, or Eucharistic Prayer I, we find a list of fifteen saints: eight men and seven women.

The first one is John. But which John? Since the three following saints are Stephen, Matthias and Barnabas, all of whom are mentioned in the New Testament, and since John the apostle was already mentioned before the Consecration, this must be John the Baptist. The argument is strengthened by the Eastern practice in the early centuries of commemorating both John the Baptist and Stephen, the first martyr, in the prayer for the dead, and the fact that the prayer where they are mentioned in the Roman Canon immediately follows the commemoration of the dead.

John is followed by Stephen, who is clearly the deacon and first martyr, whose death is described in the Acts of the Apostles (*Acts* 6:8-7:60). His feast is celebrated on December 26.

Then come Matthias, the one chosen as an apostle to replace Judas Iscariot (cf. *Acts* 1:15-26), and Barnabas, the companion of St Paul on his missionary journeys. They are both considered to be apostles, as we see in the liturgical celebration of their feast days, on May 14 and June 11 respectively.

The next saint mentioned is Ignatius, undoubtedly St Ignatius of Antioch who, on his way to Rome to be martyred in 107 AD, wrote seven letters to Churches in which he revealed his great longing to die and to be with Christ. His feast is celebrated on October 17.

Ignatius is followed by Alexander, and again there is some uncertainty about who this is. A likely candidate is the Alexander listed by some early writings as the fifth Pope, who was martyred, like St Ignatius, during the reign of the emperor Trajan (98-117). In 1855, a semi-subterranean cemetery of the martyrs Alexander, Eventulus, and Theodulus was discovered near Rome, at the spot where the tradition declares the Pope to have been martyred.

Next come Marcellinus and Peter, two martyrs whom ancient sources consider to be a priest and exorcist respectively. Although there was a Pope Marcellinus, who reigned from 296 to 304, it is more likely that the Marcellinus in the Canon is a priest of the same name, since it is known that a priest named Marcellinus and an exorcist named Peter were martyred at the time of Pope Marcellinus, during the persecution of Diocletian.

That brings us to the seven women saints, all of whom were martyrs and all well known. Saints Felicity and Perpetua were martyred in Carthage on 7 March 203. Perpetua was a 22 year-old married woman of noble birth and Felicity a slave. When she was arrested, Perpetua was nursing a young son and was pregnant with a daughter, to whom she gave birth shortly before her death. Perpetua and Felicity were martyred by being attacked by a wild cow and then being put to death by the sword. Their feast is celebrated on March 7.

St Agatha is one of the most venerated virgin martyrs of the early centuries. She was put to death for her faith in Catania, Sicily, probably during the persecution of Decius (250-253). Her feast is celebrated on February 5.

St Lucy is another virgin martyr, from Syracuse in Sicily, put to death according to the tradition in the year 303 during the persecution of Diocletian. One tradition has it that her mother Eutychia was cured of an illness after praying before the tomb of St Agatha in Catania. St Lucy's feast is celebrated on December 13.

St Agnes, another virgin martyr, was from a noble Christian family in Rome. She was put death at the age of 12 or 13 on 21 January 304, during the persecution of Diocletian, for refusing to marry the son of the Prefect. Her feast is celebrated on January 21.

St Cecilia, another much venerated virgin martyr from a noble Roman Christian family, was killed by a sword sometime towards the end of the second or first half of the third century. Her feast is celebrated on November 22.

Finally, St Anastasia was martyred at Sirmium in present-day Croatia, perhaps during the persecution of Diocletian, although little is known about the circumstances or date of her death. For a long time she was commemorated in the second Mass on Christmas day.

444 St Christopher

Some time ago you wrote about St Philomena, a saint whose feast is no longer celebrated. How about St Christopher? I have devotion to him and have a St Christopher medal in my car but his feast is not celebrated either. Is he too under a cloud?

As you say, the feast of St Christopher was once celebrated in the universal Church but is no longer. The name Christopher, by the way, means Christ-bearer and there is a very important reason why he was given that name.

Before 1969 there was a commemoration of St Christopher on July 25, the day on which the Church celebrates the feast of St James the Apostle. In the reform of the calendar in 1969, Pope Paul VI removed this commemoration since it was not of Roman tradition, it was of relatively recent origin, dating to around 1550, and its acceptance had been limited. Nonetheless, St Christopher is listed in the Roman Martyrology, and his feast may still be celebrated, for example in parishes dedicated to him and in certain dioceses and countries. Numerous cities, especially in Europe, have St Christopher as their patron saint.

What do we know about St Christopher? It seems that most of what we know falls into the general category of legend, with different and even contradictory stories about him. But obviously they have enough credibility to move the Church to allow liturgical celebrations, to dedicate parishes to him, and to allow statues and medals of him to be blessed and used. The first stories of St Christopher were in Greek around the sixth century, and by the ninth century they had spread to France. The eleventh century bishop Walter of Speyer gives one version, but the most popular ones come from the thirteenth century *Golden Legend*.

According to the tradition, St Christopher lived in the province of Lydia, in Asia Minor in the third century. He is supposed to have been of enormous size and strength and had been converted to Christianity by a hermit. He asked the hermit how he could serve Christ and was told he should do fasting and prayer. According to the story Christopher said he was unable to do this, so the hermit suggested that since he was so big, he could serve Christ by carrying people across a stream where the current was so strong that people were often swept away. Christopher then built a hut near the stream as a shelter and offered to carry across anyone who requested it.

One day a little boy appeared and asked for his services. Christopher willingly placed him on his shoulder, and started to walk across, staff in hand. But for some strange reason the child was exceedingly heavy and Christopher almost lost his balance in the strong current. When he finally reached the other side he put the boy down and said: "Child, you have put me in dire peril, and have weighed so heavily on me that if I had borne the whole world on my shoulders it could not have been more burdensome." The boy answered, "Do not wonder, Christopher, for you have borne on your shoulders not only the whole world but him who created the world. I am Christ your king, whom you are serving by this work."

To show him that this was true, the boy asked Christopher to go back to the other side and plant his staff in the ground beside his hut and soon it would blossom. Christopher did this and indeed the staff burst into bloom. Christopher then understood how wonderfully he had been blessed. News of the event spread far and wide and brought about numerous conversions to the faith. This angered the local governor, who ordered Christopher to offer sacrifice to the pagan gods. When he refused, the governor tried to win him over by promising him wealth and sending two beautiful women to tempt him. Christopher converted the women to Christianity. Finally he was beheaded and the women died as martyrs along with him during the reign of the Roman Emperor Decius (249-251).

St Christopher is venerated in the Orthodox Churches as well as in the West, the Orthodox celebrating his feast on May 9. There is some suggestion that St Christopher is identified with the Egyptian martyr St Menas who was put to death in Antioch at that time, since the details of their life and martyrdom have many common features. St Menas is the patron saint of travelers in the Coptic tradition, just as St Christopher is in the Greek and Latin traditions.

St Christopher is also invoked against storms and sudden death. In artworks he is usually depicted with the Christ Child on his shoulders and a staff in his hand, sometimes with a tree in bloom and with a river.

445 St Anthony's bread

In the school my daughter attends the chaplain recently blessed bread on the feast of St Anthony of Padua. I hadn't heard of this before. What is the origin of the custom?

Let us first remind ourselves who St Anthony of Padua was. He was born in Lisbon, Portugal in 1195 and at the age of fifteen entered the Order of Canons Regular of St Augustine. In 1219 at the Monastery of the Holy Cross in Coimbra he met a group of young Franciscan Friars who were going as missionaries to Morocco and he was greatly impressed by their zeal for souls.

In 1220 news reached Coimbra that the five Franciscans had been killed by the Moors, and St Anthony was profoundly moved. When the remains of the five martyrs were brought to Portugal for burial he was inspired to follow in their footsteps and he obtained permission from his superiors to join the Franciscans.

Soon after, St Anthony left for Morocco as a missionary to preach the faith to the Moors, but in 1221 he became ill and had to return to Europe. His boat was blown off course and he landed in Sicily, so he decided to go to Assisi to meet St Francis. While there he attended a general chapter which was then in progress, and he was assigned to the Italian province of Romagna.

St Anthony soon became known as a brilliant preacher and theologian. He was very successful in converting heretics, earning him the title "Hammer of Heretics". He died at the age of thirty-six in Padua in 1231 and was canonised less than a year later on 30 May 1232. In proclaiming St Anthony a Doctor of the Church in 1946, Pope Pius XII said he could justly be called the Evangelical Doctor, because he based all his teaching on the Gospels. St Anthony is one of the most popular saints in the Church and he is loved and respected by people of all nationalities and religions.

But what is the origin of blessing bread on his feast day, June 13? It goes back to the year 1263 in Padua, where a basilica in honour of St Anthony was still under construction. According to the most ancient account, a child fell into a barrel of water near the basilica and was drowned. The distraught mother called on St Anthony to restore the child to life and promised she would donate the child's weight in grain for the poor if her prayers were answered. While she was still praying, the child arose as if from sleep. The miracle gave rise to the pious custom of giving alms to the poor to accompany a petition or in return for favours received through the intercession of St Anthony.

The custom of blessing bread in honour of St Anthony apparently comes from a favour received by a devout woman named Louise

Bouffier in Toulon, France, in 1888. According to the account, Louise managed a small bakery and one morning she couldn't open the door with her key. Neither could a locksmith, who told her he would have to break the door open. While he went to get his tools, Louise promised St Anthony she would give some bread to the poor if the door could be opened without force. When the locksmith returned, Louise begged him to try the key once more and this time it worked.

Louise kept her promise and from Toulon the custom of giving bread to the poor in gratitude for favors received through the intercession of St Anthony spread all over the world. Pope Leo XIII, in his letter of 1898 on the Thirteen Tuesdays of St Anthony, commended the practice of giving "St Anthony's Bread" to the needy.

What are the Thirteen Tuesdays? Because St. Anthony was buried on a Tuesday and many miracles accompanied his funeral, Tuesdays are special days on which to honour him throughout the year. It is customary to pray a Novena to him on thirteen consecutive Tuesdays.

St Anthony remains today a friend of all in need, especially the poor and needy, and many people pray to him with great faith, confident that he will intercede with God to answer their prayers. The custom of blessing bread on the feast of St Anthony is just one of the many traditions surrounding the saints that make up the rich diversity of the Catholic Church. They help us appreciate the universality of the one Church founded by Jesus Christ.

446 St John Paul II

In talking with friends about the canonisation of Pope John Paul II I have found a degree scepticism, including among Catholics. They say the Church has rushed through the whole process due to popular pressure. How can I answer them?

There is no doubt that there was widespread demand for the beatification and canonisation of the beloved Pope John Paul II.

Everyone remembers seeing those placards at his funeral: "Santo subito" – "A saint quickly". They captured the sentiment of very many people. But the Church doesn't beatify or canonise someone merely on the strength of popular demand.

It is also true that Pope John Paul's cause was quicker than usual. Due to the widespread belief in his sanctity, Pope Benedict XVI waived the usual five-year waiting period after the death for the cause to begin. As a result, he was canonised just nine years after his death. But the painstaking thoroughness of the process has not been compromised in the slightest. All the normal steps were gone through, including the study of testimonies about his life and holiness, the questioning of witnesses by tribunals, the examination of his writings, etc.

In addition, a rigorous medical and theological examination was made of the miracle of the cure from Parkinson's disease of a French nun. Significantly, the cure took place in July 2005, only three months after the Pope's death. In short, his cause was not given preferential treatment. With many people working on the cause, all these steps could be gone through in much less time than usual. We should be very clear that Pope John Paul was not merely an influential and popular Pope – he was a true saint. This is why the Church has canonised him.

Among the evidence of his sanctity was his extraordinary generosity in giving his belongings to the poor. Mgr Slawomir Oder, the Postulator of his cause, tells in his book *Why he is a Saint* how on one occasion when the Pope was a priest in Poland he was delayed in arriving for his Mass one morning. The sacristan went to his lodgings to see what was wrong and found that he had given his only pair of shoes to a poor man the day before and he had nothing to wear. The sacristan gave him his shoes so that he could say Mass. On another occasion when Fr Karol Wojtyla had no warm jumper in the middle of winter, some nuns made him one but he soon gave it away. He insisted that even his underwear be mended when it had worn out rather than buying new garments.

Another important aspect of his holiness was his deep and intimate relationship with Jesus Christ. Mgr Oder, in an interview with the newsagency *Zenit* said that, in examining his life, "What came to light was certainly a mystic. A mystic in the sense that he was a man who lived in the presence of God, who let himself be guided by the Holy Spirit, who was in constant dialogue with the Lord…" He said that those who worked with him would often find the Pope in a *raptus mistico*, a rapture, "in which [John Paul II] was in such a profound dialogue with the Lord that the only thing one could do was to stand back and let him live this moment."

He was also very much in love with Our Lady. It is well known how he would take advantage of any interval between appointments or when travelling to pray the Rosary. Following St Louis de Montfort, he was totally dedicated to the Mother of God, adopting *Totus tuus*, "All yours", as his motto and putting an "M" for Mary beneath the cross on his papal coat of arms.

And from his youth when he became interested in Carmelite spirituality, he was very demanding on himself in penance. In the course of his process of beatification some of his penances became known for the first time and they even bothered some people. But, as Mgr Oder comments, "this was a sign of his profound faith, of his spiritual life." For example, those close to him said that he would lose many kilos in Lent due to his rigorous fasting.

In short, Pope John Paul II was a true saint and he is and will be always a powerful intercessor for the Church, especially for the youth. His feast is celebrated on October 22, the day of the inauguration of his pontificate in 1978.

Shrines of Our Lady

447 The Holy House of Loreto

A friend has just returned from a holiday in Italy and she visited the Holy House in Loreto, which is supposed to be the house of the Holy Family of Nazareth transported to Loreto by angels. Are we supposed to believe this?

First, I must correct your statement that this is supposed to be the house of the Holy Family. Rather, it is supposed to be the house where Our Lady received the annunciation by the angel that she was to be the mother of God. Hence it was the house of Our Lady, or of her parents Joachim and Anne.

The basilica of Loreto, with what is reputed to be the Holy House of Nazareth inside it, is one of the most revered Marian shrines in the world, attracting some four million visitors each year. Numerous Popes and saints have visited the shrine and manifested their devotion to the Holy House. The Popes have granted many privileges and indulgences associated with the shrine, and numerous miracles have been done there.

Pope Benedict XVI visited the shrine on 4 October 2012, the fiftieth anniversary of the visit of Pope John XXIII in 1962, who went there to entrust to Our Lady the fruits of the Second Vatican Council, which would open a week later. Pope Benedict had earlier been to Loreto in 2007 for a large gathering of Italian youth.

Visitors to the shrine today find a large basilica, built in 1469, inside of which is a beautiful sculpted marble structure ordered to be built by Pope Julius II (1503-1513) and designed by the Renaissance architect Donato Bramante around 1507. Inside this structure is a small stone house with three walls which is supposed to be the Holy House of Our Lady. The walls do not rest on a proper foundation, but rather on what was once a street. At the open end of the house is an altar with the inscription *Hic verbum caro factum est* – Here the Word was made flesh. According to the tradition, the house of Our Lady in Nazareth consisted of two parts: a grotto carved out of the rock, which is still venerated in the Basilica of the Annunciation in Nazareth, and an adjoining small house with walls of stone which opened onto the grotto.

Sometime after the Edict of Milan in 313, the Emperor Constantine had a basilica built over the house, in such a way that the house and grotto formed part of the crypt, or underground level, of the basilica. The basilica was destroyed when the Saracens invaded the Holy Land around the year 1090, but the house and grotto beneath it were left intact. Another basilica was built in the twelfth century, and when St Francis of Assisi visited the Holy Land in 1219-1220 he prayed at the Holy House, as did St Louis IX, King of France while leading a crusade. This second basilica too was destroyed when the Muslims defeated the crusaders in 1263. Again the house and grotto remained, buried under the ruins of the basilica.

Finally, in 1291, when the crusaders were definitively driven out of Palestine, the house was transported, supposedly "by the angels", to Trsat, in modern-day Croatia. In 1294, when the Muslims invaded that region, the house was again moved, first to two different sites near Loreto and finally to the present site on 10 December 1294. According to the official website of the *Santuario della Santa Casa di Loreto*, recent historical studies have strengthened the theory that, rather than the angels, it was members of the noble Angeli family, the name of course meaning angels, who ruled over Epiro at the time and who had the house transported by ship to Europe. Epiro was a region comprising part of modern-day Greece and Albania.

Interestingly, five crosses of red cloth, probably worn by crusaders or knights of a military order defending the Holy Land, have been found among the stones of the house. The structure of the house and the stones, as well as the way the stones are cut, are not those of the region of Loreto, but rather are similar to those of Galilee at the time of Our Lord. Also, studies of the house and of the grotto in Nazareth have shown how the walls of the house were once joined to the grotto. And over 60 graffiti carved into the stones of the house have been shown to be of Judaeo-Christian origin, similar to those found in Nazareth.

All in all, there is much reason to believe that the Holy House is indeed the house of Our Lady in Nazareth. The feast of Our Lady of Loreto is celebrated on 10 December, the day the house was supposed to have been transported to Loreto.

448 The Marian shrine of Knock

Some friends recently returned from Ireland where they visited the Marian shrine of Knock. I am completely unfamiliar with this shrine. Did Our Lady appear there as she did at Lourdes and Fatima?

Our Lady did appear at Knock, in County Mayo in the northwest of Ireland. The apparition took place on 21 August 1879 at about 8 in the evening and lasted for at least an hour and a half. This was twenty-one years after the apparitions to St Bernadette in Lourdes in 1858. The apparition in Knock was witnessed by fifteen people ranging in age from five years to seventy-five. They included men and women, teenagers and children. In addition to Our Lady, the people also saw St Joseph and St John the Evangelist standing on either side of her, outside the south gable end of the small chapel in Knock. Behind the three figures in the apparition was a plain altar on which was a cross and a lamb, with angels adoring the lamb. These figures, as they were seen then, are now depicted in statues in the Apparition Chapel, built to enclose the site of the apparition, abutting the original chapel, which still stands.

Our Lady was seen as very beautiful and standing a few feet above the ground, wearing a white cloak hanging in full folds and fastened at the neck. On her head was a bright crown which appeared to be of gold. She was seen to be deep in prayer with her hands raised and her eyes looking up to heaven. One of those who saw her went up to kiss Our Lady's feet but she felt nothing but the wall of the church, wondering why she could not feel what she could see so clearly.

St Joseph, also wearing white robes, stood to the left of the Blessed Virgin, and appeared with his head bowed towards her. St John the Evangelist stood to the right of Our Lady, also dressed in a long robe and wearing a mitre. The people thought this must be St John since he appeared in the same pose as a statue of him in a chapel at Lecanvey, near Westport in County Mayo. He appeared to be preaching, slightly turned away from Mary and Joseph, and he held a large open book in his left hand. To his right was the altar with the lamb and the cross.

When the apparition first appeared word quickly spread so that others came as well to observe it. They stood in the pouring rain, some of them praying the Rosary. Although it was still light when the apparition began, it became completely dark as the time passed, and nonetheless the figures could always be seen clearly as if lit up by a white light. They did not seem to move in any way. What is more, in spite of the drenching rain, the ground around them remained dry. When the apparition ceased the ground became wet. Unlike the apparitions at Lourdes and Fatima, there was no message as none of the figures spoke.

Some six weeks after the apparition, on 8 October 1879, the Archbishop of Tuam, Dr John MacHale, established an ecclesiastical commission to investigate the apparition. All the visionaries testified as to what they saw on the evening of 21 August and the members of the commission were satisfied that their evidence was trustworthy. They were also satisfied that there was no natural explanation for the apparition and that there was not the slightest suspicion of fraud. At a second commission of inquiry in 1936 the surviving witnesses confirmed the evidence they had given to the first commission.

The apparition immediately attracted the interest of the international media, with journalists going to Knock from as far away as Chicago. Even Queen Victoria asked her government to send her a report about the event. Over the years there have been numerous cures and favours granted through the intercession of Our Lady of Knock, and many people have left their crutches and walking sticks behind, as they have at Lourdes.

Knock has become one of the most popular shrines in Europe, visited each year by over a million and a half pilgrims. The nine-day Novena in August attracts ten thousand pilgrims every year. In 1974 Pope Paul VI blessed the foundation stone for the Basilica of Our Lady, Queen of Ireland, at Knock and in 1979 Pope John Paul II visited the shrine to commemorate the centenary of the apparition.

449 Our Lady of Walsingham

I have often heard about a shrine of Our Lady of Walsingham in England and would like to know more about it. Is it associated with an apparition of Our Lady?

The Shrine of Our Lady of Walsingham is in Norfolk and has a very long history, going back to the time of Edward the Confessor in 1061. In that year according to the Pynson Ballad, written around 1485, a devout widowed English noble woman named Richeldis de Faverches prayed that she might undertake some special work in honour of Our Lady. In answer to her prayer, the Blessed Virgin appeared to her three times in a vision and showed her the house in Nazareth where the Annunciation occurred, asking her to build a replica in Walsingham as a perpetual reminder of the Annunciation.

Richeldis then had a Holy House built, a simple wooden structure in imitation of the house in Nazareth. She entrusted the care of the house to her son Geoffrey, who arranged for the building of a priory in

Walsingham so that the monks could care for it on a more permanent basis. Although historical records from the period are scant, it is known that with papal approval the Augustinian Canons Regular built a priory there sometime between 1146 and 1174. Walsingham soon became one of the most popular shrines in Europe, especially when war and political upheaval made travel to Rome and Santiago de Compostella difficult. Over the years royal patronage helped the shrine grow in wealth and popularity, and it was visited by numerous kings, from Henry III in 1241 through Edward I and Edward II to Henry VIII in 1513. Henry VIII's Spanish wife Catherine of Aragon was a regular pilgrim.

The Reformation in England was to see the suppression of the monastery and the shrine. On the pretext of discovering any irregularities, Thomas Cromwell organised a series of visitations which led in 1536 to the suppression of some smaller monasteries, although not that of Walsingham. Even though the prior of Walsingham, Richard Vowell, signed the acceptance of the King's supremacy over the Church, the sub-prior Nicholas Milcham was charged with high treason for conspiring to rebel against the suppression of the monasteries and was hanged outside the priory walls. The priory was finally suppressed in 1538 and the buildings and shrine were looted and largely destroyed. The image of Our Lady was taken to London and burned, along with other images. A Chronicle of England of the time reported: "It was the month of July, the images of Our Lady of Walsingham and Ipswich were brought up to London with all the jewels that hung around them, at the King's commandment, and divers other images, both in England and Wales, that were used for common pilgrimage ... and they were burnt at Chelsea by my Lord Privy Seal."

In 1897, more than four hundred years after the destruction of the priory and shrine, Pope Leo XIII re-established the restored fourteenth century Slipper Chapel as a Roman Catholic shrine of Our Lady of Walsingham. The Slipper Chapel received its name from the fact that it was located about a mile from the original shrine of Walsingham and pilgrims used to take off their shoes or slippers there and walk barefoot the rest of the distance. The first post-Reformation pilgrimage was led to the shrine by the Guild of Our Lady of Ransom on 20 August 1897.

A new statue of Our Lady of Walsingham was made, modeled on the medieval statue, and it is now venerated in the Chapel. Our Lady is seated on a simple chair of state with the Child Jesus on her knee. She wears a Saxon crown as a reminder of her ancient queenship and holds the lily of purity in her hand. The Holy House too has been rebuilt as the Lady Chapel in the Church of the Annunciation at King's Lynn.

In 1922 the Anglican Church took an interest in reviving devotion to Our Lady of Walsingham and had a new statue made, based on the image depicted on the seal of the medieval priory. Devotion soon followed and pilgrimages once again became popular. In 1931 a new Holy House was built in a small pilgrimage church and the statue of Our Lady was placed there. In 1938 the church was enlarged to form the Anglican Shrine of Our Lady of Walsingham.

Over 100,000 pilgrims go to Walsingham each year, many of them visiting both the Anglican and the Catholic shrines. The feast of Our Lady of Walsingham is celebrated each year on September 24, the feast of Our Lady of Ransom.

450 Our Lady of Aparecida

When Pope Francis went to the Marian shrine of Aparecida during his trip to Brazil for World Youth Day 2013, he mentioned that some fishermen had found the statue of Our Lady that is venerated there. Can you tell me more about it? Did Our Lady appear?

The shrine of Aparecida has an interesting history dating back to the eighteenth century. The word "Aparecida", by the way, is the past participle of "appear" in Portuguese and Spanish. The name was applied to a statue of Our Lady which had quite miraculously appeared.

According to the official account, in October 1717 Dom Pedro de Almeida, Count of Assumar and Governor of the Province of São Paulo and Minas Gerais, was passing through the area of Guaratinguetá, a small city in the Paraíba river valley near São Paulo, Brazil. The local people decided to celebrate a feast in his honour with a banquet in which fish would be served. Three fishermen then went out to fish on the river, having prayed to Our Lady of the Immaculate Conception for a good catch as they had the custom of doing. It should be noted that their devotion preceded the proclamation of the dogma of the Immaculate Conception by over one hundred years (cf. J. Flader, *Question Time 1*, q. 32).

After many hours of fishing they had caught nothing and were very discouraged. They cast their nets once more and instead of fish hauled in a clay statue of Our Lady without its head. One more cast netted the head of the statue. They washed the statue and recognised it as a dark-skinned representation of Our Lady of the Immaculate Conception. They wrapped it in cloth and named it *Nossa Senhora da Aparecida Conceição*, Our Lady of the Conception which has Appeared.

The statue was less than a metre high and after a long time in the water it had lost its polychrome colouring. It is believed to have been made around 1650 by Fray Agostinho de Jesus, a monk from São Paulo known for his sacred images in clay. Buoyed up by hope in the image they had found and having entrusted themselves once more to Our Lady, the fishermen went back to their fishing. This time they were successful, filling their nets completely. They attributed the miraculous catch to Our Lady's intercession.

One of the fishermen, Felipe Pedroso, took the statue to his home, where his family and friends began to venerate it. For the next fifteen years the statue remained in his home and devotion to Our Lady increased. People were coming from far and wide, having heard of the many favours and miracles attributed to Our Lady. The Pedroso family built a small chapel for the statue but this soon became too small for the many visitors. In 1732 the Pedrosos moved to Porto Iguassu, taking the statue with them. There a larger chapel was built on the Morro dos Coqueiros (Hill of the Palm Trees), and it was opened in 1745. With the number of visitors increasing constantly, work on a larger church began in 1834. It was granted the title of Minor Basilica in 1908.

In 1904, the fiftieth anniversary of the proclamation of the dogma of the Immaculate Conception, the statue was adorned with a gold crown following a decree of Pope Pius X. The statue at present is dark brown in colour and is clothed in a dark blue robe of richly embroidered cloth, with gold clasps. Only Our Lady's face and hands can be seen. In 1930 the Blessed Virgin Mary, under the title Our Lady of Aparecida, was proclaimed Queen and Principal Patroness of Brazil by Pope Pius XI.

In 1955 work began on the present Basilica, which is in the form of Greek cross and can hold up to 45,000 people. It is the largest Marian temple and the second largest Basilica in the world, second only to St Peter's in Rome. It was consecrated by Pope John Paul II in 1980 and given the title of Minor Basilica. Due to the growth of the town of Aparecida and the importance of the shrine, the Holy See in 1958 created the new Archdiocese of Aparecida.

Since the nineteenth century the feast of Our Lady of Aparecida has been celebrated on October 12. In Brazil it is a holy day of obligation and since Pope John Paul II's visit to the country in June 1980, it has been a national public holiday. Some five million pilgrims visit the shrine each year.

INDEX

acolytes 115, 136, 142-3, 150-1
adultery 58, 203, 205-6, 208, 215, 219, 240, 260-1, 263
Advent wreath 300-2
Akathistos 290-3
Ambrose, St 48, 139, 144
angels 17, 88, 90, 94, 100, 114, 120, 289-90, 296, 298, 325, 337, 348-50
    fall of 12-14, 326
    guardian angels 16
    St Michael, Archangel 325-6
Angelus 284-5, 290, 305, 313
Anglican Ordinariates 320
Anselm, St 234, 302
Anthony of Padua, St 159, 343-4
Apostolicae Curae 156
Aquinas, St Thomas 4, 58, 88, 91, 193, 200, 310
Athanasian Creed 303
Athanasius, St 35, 304
atheism 6-7, 85-6
Augustine, St 21, 31, 48, 127, 193, 198-9, 221, 237, 310, 313-4, 335, 343

Bacon, Francis 6, 8
Basil the Great, St 334
Bede, St 316

Benedict XV, Pope 20
Bernadette, St 282, 350
Bernardine of Siena, St 64
blasphemy 52, 205, 207, 239-41, 307
blessings 75, 101, 103, 121, 134, 143, 150-2, 169, 274-5, 282, 299, 301
    who can give blessings 105-7
    Jesus' blessing in the Last Supper 108-9
body piercing 249-51
Boethius 87
Bonaventure, St 284
Boniface VIII, Pope 52

Campion, St Edmund 232
canonisation 239, 336, 345
    history of 334
Casti connubii 260
Catherine of Genoa, St 96
celibacy 264
    Is it too hard? 179-80
    Why only in the West 181-3
chastity 35, 61-2, 182, 204-5, 208, 220, 259-60, 262, 265-6, 323, 333
Christian unity, Octave of prayer for 320-1
Christmas 35, 37, 46, 99, 104, 287, 300-2, 307-8, 333, 341

importance of 302-4
Nativity scenes 304-6
Christopher, St 341-3
Chrysologus, St Peter 138
Chrysostom, St John 31, 33, 41, 120, 274, 293, 335
Communion, in Mass 107, 114
    blessings in 150-2
    denying Communion 146-8
    extraordinary ministers 107, 142-4, 151
    how to receive Communion 148-50
    taking to the sick 152-4
    who may receive Communion 139-41, 144-6
conclave 70-1, 73-4, 77
Constantine, Emperor 326, 338, 349
consubstantial 43, 64, 121-3
cosmetic surgery 251-3
Credo of the People of God 80
Cyril of Jerusalem, St 31, 127, 238

Damascene, St John 14, 324
Darwin, Charles 6-9
De Benedictionibus 107, 151
Denton, Michael 4
design in nature 3-6
devil 12-18, 27, 94, 131, 201, 221, 273, 278, 325-7
    forms of diabolical activity 15-16, 245
    reality of 14-15

Didache 144
Dignitas personae 256-7
Directory on Popular Piety and the Liturgy 301, 306
divorce 151, 246-7, 260-1
Donum vitae 254

Easter 99-101, 291, 298, 319
    date of 315-7
    spirit of 313-5
Eastern Catholic Churches 138, 140, 180-3, 185, 290-1, 293-4, 314, 317, 320, 339
Einstein, Albert 3, 7
Emmerich, Blessed Anne Catherine 52, 60
Epiphanius, St 31, 35, 48
Epiphany 99, 106, 311-3
Eucharist 23, 78, 108, 111, 119, 121-2, 124-5, 129, 133-4, 142, 144-5, 148-9, 154-6, 164, 194, 197, 201, 207, 234
    Eucharistic miracle of Bolsena, Italy 159
    Eucharistic miracle of Buenos Aires 157-9
    Eucharistic miracle of Lanciano 161-3
    Eucharistic miracle of Poland 159-61
    Real Presence 23, 78, 125, 155-7, 159, 161-2
Eusebius 31, 65, 315

evangelicals 81
evolution 4, 7-9, 233

faith 20, 22, 25, 33-4, 36, 61, 91, 118-9, 121, 125, 130, 162, 164, 201, 227, 234-5, 275, 279, 281, 305, 335-6, 340, 344
   and Church teaching 230-2
   can it be lost 235-7
   two kinds of faith 237-9
   why study the faith 233-5
Familiaris Consortio 151
Fatima 95, 282, 350-1
Flavius Josephus 41, 310
Fleming, Fr John 257
Flew, Antony 7, 86
Francis of Assisi, St 304, 344, 349
Francis, Pope 15-18, 157-9, 315, 354
General Instruction of the Roman Missal 105, 113-4, 127, 148
grace 13, 62, 86, 89, 92-3, 95, 120-1, 139-40, 145, 147, 178-9, 194-7, 206-7, 221, 226, 235, 238, 247-8, 263, 277-8, 324, 334
   actual 195-6, 198, 200-1
   charisms 200
   graces of state 200-2
   sacramental 168-9, 171, 195-6, 200-1
   sanctifying 170, 195-7, 202
Gregorian calendar 317
Gregory of Nazianzus, St 31

Gregory of Nyssa, St 334
Gregory the Great, St 216, 219, 295, 297-8, 335-6
Grisez, Germain 253

habits 92-3, 205-6, 218, 222-6
Hahn, Scott 261
Hail, Holy Queen 286-8
halal meat 241-3
Halloween 244-6
heaven 12, 35, 68, 88-9, 91-3, 120, 127, 138, 141, 195, 202, 204, 224, 228, 247, 274, 280, 289, 292, 297, 308, 332-4
   and time 120
   pets in 89-91
Helena, St 43, 313
hell 12-13, 90, 203-4
   God's mercy and 94-6
Hermann the Cripple 286-7
Holy Innocents 309-10
Holy Orders 125, 137, 155, 157, 179, 184, 201
   validity of Anglican orders 156-7
Holy Week 106, 291
Hoyle, Sir Frederick 5
Humanae vitae 254

Ignatius of Loyola, St 64-5
in-vitro fertilisation (IVF) 253-5
Irenaeus, St 31-2, 337

Jerome, St 22, 24, 29, 33, 48, 140, 327

Jesus Christ 16, 66-7, 79-81, 84, 91, 95, 120, 125, 131, 178, 227-8, 230-1, 234, 240, 298, 303-4, 320, 345, 347
    "brothers and sisters" 46-8
    "hour" of 39, 49-51
    circumcision 44-6, 330
    humanity 35, 298
    place of birth 38-44, 104, 304-6, 309, 311
    time of birth 39
    Veronica and the face of 51-3

Jesus of Nazareth 38, 40, 112, 129

John Damascene, St 14, 324

John Paul II, Pope St 23, 49, 53, 60, 71-3, 78, 157, 169, 297, 321, 345-7, 352, 356

John Vianney, St 335

Josemaría Escrivá, St 225

Joseph, St 294, 298, 337, 350-1
    betrothal of 54-6
    chastity 61-3
    dilemma of 56-9
    flowering staff 59-61
    sorrows and joys of 329-31

Kepler, Johannes 6, 41

Knock, Marian shrine of 350-2

Kreeft, Peter 91

Last Supper, and the Passover 50, 108-12, 124, 196, 320

Lefebvre, Archbishop Marcel 156

Lent 100, 115, 169, 195, 291, 294, 301, 313, 347

Leo XIII, Pope 22-3, 26, 52, 156, 326, 333, 345, 353

life, origin of 5

Linoli, Odoardo 162-3

Litany 290
    of Loreto 63, 295-7
    of the Saints 294, 297-9
    What is a litany? 292-4

Liturgiam Authenticam 118

liturgy 118, 120, 122, 131, 133, 135-6, 138, 186-7, 289-90, 293, 310, 313, 324, 335
    applause in 101-3
    Liturgical year 99-101
    silence in 103-5

Loreto, Holy House of 348-50

Lourdes 282, 350-2

Lumen gentium 36, 86, 155

magi 38, 41-3, 311-3

Mamertus, St 294, 297

Marie of St Peter, Sister 52

Mary of Agreda, Venerable 323

Mary, Blessed Virgin 28, 35-6, 60, 241, 298, 313, 328, 333, 351-2, 356
    betrothal of 54-6

Lady of the Rosary 281
Our Lady of Aparecida 354-6
Our Lady of Knock 48-50, 352
Our Lady of Loreto 350
Our Lady of Ransom 354
Our Lady of Walsingham 352-4
Presentation in the Temple 322-4
Star of the sea 327-9
virginity 36, 48, 55, 61
Mass
   Communion 107, 114, 144-6
   extraordinary ministers of Communion 107, 142-4, 148-51
   homily 101-3, 115-7, 120-1, 168, 281, 315
   penitential rite 105, 112-4, 119, 175, 294
   Roman Canon 131, 298, 335-41
   why a new translation 117-9, 121, 125-41
Memorare 290
Memoriale Domini 149
Metaxas, Eric 5
Mysterium Fidei 78
Mystici corporis 265

natural law 84, 191-3, 205
Newton, Sir Isaac 4, 6
Nicaea, Council of 43, 122-3, 182, 316

Origen 31, 43, 325
Orthodox Churches 183, 291, 320, 343

Passover 49, 110-2, 133, 140, 315, 318-9
Paul VI, Pope 34, 78-80, 93, 136, 142, 254, 341, 352
Penance, sacrament of 95, 114, 145, 165, 169, 195, 197, 201, 222
   absolution without prior confession 174-6
   benefits of confession 170-2
   general absolution 167-9
   importance of individual confession 167-9
   retaining sins 165-7
   seal of 172-4
Pentecost 100, 267, 279, 281, 313, 317-22
Pius VII, Pope 331
Pius X, Pope St 31, 156, 260, 265, 321, 344, 356
Pontifical Biblical Commission 23, 26, 31, 34
Pope
   abuses in election 75-7
   election of 71-3
   resignation of 68-71
Porta Fidei 78-9, 234
prayer 197, 199, 221, 228, 239, 241, 248
   contemplative 279

distractions in 275-7
in tongues 279-81
mental 180
struggle in 277-9
pride 13, 216, 219, 224-6, 248
Providentissimus Deus 22
Purgatory 10, 90, 92-3, 171, 195, 210, 228, 332, 337

Ratzinger, Cardinal Joseph 102, 134, 254
Redemptionis sacramentum 115, 143
Rosary 154, 180, 274, 276-7, 281-4, 286, 290, 294-7, 334, 347, 351
Rosicrucians 82-4

Sabbatine privilege 332-4
sacramentals 106-7
Sacramentum caritatis 115, 143
Sacrosanctum Concilium 117
scandal 213-5, 264
scapular 106, 332-4
Scripture, sacred 79, 116, 135, 186, 238, 260
historicity of the Gospels 32-4
interpretation of 21-3
unity of 19-21
Second Vatican Council 19, 33-4, 36, 57, 62, 78, 80, 86, 117, 119, 131, 135, 155, 198, 321, 324, 348
secrets 267-9

Seewald, Peter 69
Sheehan, Archbishop Michael 4
Sign of the Cross 106, 273-5
sin
cooperation in 211-3
deadly sins 216-220
diminished guilt for 204-6
mortal 92, 94, 96, 114, 145-6, 167, 171, 197, 204-8, 214, 219, 235, 262-3
occasions of 202-4
punishment for 10, 58, 91-5, 193, 210, 241, 268
venial 92-3, 114, 145, 170, 175, 263
Sistine Chapel 73-4, 77
Slipper Chapel 353-4
Spe salvi 89-90
spiritual dryness 277-9
St Michael, Archangel 16-17, 325-7
Stephen, St 306-9, 311
Stickler, Cardinal Alfons 181-2
suffering 11, 14, 49-50, 57, 94-5, 125-6, 129, 206, 210-1, 227-9, 235, 252, 263, 265, 283, 293
symbols, early Christian 64-8

tattoos 249-51
temptations 15, 199, 201, 215, 220-2
Teresa of Avila, St 224, 278
Teresa of Calcutta, Blessed 277
Tertullian 273, 312, 337

INDEX

Tesoriero, Ron 157-9
The Case for Clerical Celibacy 181
The Spirit of the Liturgy 102
Tradition, sacred 12, 21-2, 31, 42, 48, 59, 70, 169, 260, 273, 297, 301, 312-3, 322, 326
Trent, Council of 20, 22-3, 30, 182, 260
Tridentine Rite 117
Trisagium Angelicum 288-90

Verbum Domini 21-2, 33, 116, 186, 302
virtues 57, 59, 62, 171, 219-20, 223, 226

Walsingham, Our Lady of 352-4
weddings 185-7
    hymns in 186
    readings in 186
    signing the register 187
Whitehead, Sir Alfred North 6
Wickramasinghe, Chandra 5
Willesee, Michael 158

Year of Faith
    of Pope Benedict XVI 78, 80, 234, 236
    of Pope Paul VI 78-80

www.ingramcontent.com/pod-product-compliance
Lightning Source LLC
Chambersburg PA
CBHW050159240426
43671CB00013B/2179